Marie Caroline Watson Hamlin

Legends of le Détroit

Marie Caroline Watson Hamlin

Legends of le Détroit

ISBN/EAN: 9783337150778

Printed in Europe, USA, Canada, Australia, Japan

Cover: Foto ©ninafisch / pixelio.de

More available books at **www.hansebooks.com**

LEGENDS OF LE DÉTROIT.

MARIE CAROLINE WATSON HAMLIN.

ILLUSTRATED BY

MISS ISABELLA STEWART,

DETROIT:
~~THORNDIKE~~ NOURSE.
1884.

DEDICATION.

To the Loved Ones at "Tonnancour," on the Banks of Lake Sainte Claire, where Under the Grateful Shade of a Majestic Willow I Have Listened to Many a Tale of the Mystic Past,

These Legends Are Most Affectionately Dedicated.

M. C. W. HAMLIN.

Detroit, December, 1883.

INTRODUCTION.

The word "Legend" explains itself. Historical and romantic souvenirs hang like tattered drapery around the fair City of the Straits. Interest and curiosity have only to shake its venerable folds to scatter fragmentary history and legendary lore.

These weird tales, quaint customs and beautiful traditions have been handed down from generation to generation as sacred trusts. Originally brought from their cradle in Normandy, they are still tenderly cherished in the homes of the old families of Norman descent settled along "le Détroit."

It has been my good fortune to hear many of them from loving, though aged lips of ancestors whose memories extend back into the last century.

It seems a befitting tribute to these noble and hardy pioneers that a descendant of theirs should gather and preserve in an imperishable form these mementoes they valued so highly.

For my interest in the subject, and for the historical facts, in the writing of which I have tried to be strictly accurate, I am indebted to Charlevoix, La Hontan, Lambert, Margry's Collections, Parkman, Rameau, Lemoyne, Campbell, Sheldon, Lanman, and others. The Pontiac Manuscript, Morris' Diary, the Cass, Trowbridge and Roberts' Memoirs have also furnished material.

For the data made use of in the articles on the "French Families" I am under much obligation to the records of Old Ste. Anne's Church, to the researches of my friend L' Abbé Tanguay, and to the brilliant essayist, poet and historian, Benjamin Sulte, of Ottawa.

LEGENDS OF LE DÉTROIT.

CHRONOLOGICAL SEQUENCE.

	DATE	PAGE
1.—The Cross and the Manitou	1669	1
2.—The Baptism of Lake Ste. Claire	1679	8
3.—The Nun of Ste. Claire	1690	17
4.—The "Nain Rouge"	1701	22
5.—The May Pole	1704	30
6.—The Phantom Priest	1705	40
7.—Francois and Barbe	1710	49
8.—The Devil's Grist	1712	57
9.—Jean Chiquot	1721	64
10.—The Widow's Curse	1735	71
11.—Le Lutin	1746	77
12.—The Warrior's Love	1747	85
13.—The Miami Seer's Prophecy	1758	91
14.—The Bones of the Prophet	1761	97
15.—The Bloody Run	1763	103
16.—Le Loup Garou	1770	113
17.—The Old Red Mill	1775	122
18.—La Chasse Galerie	1780	126
19.—Le Feu Follet	1785	134
20.—The Feast of St. Jean	1790	143
21.—Hamtramck's Love	1793	151
22.—The Haunted Spinning Wheel	1795	161
23.—The Cursed Village	1800	169
24.—San Souci and Okemos	1805	180
25.—The Sibyl's Prophecy	1806	189
26.—Captain Jean	1807	197
27.—Kennette's Vision	1808	205
28.—The Fisherman of Grosse Pointe	1810	213
29.—The Ghost of Mongaugon	1812	220
30.—The Eve of Epiphany	1813	228
31.—Kishkaukou	1815	237

INDEX TO EARLY FRENCH FAMILIES.

		PAGE.
1.	INTRODUCTION TO THE FAMILIES	263
2.	STE. ANNE'S CHURCH	264
3.	OFFICERS OF THE FORT	369
4.	ADHEMAR DE ST. MARTIN	569
5.	ASKIN—see *Barthe*	272
6.	BABY	271
7.	BARNARD—see *Desnoyers*	294
8.	BARTHE	272
9.	BEAUFAIT	275
10.	BRUSH—see *Barthe*	272
11.	CAMPEAU	275
12.	CHABERT	281
13.	CHAPOTON	281
14.	CHESNE	283
15.	CICOTTE	284
16.	CUILLERIER DE BEAUBIEN	289
17.	COLE—see *Desnoyers*	294
18.	DE MERSAC	290
19.	DE QUINDRE	290
20.	DESCOMPTES LABADIE	291
21.	DESNOYERS	294
22.	DOUAIRE DE BONDY	296
23.	DUBOIS	297
24.	GAMELIN	297
25.	GODE DE MARANTAY	298
26.	GODFROY	299
27.	GOUIN	304
28.	GRANTS—see *Barthe*	272
29.	HALL—see *Godfroy*	299
30.	HAMLIN—see *Godfroy*	299
31.	LOTHMAN DE BARROIS	305
32.	MORAND	305
33.	NAVARRE	307
34.	PALMS—see *Campeau*	275
35.	PELLETIER	311
36.	PIQUETTE—see *Campeau*	275
37.	REAUME	313
38.	RIOPELLE	314
39.	RIVARD	314
40.	ST. AUBIN	315
41.	VAN DYKE—see *Desnoyers*	294
42.	VILLIER DIT ST. LOUIS	316
43.	VISSIER DIT LAFERTE	317
44.	WATSON—see *Godfroy*	299

ERRATA.

Page 23—For 1674, read *1694*.

" 44— " Grandmensil, read *Grandmesnil*.

" 50— " Rancée, read *Renée*.

" 213— " Diplomate, read *diplomat*.

" 226— " (Note—Arpent), for 19 read *192*.

" 231— " Onto (in seventh line) read *into*.

ERRATA

Page 89.—For 1078 read 1098.
" " 117. " Grandinentii, read Grandineneii.
" " 191. " Elfanhos, read Fanho.
" " 231. " Diplomata, read Diplomat.
" " 376. " Wolja—Argius, read Argius Wo-
" " 391. " Canalis ew th. line, read em.

PONTIAC TREE.

THE CROSS AND THE MANITOU.

A Legend of Belle Isle.

OW frequently, as we sail on the beautiful Detroit River, or tread the busy streets of the prosperous city, does the mind go back to the remote past, wondering what kind of men were those brave explorers who first visited the wilds of these regions and gazed upon them in all their virgin loveliness. History has preserved to us the names of two of these.

Francois Dollier de Casson had served as a cavalry officer of renown under Turenne, and laid aside, in his ancestral halls in Brittany, his sword, sheathed in laurels, to take up the cross which was to lead him through the trackless forests of the new world.

Abbé Bréhant de Galinée was a student whose knowledge of surveying and geography made him a valuable acquisition to the explorers of a new country, and to his graphic pen are we indebted for a detailed account of the visit of the missionary explorers to Detroit.

They arrived in Montreal from France at the time when La Salle's great project for the exploration of the far West was the theme of every tongue. So thoroughly were all imbued with the spirit of adventure, the desire of gain and the glory of extending the arms and name of France, that even enlisted soldiers were allowed to apply for a discharge if they wished to accompany him.

La Salle had just received the necessary permission and orders from De Courcelles, then Governor of Canada, to fit up his expedition for the exploration of that great river called by the Iroquois, Ohio, by the French, Belle Rivière, really an arm of the Mississippi, of which such marvellous things were told by the Indians, who came each season to trade at Quebec and Montreal.

Numerous tribes who had never been visited by the "black gown" were said to people its shores. So Dollier and Galinée determined to carry to these nations the knowledge of the true God.

On the 6th of July, 1669, the little fleet of seven birch bark canoes, each manned by three men, and laden with the necessary merchandise to exchange with the Indians along their route for provisions, beaver skins and other furs, bade adieu to Montreal amid the joyous notes of the Te Deum and the sound of the arquebus. They reached Lake Frontenac (Ontario) August 2, and the 24th of September an Indian village called Timaouataoua, where they remained some time waiting for guides. There they overtook Louis Joliet, who was on his way to Lake Superior in search of a copper mine, wonderful specimens from which had been sent to Montreal by the Jesuit Allouez. The latter was then at Sault Ste. Marie, whither he had gone through the Ottawa River, Lake Simcoe, and with numerous portages into Georgian Bay. It was also Joliet's object to discover a shorter route, and one which could obviate the necessity of so many tedious portages. Accident had revealed this route to La Salle. Being out hunting one day he found an Iroquois exhausted by sickness and travel worn. He tenderly cared for him, and the Indian repaid his kindness by sketching on a clean sheet of bark, with a piece of charcoal, the position of the lakes and the route to the Ohio and Mississippi. This crude chart proved a precious legacy to the energetic and intrepid La Salle. Unfortunately he was taken ill, and his malady was of so severe a nature that he was forced for the time to give up his cherished project. But Dollier and De Galinée, urged by Joliet, determined to abandon the expedition to the Ohio and Mississippi, and go in search of the tribes along the lakes. They bade adieu to Joliet and La Salle and started on their perilous journey, accompanied by seven men. They wintered at Long Point on the northern shore of Lake Erie. From the mildness of the climate when compared with that of Lower Canada, the quantity of its game, the purity of its waters, the abundance of its fruit, especially the grape from which they made sufficient wine to use for the Holy Sacrifice of the Mass, they called it "The Terrestrial Paradise of Canada."

It was in the early spring of 1670 that their canoes landed at Detroit. It was an enchanting scene, which unfolded like a coy maiden, its rare loveliness to the admiring eye of the European. He saw the fresh virgin forests clad in the vestments of spring, the broad sweeping river, with its graceful curves in whose limpid waters thousands of fish could be seen, along the banks teeming herds of bison, and droves of deer gazing with wondering eyes on the stranger. The air was perfumed by woodland flowers which scattered their sweet incense to the music of the birds, whose gorgeous plumage almost rivaled the flowers in hue. Above all was present that grand solemn silence only found in the heart of the forest, resting like a hushed benediction. After wandering about some time in this fair region, and with hearts overflowing with emotions of love and gratitude towards Him who had led their footsteps here, they came upon an open clearing in the center of which arose a grassy mound crowned by a rude stone idol. It was a crude production of nature, created by her in a fit of abstraction and which the Indians had attempted to convert into the semblance of a deity by touches of vermillion. Offerings of tobacco, skins of animals, and articles of food were scattered in reckless profusion at its feet. This, then, was the great Manitou, of whom their guides had spoken, who held in his hand the winds, and whose mighty voice was heard in the storm that swept over the lakes. He was held in great veneration, and as the Indian launched his frail bark on the treacherous waters of the lakes he would come with his offering of propitiation to this wayside place of pilgrimage. The missionaries, indignant at this exhibition of idolatry, broke the statue in a thousand pieces, and in its place erected a cross, at whose foot they affixed the coat of arms of France with this

INSCRIPTION :

In the year of grace 1670, Clement IX. being seated in the chair of St. Peter, Louis XIV. reigning in France, Monsieur de Courcelles being Governor of New France and Monsieur Talon being the Intendant of the King, two missionaries of the Seminary of Montreal, accompanied by seven Frenchmen, arrived at this place and are the first of all the European people who wintered on the land bordering on Lake Erie, which they took possession of in the name of their King, as a country unoccupied, and have affixed the arms of France at the foot of this cross.

  (Signed)   FRANCOIS DOLLIER,
    Priest of the Diocese of Nantes, Brittany.
         DE GALÍNÉE,
    Deacon of the Diocese of Rennes, Brittany.

Taking the largest fragment of the broken idol, the missionaries lashed two canoes together and towed it to the deepest part of the river so that it should be heard of no more. But the tradition says that after the fathers were far away, a band of Indians coming to offer their homage to the deity found only its mutilated remains. Each took a fragment which he placed in his canoe as a fetish, and it guided them to where the Spirit of the Manitou had taken refuge under the deep, sombre, shadow of Belle Isle. He bade them bring every fragment of his broken image and to strew them on the banks of his abode. They obeyed his order, and behold! each stone was converted into a rattlesnake, which should be as a sentinel to guard the sacredness of his domain from the profaning foot of the white man. To the answering call of those who came to his leafy retreat he would mockingly re-echo their words. Many a laughter loving party as they lazily float on the moonlit waters of the Detroit, amuse themselves in awakening the angry spirit of the Indian god as they test the echoes of Belle Isle.

Belle Isle has changed name four times.
1. It was first called Isle Ste. Claire (Charlevoix).
2. Rattlesnake Island from the number of these serpents which infested it.
3. Hog Island, (Isle Aux Cochons,) by the French from the number of these animals put there to destroy the snakes.
4. Belle Isle, in 1845, after Miss Belle Cass, daughter of General Cass and afterward the wife of Baron Von Limburg.

II

THE BAPTISM OF LAKE SAINTE CLAIRE.

A Legend of the Griffin's Voyage.

DURING the long winter months of 1678-9 there might have been witnessed on the banks of the Niagara River, some five miles above the Falls and near the mouth of what is now known as Cayuga Creek, an undertaking new and unheard of in that locality, and well calculated to excite the wonder and amazement of the savage denizens of the surrounding forests.

It was the building of a ship by the daring band of French explorers under the Sieur de La Salle—the first sailing vessel that ever navigated Lake Erie and the upper lakes, and the pioneer of the vast commerce that now plows these waters.

Through the dreary winter the little band of

workmen toiled assiduously, though their food at times was only parched corn, and they had to depend to a great extent on the uncertain supplies of fish and game furnished by the Indians, while spikes, chains, anchors and even cannon had to be carried up the rocky steeps from the level of Lake Ontario. The undaunted energy and iron courage of their commander, La Salle, aided by the pious exhortations of the Recollêt Chaplain, Louis Hennepin, bidding them to labor for the glory of God and the honor of France, made them indifferent to the taunts and jeers of the jealous Indians. Their imaginations were inflamed and their enthusiasm aroused by glorious pictures of the new discoveries to be made in the far West; of the great honors and fortunes all were to acquire; of the new traffic that was to be opened in the hides of the wild cattle that roamed in countless numbers over the plains; of the inexhaustible supply of furs they could draw from the rich mines of Mexico, and of the outlet for all this wealth which was to be found at the mouth of the great Mississippi that La Salle was to open to the ships of France.

The shadows of the summer of 1679 had deepened before the little brigantine of forty-five tons approached completion. The commander had decided to name her the "Griffin," in allusion to the arms of the Comte de Frontenac, whose supporters were "Griffins." An expert wood carver from Rouen had carved for the ship's bows a wonderful image of the fabled monster, half lion and half eagle, with ears erect, emblematic of strength, swiftness and watchfulness. But among the more pious of the band the name was deemed an evil one, and their superstitious natures conjured up disasters to come, "For," they said, "a vessel constructed for such an enterprise ought to be named after the Blessed Lady, or at least after one of the saints." La Salle laughed at such notions, and tried to impress on the minds of the Frenchmen and Indians that the Griffin was a powerful Manitou, who would protect them from all harm, and guide them safely to their destination.

At last all was ready for the launch—the crew were assembled and the notes of the "Te Deum" floated on the air. A bottle of brandy was broken over the bows of the vessel, and liberal potations distributed among the Indians. A salute was fired from the seven guns, ranged along the decks, and amidst the enthusiastic shouts of "vive le Roi," the vessel glided from her ways, and floated on the waters of the Niagara River. The indignation of the Indians who were watching, and who had never dreamed it possible to launch her, knew no bounds. At last she was beyond their power to destroy by fire, which they had several times attempted. La Salle, with a number of his men, had returned to the shore and noticing the chagrin of the savages, pointed to the flag with a Griffin emblazoned thereon, proudly waving from the masthead, and tauntingly exclaimed:

"Now you can see the eagle flying above the crows," alluding to the black-gowned Jesuits whom he deemed his enemies and what was worse, entirely too friendly with the Iroquois.

On this the noted prophet Metiomek could no longer contain himself, and exclaimed: "Great Chief, you are too proud. You have shown contempt for the Great Spirit who rules all things, and you have set up an evil spirit on His throne. You seek the tribes of the west to trade with them and to destroy them with your cursed fire-water. You sneer at the "black gowns" Onontio sent us, who have taught us to worship the Great Spirit and till the ground. But Metiomek, the prophet of his race, bids you beware; darkness, like a cloud, is ready to envelop you—the Christian Indian's curse rests on you and on your great canoe. She will sink beneath the deep waters and your blood shall stain the hands of those in whom you trusted!"

As Metiomek gave utterance to this prophecy in

deep and impressive tones, amidst the most solemn silence, Fathers Hennepin and Zenoble looked serious, and the sailors ominously whispered to each other their apprehensions, but La Salle, with his usual exuberance of spirits, carelessly laughed away the rebellious mutterings which fluttered like a light cloud over the assembly.

On August 7, 1679, the great square sails of the brigantine were set, and La Salle, mounting the lofty stern, gave orders to take a course of west by south, and sailed away on the unknown waters.

Despite the prophecy, the voyage was most prosperous, and favorable winds carried them twenty leagues the first night. On the 8th they made forty-five leagues and passed a point which they named St. Francis (now Long Point). On the 9th they passed Point au Pelée; and on the 10th, the feast of St. Lawrence, they saw the Trois Sœurs (Three Sisters' Islands), standing like the three Parcæ, guarding the terrestrial paradise of le Détroit.

As they sailed by Grosse Isle and the adjacent island, their spirits were wonderfully exhilarated.

"We found," says Father Hennepin in his journal, "the country on both sides of this beauful strait, adorned with fine open plains. Any number of stags, deer, bear (by no means fierce, and very good to eat) poules d'indes‡ in abundance, and all kinds of game. The vessel's guys were loaded and decked with the wild animals our French and Indian hunters shot and dressed. The islands on both shores of the straits are covered with primeval forests, fruit trees, like walnuts, chestnuts, plums and apple trees, wild vines loaded with grapes, of which latter some were gathered, and a quantity of wine was made. The vast herds of deer surprised us all, and it appears to be the place of all others where the deer love to congregate." And so the pioneer ship sailed up "le Détroit," or the strait now called the Detroit River* and passed the site of the present great city. They noticed on shore the spot where ten years before Dollier and Gallinée (who had visited these regions in a birch bark canoe) had broken in pieces the painted stone idol, worshiped as a Manitou by the Indians. They saw on the border of the forests the Indian village of "Teuscha Grondie," and, to impress the fleeing savages, gave them a grand salute from the guns—but the boat glided too rapidly for them to hear the imprecations hurled after them by the Indians, and the winds kindly wafted them away from the

---

‡ Wild turkey.
* Wa-we-a-tu-nong. Indian name for Detroit River.

European ears. "May the Manitou whom we worship," they shouted, "and Wis Kin, who guards the gates of the lakes, devour the evil pale face who comes among us with his white winged bird vomiting forth fire, smoke and thunder; and may the Manitou whom the black gowns cast in the lake many moons ago so trouble the waters, that their canoe shall find no rest thereon and be drawn down to the home of the evil spirit at the bottom] of the lake." Unconscious of the malediction evoked by the savage foes, the Griffin passed Belle Isle into a circular-shaped lake at the head of the river.

The summer sun was setting and flooding the waters with its golden hues—the soft sound of the vesper bell died away in sweet cadences. The little band of hardy explorers fell on their knees giving thanks to Heaven for their prosperous voyage. On the lofty stern of the vessel was Robert Cavalier de la Salle, future explorer of the Mississippi; by his side Henri de Tonty, his captain of brigade; near by, his partners in the enterprise, the Sieur de Boirondet and the Sieur d'Autray, and also the notary Jacques La Meterie and Jean Michel the surgeon. Sixteen French voyageurs and a small number of Indians comprised the crew. As they rose from their devotions Father Louis Hennepin addressed them a short discourse, and concluded by saying: "This is the feast of Ste. Claire, let us commemorate it by bestowing her name on this beautiful sheet of water. I hereby solemnly baptize it Lac Sainte Claire, by which it will be henceforth known." Then all pledged the newly christened lake in many a bumper of wine made from the Detroit River grapes.

The Griffin's journey to Lake Michigan where La Salle left her in order to pursue his discoveries, his vain effort to find the mouth of the great river he had explored while on his second expedition from France, and the closing of his adventurous career by the murderous hands of his men are events which have illustrated many a glorious page of our history. The attempt of the vessel to return loaded with a precious cargo of furs is mentioned, but uncertainty throws its melancholy shadow over its subsequent fate and that of its daring crew. But Indian tradition sees the angry Manitous of the water surround the ill-fated ship and drift her into unknown realms, and on bright moonlight nights they hear a full chorus of manly voices* chanting the evening hymn, and frequently the image of a phantom ship is seen in the clouds.

---

*These voices are no myths. Science has examined into the cause and says they are produced by the beating of the waves on a peculiarly sonorous shingle. Along the northern coast of certain islands in Lake Superior is a low cliff of compact, fine-grained limestone which clinks like steel under the hammer. When the wind blows from the northeast, the waves beating at the foot of the cliff dash the fragments of stone against each other, causing them to give forth peculiar sounds. It is an Eolian harp of stone.

III

THE NUN OF STE. CLAIRE.

A Legend of the "Coureur des Bois."

LONG before Cadillac had founded our beautiful city of Detroit, certain bold rovers called coureurs des bois had already pitched their tents on the shores of Lake Ste. Claire. Among them was Jean Parent, whose stern, silent face like a tomb seemed to hide the dust of dead and buried hopes. He had left beneath Canada's skies the graves of wife, parents and kindred. One tender rootlet remained to try to win him back to life—little Genevieve, his daughter, whom he had brought with him to Grosse Pointe, whose happy, sunny disposition caused joy to reign in the fullness of her grace. As the father gazed upon his growing child he would smile, as if some far-gone memory came back to surprise his heart.

An expression of gentleness would flash on his face, and his voice would soften like the winds when the storm is o'er. Others soon found this wild forest flower and offered her their simple homage. Shyly she turned away from them; the tremulous wings of her heart were still furled, and she waited only to fly from the world to rest on the bosom of her Saviour. She was anxious to devote her life to the service of God, and had written some time previous to the opening of our story to her aunt, the superior of the Ursuline convent at Three Rivers, to be admitted as a nun in her community.

Jacques Morand one day met Genevieve, and was charmed as if by a vision. He was one of the fifty men who had come with Duluth in 1680 to found a fort near the present Fort Gratiot, to which they gave the name of Fort St. Joseph. Genevieve tried by every gentle art to make him understand that his efforts were in vain. Seeing him still persistent, and knowing that vanity plucks from her quiver her barbed arrows only when rivalry enters the field, she told him the desire of her heart was to become a nun. This resolution on her part only inflamed his wish to possess her either by fair or foul means. He appealed in his desperation for assistance to an old Indian witch who practiced her incantations in the darkest part of the forest, untenanted save by the ghosts of gloom. On his promising to sell his soul to the devil she gave him the power to change himself into the form of a wolf or Loup Garou (wehr-wolf), so he might more easily carry away his victim.

The postal system of those primitive days was not as perfect or expeditious as at present, so Genevieve had many long vigils to keep ere an answer would arrive. She spent most of her time in preparing herself for her new vocation by prayer and fasting. Some pious hands had raised, on the border of the forest, beneath an ancient oak whose acorn had been cradled ages before, an altar to Notre Dame de Bonsecour. Genevieve wished to erect one on the beach. So, assisted by her father, she formed one of the rocks cast there by some great Manitou, whereon she placed a statue of the Blessed Virgin. She frequently visited the forest shrine, but long were the hours spent at the one on the beach. The waves would lazily sing as they crept upon the shore, and the birds catching the refrain would chant it to the rustling leaves. It was but a note in the grand harmony of nature to which the girl's yearning soul responded in the same mystic key. Early in the springtime when the earth blossomed with new hopes, Genevieve sent forth her petition to Three Rivers. Late in the fall, when the waters chased by the east wind had nestled at the foot of the rocky shrine, the answer came to Genevieve that her wish was granted. With a heart aglow with happiness, which lent buoyancy to her tripping feet as they crushed the autumn leaves, she visited the sylvan shrine of Bonsecour. This child of the wilderness poured forth her simple thanksgiving, borrowing unconscious pathos from the dead leaves, frost-bitten shrubs and bare trees, mute types of mortals' doom.

As she prepared to go towards the beach her lover Jacques, in the form of a Loup Garou, with gleaming eyes, sprang out into her path. But the cross which she held in her hand disconcerted him. Like a fawn Genevieve leaped aside and flew swifter than the wind toward the lake. The evil beast came bounding in hot pursuit. Genevieve finding her strength failing sought refuge in the little grotto of rocks on the beach. She threw herself at the feet of the Virgin, imploring aid and protection. She felt the fiery breath of the brute and, with a despairing cry for mercy, fainted. The appeal was heard ; as the Loup Garou leaped on the rocks he was instantly transformed to stone. The passer-by to-day may see at *'Tonnancour this old legend embodied in stone.

---

*Tonnancour is the name of Mr. T. P. Hall's summer residence at Grosse Pointe, so called from a title and seigneurie in the God-

The fashionable worldlings who drive past merely see a pretty rustic retreat, but the descendants of the old habitants say, "Voila le Garou!" and raise their hats piously to Notre Dame de Ste. Claire.

---

froy family of Three Rivers, Canada, bestowed by Louis XIV. September 15, 1668.

IV

THE "NAIN ROUGE."

A Legend of the Founding of Detroit.

OFT strains of music mingled with sounds of revelry and joyous laughter issued from the banquet hall in the grand old castle of St. Louis, Quebec, on the evening of the 10th of March, 1701. Subdued, shaded lights bathed the room in mellow radiance, where, around a table resplendent with costly silver and sparkling glass, sat a gay party of French officers.

At the head was Hector Louis de Callieres, Governor of New France, and on his left the Intendant le Chevalier Bochart de Champigny. Amid the brilliant group were those bearing names which stood high in la belle France—De Montigny, Le Gardeur, Le Moyne, Dagneaux Douville, De Tonty, Godfroy de Tonnancour, etc. The post of honor was occupied by Monsieur La Mothe Cadillac, Sieur de Douaguet and Mont Désert.

He had just returned from France, bringing with him from Count Pontchartrain, the Colonial Minister, a commission of Commandant, and the grant of a tract of land fifteen acres square, wherever on "le Détroit" he should see fit to locate a colony and build a fort.

Whilst they are toasting Cadillac in many a bumper, let us turn for a brief review of the eventful career of the founder of Detroit.

Antoine de la Mothe Cadillac, son of Jean and Jeanne Malenfant, first saw light at Toulouse in 1661. At the age of 16 he entered the service, and became a Lieutenant at 21. He came to Quebec with his regiment, in which were many of the scions of noble houses. Here he met and wedded the beautiful Marie Thérèse Guyon, the daughter of an influential and wealthy bourgeois. Shortly afterwards the stern decree of war compelled him to leave his bride. He was sent to Acadia, where his bravery won him distinction and a commission from the French Government to make a report of the condition of the English colonies at that epoch. Count Frontenac in 1674 complimented Cadillac as the most efficient and energetic officer at his disposal, by giving him the command of Fort Buade, Michillimackinac, a post he retained for five years. His treaties with the Indians displayed such thorough experience and ability that he was rewarded by the government with a concession of the Island of Mont Désert (now a watering place on the New England coast), also a grant of a tract on the main land near the River Pentagoet, called Douaguet, from whence he took his titles. He had several times passed through "The Strait," (Detroit River) and noted with his quick eye, the wonderful advantages it possessed. As a military post it would be a barrier to the wily Iroquois; to the English a gate, shutting them off from commerce with the Indians of the far West, and to France, the center of the fur trade in this section of the country. His earnest representations on the desirability of establishing a post on "le Détroit," added to his renown as an able soldier, had gained the consent of the Colonial Minister to his daring scheme.

Let us return to the festive dinner party, where the swiftly passing hours were enlivened by the sparkling repartees which flashed from lip to lip and the brilliant jeu d'esprit, which drew their inspiration from the rare, generous wine of the noted cellars of the castle.

Whilst merriment was at its height, a servant whispered something in the host's ear, and he, turning to the guests, said: "Messieurs, an old fortune-teller craves to enter; shall I bid her do so?" All were in that happy frame of mind eager for any diversion, and a full chorus of "Oui, Monsieur" was the response. One of the gentlemen proposed to change places so as to puzzle the old witch if she had heard anything from the servants. The party had barely changed when the door opened and the figure of an old woman entered.

So strange, so bizarre, was her appearance that a murmur of surprise greeted her. A woman of unusual height, a dark, swarthy complexion, restless, glittering eyes,—strangely fashioned garments yet in harmony with her face. Some one said, "What is your name?" In a deep, sonorous voice, with a slight foreign accent, she answered, "They call me Mère Minique, La Sorcière." On her left shoulder was perched a black, meagre cat. Half a dozen palms were stretched forth for her inspection; one after another she read. When she hesitated the cat would lick her ear, and the more superstitious thought it the devil giving information. Many were the lively sallies as she betrayed some marked peculiarity of the guest, and whisperings of amazement, as at times her knowledge seemed almost supernatural. At last she came to La Mothe Cadillac, who, naturally skeptical, said, "Ma bonne Mère, see what you can tell for me of the future, I care not for the past."

Earnestly scanning his bold, energetic face, she took a brazen basin, into which she poured from a curiously carved silver vial, which she drew from her breast, a clear, heavy liquid like quicksilver, and holding La Mothe Cadillac's hand, gazed into the basin. "Sieur," she said, "yours is a strange destiny. A dangerous journey you will soon undertake; you will found a great city which one day will have more inhabitants than New France now possesses; many children will nestle around your fireside." She paused and Cadillac, thoroughly interested, bade her continue. "Mon Chevalier, I wish you had not commanded me to go on, for dark clouds are arising and I see dimly your star. The policy you intend pursuing in selling liquor to the savages, contrary to the advice of the Jesuits will cause you much trouble, and be the cause of your ruin. In years to come your colony will be the scene of strife and bloodshed, the Indians will be treacherous, the hated English will struggle for its possession, but under a new flag it will reach a height of prosperity which you never in your wildest dreams pictured.

You will bask in a sunnier climate, but France will claim your last sigh."

"Shall my children inherit my possessions?" asked Cadillac, unconsciously giving utterance to the secret desire of his heart.

"Your future and theirs lie in your own hands, beware of undue ambition; it will mar all your plans. Appease the Nain Rouge* (Red Dwarf). Beware of offending him. Should you be thus unfortunate not a vestige of your inheritance will be given to your heirs. Your name will be scarcely known in the city you founded."

All were deeply impressed by the prophecy of the sibyl, save him to whom it was addressed. Shortly afterwards the party separated and Cadillac amused his wife by giving her a humorous account of the old prophetess, but, to his amazement, she too, seemed to look upon the event as of grave import.

On the following day La Mothe Cadillac bade farewell to Quebec and left with his expedition of fifty soldiers and fifty artisans and voyageurs. Alphonse de Tonty, a relative of the Guyons, was his captain; Dugué and Charconale his lieuten-

---

*The Nain Rouge was the demon of the Strait, and in the old traditions is described as most malignant, if offended, but capable of being appeased by flattery.

ants; Jacob de Marsac, Sieur de L'Ommesprou his sergeant; Francois and Jean Fafard his interpreters; Father Constantin del Halle, a Recollêt, and Father Vaillant, a Jesuit, the chaplains. La Mothe Cadillac was not fond of the Jesuits, as they were powerful and strongly opposed to the sale of brandy to the savages, this traffic being an immense source of revenue to the early colonists. The Jesuit was sent by the Governor at the solicitation of the Superior of the Jesuits, and was nicknamed by La Mothe Cadillac as "Monsieur de Trop."

Cadillac wished to go by way of Lake Erie, but the Governor decreed otherwise. They left the Lachine Rapids the 5th of June, the trees were just budding and game and fish furnished an abundance of food. In July they arrived at Georgian Bay, via the Grand River of the Ottawas, and coasting down the eastern shore of Lake Huron they reached, on the 20th, the river Ste. Claire and the old Fort St. Joseph, at the foot of Lake Huron abandoned by Duluth thirteen years before.

On the 24th of July, 1701, the head of the expedition rounded Belle Isle and soon landed at a little cove at the foot of the present Griswold street. The Ottawas and Hurons, whose villages were near, rushed down to welcome them, as did also a few French "coureurs des bois," who lived here. Two of their names are still preserved; Pierre Roy and Francois Pelletier.

On the following day, with great ceremony, pickets for a new fort on the site of an old stockade were erected and a store house built on the foundation of an abandoned one, previously constructed by the coureurs des bois for their winter supplies.

A salute was given from the guns brought for the new fort, which Cadillac christened Fort *Pontchartrain. On the 26th, Ste. Anne's day, with clerical ceremony, the foundation of the first church west of the Alleghanies was laid. Soon the stockade, which enclosed about an acre,† was finished, and the streets of Ste. Anne and St. Louis laid out and lined with the barracks for the troops and with houses constructed of hewn logs. Detroit was founded, and its prospects for a successful colony bright.

The fortune-teller's prediction, or at least part of it, was verified.

---

* Royal sanction for this name was received by Cadillac a year later, July, 1702.

† An acre of ground at the foot of a hillock on the river bank.

V

THE MAY POLE.

A Legend of "Faith and Homage."

SIX years had passed since the founding of Detroit. The frontier settlement began to assume a civilized aspect, and everywhere the touch of woman's hand had left its impress of comfort and refinement in the rude pioneer homes, which already extended along the Coté du Nord Est to La Rivière Parent (Bloody Run).

The undaunted energy of Cadillac was rewarded by a yearly increase of settlers, and the records of Ste. Anne's Church, the most accurate and authentic census of those early days, show from 1704 to 1707 an annual birth rate of fourteen.

La Mothe Cadillac made his first grant of land to his interpreter, Fafard, on the 10th of March, 1707. It was of a tract adjoining his domains, stipulating as usual for all his feudal rights, including the acknowledgment of faith, homage, and the planting of a May pole each year.

There was great commotion in the little colony on that bright May morning in 1707. The very atmosphere seemed pregnant with excitement, for so does a gala day drape itself around everything, clothe all in its vague fancies, and unconsciously communicate to us more or less of its color. We wear its cockade and favor in our dress and humor.

In front of the Seigneur de Cadillac's manor a great crowd had assembled, and from the eager expectancy written on every face, it was evident that some unusual event of interest was to take place. Slowly the form of Monsieur Fafard, the interpreter, was seen approaching with a stately, dignified step, each movement measured by the importance of the act of which he was to play the part of chief actor. The French understand perfectly that delicate art of investing even a trifling circumstance with an *entourage* of interest and display which gratifies their national vanity and love of glory.

Monsieur Fafard knocked at the Seigneur Cadillac's door, which was opened by the major domo. He inquired for Monsieur la Mothe Cadillac, who immediately stepped forth arrayed in his blue uniform and cavalier hat with white plumes. Monsieur Fafard uncovered his head and falling on his knees rendered fealty in the following manner: "Monsieur du Détroit, Monsieur du Détroit, Monsieur du Détroit, I bring you faith and homage which I am bound to pay you on account of my fief of De Lorme, which I hold as a man of faith, of your Seigniory of Détroit, declaring that I offer to pay my seignorial and feudal dues in their season, and demanding of you to accept me in faith and homage as aforesaid." As he saluted la Mothe and turned away, Francois Bosseron and others who had been granted fiefs offered their homage in turn.

Cadillac's house stood on the line of the present Jefferson Avenue before it had been sloped down to the Chemin du Rond.* A spacious "gallerie" adorned the front of the manor overlooking the smooth cut lawn and majestic river. A hole had been dug in the center of the lawn, and a tall, stately pole lay ready for raising. The branches had been trimmed off, except a little clump at the top called "the bouquet." And to this had been nailed a parti-colored pole, from which the royal flag with the fair Fleur de Lis of France floated. Smooth and white was the pole and to its sides

---

*Near the old Campau homestead.

blocks were nailed to allow a person to ascend. The firing of a gun was the signal to begin the ceremony. The Seigneur Cadillac had seated himself on the "gallerie," surrounded by his wife, children and officers. A delegation from the habitants approached and bowing low asked him permission to plant the May pole in front of his house. The request was graciously acceded to and Father Deniau knelt and offered up a prayer that the festivities might pass without accident. The pole impelled by strong, sinewy arms slowly rose, while the voyageurs broke out in their wild and inspired song, "Vive la Canadienne et ses jolis yeux doux."*

'The Seigneur de la Mothe Cadillac then advanced hat in hand and smilingly accepted the pole, and asked all to join him in watering it that it might flourish. A cask of *eau de vie* was tapped; cups and flasks of every design and shape were passed around, and Cadillac raised his silver goblet and pledged the King and the health of all present. An agile youth ascended the pole and

---

*The favorite boat songs of the voyageurs were "La Jolie Canadienne," and "A la Claire Fontaine." Mr. Marinier in his work, "The Songs of the North" ("Chants du Nord"), publishes nearly line for line these songs as belonging to his country, Franche Comté.

shouted, " Vive le Roi, Vive le Seigneur Cadillac du Détroit!" Then all caught the refrain :

"Grand Dieu sauve le Roi,
Grand Dieu venge le Roi,
   Vive le Roi !
Que toujours glorieux,
Louis Victorieux,
Voye ses ennemis,
   Toujours soumis,
      Vive le Roi !"*

The air was filled with cheers, the drums rolled, the trumpets sounded, and the guns completed the crescendo of acclamations. The pole was then ready to be blackened. This was done by Cadillac taking a gun loaded with powder only, and firing at the pole. Then Madame and Antoine, Jr., a cadet of fifteen, took their turn, followed by the members of the family and officers, and finally each of the habitants until the clean pole was blackened its whole length. It was usually left standing several months, to remove it being considered unlucky. Tables were spread under the shade of the trees, and refreshments in abundance served to all.

Then followed " La dance ronde " on the green sward. Cadillac gazed musingly on the pretty scene before him. The picturesque dress of the

---

*Vive le Roi. Handel appropriated this song for the House of Hanover. It was sung by the girls of Saint Cyr before Louis, 1652.

habitants and voyageurs, clad in their blue tunics and elk skin trousers, (whose seams were adorned with yellow fringe,) their buckskin moccasins ornamented with beads, their scarlet sashes, in which were kept the hunting knife in its silver case, blended with the soldiers' dress of blue, with its white facing. The officers wore gay uniforms and cavalier hats, with the showy ostrich feather, their hair hanging in long powdered queues tied with ribbon. The ladies, in their coquettish costumes, dashed with bright ribbons, resembled birds of paradise as they swayed to the graceful movements of the dance. Each lady's head was surmounted with a gay "fontange" or top-knot. It was a gay, light-hearted community, with few taxes to pay, simple tastes to gratify, friendly with the neighboring Indians. Peace, contentment and quiet happiness seemed to reign over this little Arcadia.

So thought Cadillac as at twilight, after the people had dispersed, he strolled with his wife in the King's Garden.* Human nature grows more communicative at this hour, thoughts which find no utterance in the broad light of day now glide forth from the heart. He told her that his dreams

---

* The King's Garden was between Jefferson avenue and Woodbridge street, near the site of the present Chamber of Commerce.

of ambition were about to be realized, notwithstanding the obstacles of his enemies. His colony was prosperous and his children would inherit a princely portion ; that his name would become historic and illustrious. Thus were they talking when two weary revellers homeward bound passed so near them that fragments of their conversation fell on their ears. "Yes," said Jean Baptiste, "our Seigneur and the Dos Blanc* carry themselves very high, with their silver plate and fine clothing, whilst we poor habitants must pay double for everything, even our petit coup 'd eau de vie ;" expressing a little of the communistic sentiments of the present time.

"Things cannot run very long thus," answered his companion. "My wife saw a few days ago 'le petit homme Rouge' and—" The rest was lost as the speakers disappeared. Cadillac's wife grasped her husband's hand convulsively and said: "Did you not hear ? 'Le petit homme Rouge' is the dreaded 'Nain Rouge.'"

"What of that?" said Cadillac.

"'Beware of the Nain Rouge' was what that

---

* Dos blanc. Literally "White backs." The officers powdered their wigs, and the powder falling on their coats whitened the backs. Many of the habitants encased their queues in eelskin to prevent the powder from ruining their dress.

prophetess told you; when he should come misfortune was nigh."

"Bah!" laughed Cadillac, "have you not forgotten that nonsense of a silly old fortune-teller? Let us return home."

Annoyed himself at the remembrance, and doubly so at his wife for unconsciously giving utterance to his vague uneasiness, they proceeded in silence.

Suddenly across their path, trotting along the beach, advanced the uncouth figure of a dwarf, very red in the face, with a bright, glistening eye; instead of burning it froze, instead of possessing depth emitted a cold gleam like the reflection from a polished surface, bewildering and dazzling all who came within its focus. A grinning mouth displaying sharp, pointed teeth, completed this strange face.

"It is the Nain Rouge," whispered Cadillac's wife.

Before she had time to say more, Cadillac's ill-nature had vented itself in striking the object with a cane he held in his hand, saying:

"Get out of my way, you red imp!"

A fiendish, mocking laugh pierced the still night air as the monster vanished.

"You have offended him," said Madame. "Your impetuosity will bring you and yours to ruin.

You were told to coax him—to beware of annoying this demon—and in your ungovernable temper you do just otherwise. Misfortune will soon be our portion."

Cadillac shortly afterward visited Montreal, was arrested through the intrigues of his enemies, and was compelled to sell his seigniory in Detroit to pay for his trial. He was removed to Louisiana as Governor, but died at Castle Sarasin, in France. His children never inherited an acre of his vast estates. His colony for the next hundred years was the scene of strife, war and massacre. Its flag changed five times; under that of the Republic it reached that glorious prosperity which the fortune-teller had predicted.

The Nain Rouge in the mystic past was considered the banshee or "Demon of the City of the Straits," and whenever he appeared it was a sure sign of impending evil. The night before Dalzell's ill-fated attack at Bloody Run, he was seen running along the shore. And in 1805, when the city was destroyed by fire, many an old habitant thought that they caught a glimpse of his malicious face as he darted through the burning buildings. On a foggy morning before Hull's cowardly surrender of Detroit, he was seen; but since then he has never reappeared, having, it is to be hoped, accomplished his mission. But the tradition still lingers among the old habitants that should misfortune ever threaten the bonnie City of the Straits, the Nain Rouge will again appear to give the signal of warning.

VI

THE PHANTOM PRIEST.

A Legend of Sainte Anne's Church.

ENEATH the sunny skies of Italy, on the banks of the Arno, not far from "Florence the Beautiful," the guide points to an old monastery as the last relic of an order now almost extinct, the Recollêts. With the deep feeling of interest which the slightest relation with home awakens in a foreign land, we turn with kindling eyes and tender emotions surging through our hearts, to gaze reverently upon the building as on the face of an aged friend. For from beneath that massive archway came forth a brave, courageous band, who first left the impress of their footsteps on the

virgin soil of our fair city. Within those gloomy walls they were trained by an austere and ascetic rule to meet those dangers and hardships inseparable from the explorations of a new country; and their heroic and almost supernatural efforts to convert the savage, have challenged the admiration of every age. Wherever the lily of France unfurled itself to the new breezes of America, the cross became its flag-staff, and the rude birchen chapel the mile-stone to record the missionaries' progress.

In 1670 there resided in Florence an ancient family of wealth and distinction named Del Halle. Its heir and last representative belonged to the "jeunesse dorée" of the day. He blended in his character that happy union of manly qualities which satisfied his haughty father's ambition, with those gentler accomplishments which made him the idol of his mother's heart. Early betrothed to Adelina, the daughter of a princely house, to whom he was endeared by the sweetest links of childhood, their future promised to be as unclouded as the sunny sky of their native land. But, like the simoon which blackens and lays low all over which it passes, the fell destroyer, "the black death" of the fourteenth century, again visited Florence, converting its palaces into charnel houses, its laughter into wails, its music into funeral dirges, leaving mourning and desolation hanging like a pall over the doomed city.

One morning young Del Halle awoke to find no response to his faint call of father or mother, no anxious, loving bride to catch the first dawn of returning consciousness. All had been swept away by the dreadful scourge, and he sat alone in his deserted halls, with memory and grief as his companions. The recollections of other days with their bright pictures and melodies would come surging up with their mocking delusions. But ever and anon the holy face of an aged Recollêt monk, at whose knee he had listened in early boyhood to the marvelous tales of the missionaries of his order in the wilds of Canada, came like refreshing dew to cool his parched soul. A few weeks afterward he knocked for admittance at the monastery gate, willingly leaving behind the pleasures, the refinements, and the brilliant prospects so alluring to his years. He exchanged the costly robes of the Florentine noble for the serge; the sword for the breviary, and thus at the early age of twenty did the heir of the Del Halle become the humble Frère Constantin. Ten years later he was sent to France and from thence sailed to Montreal. It was in Montreal he met La Mothe Cadillac, a young French officer, who was enthusiastic over a scheme of founding

a colony in the beautiful "Détroit du Lac Erie."
The frank, easy manners of the officer, his keen
intellect and his undaunted energy won the affection of Frère Constantin, who entered with all
ardor into the project of his friend.

Owing to various political causes, the necessary
permission and grants were slow in coming, but
Cadillac's patience and perseverance were at last
rewarded, and on the 5th of June, 1701, with his
little band of fifty soldiers and fifty Canadians,
with M. de Tonty as captain, Messrs. Dugué and
de Chacornacle as lieutenants, he sailed from Montreal. Frère Constantin Del Halle accompanied the
troops as chaplain, with Father Vaillant, a Jesuit,
who was going as missionary to the different tribes.
They arrived at Detroit July 24, 1701. Shortly
afterwards the tinkling sounds of the bell summoned the garrison to early mass and told that
the chaplain had already begun his work. By the
simplicity of his manners, the uniform sweetness
of his disposition and his austere life, he gained
the respect and affection of all. The deep shade
of melancholy which tinged his features told the
unfortunate that here was one who had known
sorrow, and who would lend a sympathetic ear to
the tale of their misfortunes and give the balm of
comforting words to their bruised hearts. The
little children drawn by the sympathetic instincts

of childhood would nestle their heads against him and shyly put their tiny hands in that of "le bon Frère."

Among the officers who were stationed at Fort Pontchartrain (as Cadillac had called his post, in honor of Jerome Phelyppeaux, Count Pontchartrain), was Etienne Veron de Grandmensil, keeper of the King's storehouse, who had become enamored with the dusky daughter of a Pottawatomie chief. This tribe, though friendly to the French, had resisted every effort to convert them to Christianity. A prophet of their nation had foretold that as soon as they should desert their Manitou for that of the white man, their lands would pass away, their wigwams be burnt, and their tribe scattered. Young de Veron, unable to overcome the obstinate prejudice of the old chief against Christianity, in the ardor of youth and passion, thought of allying himself to his Indian sweetheart by the Indian rights and betaking himself to the lodges of the Pottawatomies. Frère Constantin remonstrated with de Veron, who belonged to a noble family of Quebec, spoke of his father's hopes in him, his mother's love and of his duty as a soldier of France, told him to be patient, and the old chief would relent; but threatened, if he persisted, that he should incur the severest penalty of the church—excommunication. The

Indian maiden, worried by her father's command to wed a warrior of her nation, and stung by the apparent indifference of her lover, determined to put an end to her sorrow. Stealing away from her wigwam one stormy night under the kindly protection of the darkness, she plunged into the turbulent waters. An agonizing cry brought succour to the shores but she sank away before aid could reach her and a few days later her body was found floating in the Detroit.

Shortly after Frère Constantin was called temporarily away to another mission, and as days passed and he still lingered, although the coureurs des bois had reported his leaving the mission before them, Cadillac became uneasy; for time and the constant dangers and perils of those days only served to cement the links of a friendship so happily begun years before in Montreal. It was noticed that a cloud rested on Cadillac's brow which the tender solicitation of his wife, the fair Therese Guyon, could not chase away nor the infantile graces of his favorite child, the little Therese, the pet of the colony—as she was the first born and baptized in the fort—soothe by her caresses. Strange stories were whispered by the Indians to the soldiers, of a haunted spot on the Savoyard.*

---

*A beautiful stream which meandered above the present Russell

These reaching Cadillac's ear seemed to lend a color to his own sad forebodings of the fate of his friend. It was said that at dawn every morning faint sounds of a bell might be heard, and different parts of the mass distinctly made out, and that a voice, as mournfully sweet as if it had its source in unshed tears, would float on the midnight air chanting in Latin the Miserere.

It was noticed that for some time Churlioa, the Pottawatomie chief, sat before his wigwam, occasionally muttering to himself, then drawing his blanket over his head would vanish for days in the forest. The medicine men sadly shook their heads, and pointed significantly to their foreheads, saying the great Churlioa was bewitched.

One evening an Indian presented himself at the gate of the fort and asked to see Cadillac. Admitted to the commandant's presence, he stated that Churlioa had sent for the chief of the white men; that when the young men returned from hunting that day they had found their great chief lying as one dead in the forest. Cadillac followed his guide and soon stood by the dying warrior. He confessed having murdered Frère Constantin to revenge himself for his daughter's death. He feared to take his scalp as it might

street, crossed Congress and Larned streets and emptied into the Detroit near the Michigan Central Depot.

betray him, and bring upon his tribe the vengeance of the French. He had known no peace since, for the spirit of the priest seemed to haunt him in the moaning reeds. He heard his voice in the rustling leaves, and a strange fascination led his footsteps to the spot where the murder occurred. That the previous night he wandered there, the bright moon illuminated the forest and he could see as in the daylight, that the tall form of his victim stood in his path, and with outstretched arms besought him to have his bones lie in consecrated ground—that until then the Indian would be haunted—and with the sound of rushing waters in his ears the chief knew no more until he awoke in his wigwam and sent for Cadillac.

The sad news was soon known in the colony, and Cadillac went to the spot indicated by the Indian. In the hollow of a tree, covered by leaves, they found the body of Frère Constantin. They placed it on a litter formed of the fragrant boughs of the spruce. Father de la Marche came to meet the body, which was borne by the officers of the Fort followed by the weeping people. Tenderly they laid it to rest in the consecrated earth as he had so earnestly desired. The last of a princely race rested in the forest of a new world. No stately mausoleum received his remains; no pompous tablet told his lineage, or recorded his deeds.

The pines chanted his requiem, the tears of his flock were his epitaph, and the innocent hands of children strewed his grave with the wild flowers of the woods.

In 1724, when the new Ste. Anne's Church was built, Alphonse de Tonty had the remains removed from the humble grave and placed in a vault which he had himself prepared beneath the altar, in the presence of all the people of the colony, to whom Father Bonaventure related the edifying life and death of the saintly priest, Frère Constantin del Halle.

FRANCOIS AND BARBE.

A Legend of the Habitants.

IT WAS in the early days of the colony that Barbe Loisel sat alone with her little children in the rude settler's cabin on the banks of the Detroit. Without raged the fierce winter's blast. In the huge fireplace the flames danced merrily above the hickory logs, and the iron crane held the steaming pot-au-feu. She was waiting for her husband's return from a distant expedition, whither he had been sent by de la Forest, Commandant of Fort Pontchartrain. It was Francois Fafard, dit Delorme, a noted interpreter. Theirs had been among the first marriages recorded in the register of the little church of Ste. Anne, and their signatures, with their quaint characters, are still to be seen to-day. She had been the widow of Francois Gautier, Sieur de la Vallée Rancée, a French officer of high rank, who was killed in 1710. Her youth, beauty and unfortunate condition appealed to the manly heart of Delorme, who won her, and his strong arm shielded her from many dangers inseparable from a frontier life. To-night he had promised to return, and she knew it could only be an insurmountable obstacle that could cause him to break his word.

The blood-curdling howling of wolves were doleful symphonies to ears strained to catch the first sound of familiar footsteps. At each weird note of the storm the little ones would nestle closer to the mother, drawing in security even from the touch of her garment such is the wonderful witchery of maternal affection. To quiet them and to lull the beating of her own anxious heart, she told them many Indian legends of the past.

Of the great rivalry which once existed between the east and west wind. How the east wind, being victorious, prevailed for seven years, until the waters of the rivers and lakes had risen to such a height as to threaten inundation to the lodges and corn-fields of the tribes living on the banks, when the Great Spirit, seeing the misery of his children, and listening to their petitions, recalled the west wind from behind the moun-

tains whither it had been driven, and caused it
to reign for seven years, thus forcing back the
waters into their original channel. Many to-day
notice the fact relative to the waters of the Detroit, and we find a memorandum of it in the journal of Capt. Morris, of her Majesty's Eighteenth
Infantry, who visited Detroit in 1764: "That the
waters of these lakes rise for seven years and fall
for seven years; in fact there is a seven years'
tide; and Gen. Bradstreet whilst encamped on
the shores of Lake Erie, lost a great many boats
and a large quantity of provisions and baggage
by a sudden washing of the waves against the
shore. What struck him as a strange phenomenon was that during the heaviest part of these
swells no wind was perceptible, a fact he fully
illustrated by placing soldiers along the banks
with lighted candles, not one going out."*

Then the good Barbe told them how severely
the Great Manitou had punished disobedient
children in days gone by. He had condemned
them to flit about in a circumscribed space as

---

*Considerable doubt still exists as to the cause of the periodic
rise and fall. The floating ice from Lake Huron one spring so
blocked up the channel of the Ste. Claire River that Lake Ste.
Claire and the Detroit River were almost drained. The water
had receded from the shore of Grosse Pointe nearly four miles.
A similar freak of nature occurred in 1818. In winter the ice
seems to have some effect.

little winged insects and guarded by a stern old Manitou. That one day a little brother of these naughty children had resolved to go in search of them. He started out bravely, walked all day, and towards night becoming exhausted, fell asleep beneath the leaves of the aspen tree. The spirit which is believed to inhabit it appeared to him and said: "Follow me and I will lead you to your brothers and sisters." He awoke and found himself going up higher and higher until he reached cloud land. His guide then gave him a bow with a quiver full of arrows, and said: "Always shoot towards the north; keep one arrow to return with; as soon as you reach water throw some on your brothers and sisters and they will return to their natural shape, and the evil spirit will never be able to molest them again." At each flight of a magic arrow a long, solitary streak of lightning appeared like a golden rent in the sky, through which the child could catch glimpses of the beauties hidden there. At last he saw where his brothers and sisters were confined and, aiming straight, soon opened the door to the imprisoned ones, who came through the golden crevice in the form of myriads of little insects which flitted around him joyfully. During his delight he forgot the injunction of the fairy and sent his arrow away from the north, when suddenly a distant sound like thunder was heard and a fearful voice full of majesty and passion, said: "Presumptious one, for having dared to invade the kingdom of the Manitou, you shall be made an example to deter others from such profane ambition." He was turned into the heat lightning which is always seen on the northern skies on summer evenings. And the little insects, paralyzed by that dreadful voice, perished in one night. How frequently on a summer's night we see countless numbers of these insects, the familiar "June flies" of the Detroit, hanging to the lamp-posts, apparently dazed from some unknown cause, and strewing the sidewalks to be crushed under foot. The Indian mother never whips her child, but always throws cold water in its face, thus punishing it and preventing its being changed into an insect or bug.

In this way the pioneer's wife was wont to hush her little ones to sleep; the Indian legends were their lullabys. It was growing late, and still Delorme returned not. Barbe shaded her eyes and gazed out into the night,—darkness everywhere; the voices of the storm were whispering their doleful cadences, but it seemed as if above these she heard the loved one calling her. Thinking her imagination had been overwrought by the stories she had related, she closed the door. But an impulse stronger than herself bade her open it again and distinctly came the words, in a mournfully sweet voice, "Barbe, come to my assistance!" (Barbe viens à mon secours.) The dogs broke out in a desponding wail, as if they felt the passage of some unseen phantom.

She no longer hesitated, the woman's sublime unselfishness conquered the natural timidity of her sex. Taking the musket from the wall, throwing the powder horn and bullet bag over her shoulder, she boldly stepped out into the Thebaïd darkness. Bravely she went on, though fancy sketched everywhere frightful spectres in the trees, imagination draped phantoms in the swaying branches, to which fear lent the finishing touches. The howling of the wolves gave voice to the desolation of the scene. There are times when nature, weary of her muteness, seems to lend tongues to stones, voices to the reeds and to the winds, language to the articulate lamentations of the brute creation. That voice which ever and anon arose flute-like through the frightful orchestral recital of nature's woes was her compass. The howling sobs of the dogs, so allied to terror of the supernatural, warned her that she had neared her destination. She fired her musket upward, and by the flash saw that a giant tree had been felled by the strong arm of the tempest. Moans issued from near, and she soon learned that her husband lay beneath it. Powerless alone, she flew to the fort, returning shortly with several brave soldiers who extricated Delorme from his perilous position. He was tenderly carried to his home and his injuries examined and fortunately pronounced not fatal. His companion was dead, his skull having been fractured. They asked how it was that his voice had reached Barbe. He could not explain save that he had implored the spirit of his friend to send Barbe to him, as it would pass near her home, only a short distance away. And the strong bond of friendship which even death could not sever, sent its message to Barbe as it glided towards the spirit land.

VIII

THE DEVIL'S GRIST.

A Legend of Wind Mill Point.

FORT Pontchartrain from its advantageous position as key to the Upper Lakes, was coveted by the English, who finding all their efforts futile whilst so jealously guarded by France, determined to wait until the rigid watchfulness of the garrison should relax by apparent security. In the early spring of 1712 the opportunity seemed to present itself. De la Forest, the successor of La Mothe Cadillac, was detained in Quebec; the Hurons, Ottawas and other Indian allies of the French had not returned from their winter hunting in the gloomy recesses of the forest, whilst the fort was manned by a small number of men with Du Buisson as its temporary commander.

A band of Macoutins and Outagamies* or Foxes, were sent by the English, who lit their camp-fire beneath the shadow of the fort, and pitched their tents in seeming confidence almost within the range of its guns. But Du Buisson was too well versed in the craftiness of the Indians, and too experienced in their peculiar mode of warfare to be deceived by this semblance of friendship. Nor did he neglect those measures of prudence and forethought necessary to secure him against a siege. Under pretext of fearing an attack from the Miamis, he ordered all the grain to be brought into the fort from the storehouses, which were built outside of the fortifications, and caused the buildings to be destroyed as a precautionary measure against fire. He sent word to the Hurons and Pottawatomies that he was in danger, and to hasten to his assistance. Daily the number of the Foxes seemed to increase, and seeing that their lawless acts met with no punishment, they became more and more insolent. The little fort held bravely on, and though a powerful and merciless foe lay crouching at its gates, watch-

---

*Outagamies. The ancient spelling for Ottawa was Outaouas; Pottawatomie, Pouteouatamie; Iroquois, Iroquese.

ing its every movement, and ready to pounce on its prey, the garrison seemed not to notice it, and went along its daily routine.

But beneath that calm and indifferent exterior many were the sad and weary hearts ; for all were under the influence of a feeling which was calculated to paralyze the energies of the boldest, since, unless succor should soon arrive, their loved lily of France, crimsoned by their hearts' blood, would be replaced by the cross of St. George, and their reeking scalps, hung at the savage's belt, would record the fearful history of Fort Pontchartrain. The brave Du Buisson would try to rouse them by his example, relating the deeds of French soldiers at other far and desolate forts, whilst the gentle chaplain, Deniau, would tell them to place their trust in God, to remember their distant homes and their loved ones. A new light would come to their eyes, heavy from long, weary vigils, and new courage steal into their hearts and nerve their arms to deeds of daring.

At last Saguina, Chief of the Ottawas, and Makisabe, Chief of the Pottawatomies, with their dusky warriors in all the full regalia of war and the haughty waving crests of the eagle and bright sashes of vermillion, lit up the landscape, while their savage war whoops awoke the echoes of the forests, and found a response in the anxious

hearts of the besieged garrison. Branches of the
Sacs,* Illinois, and even Osages and Missouris,
had hastened to the relief of the fort, borne along
by a spirit of hereditary warfare against the
restless Foxes and Macoutins, or "dwellers in the
prairies," who were the roaming brigands of the
wilds of America. Saguina presented himself at
the fort and said to Du Buisson : "Father, behold
thy children compass thee round. We will, if
need be, gladly die for our father, only take care
of our wives and our children, and spread a little
grass over our bodies to protect them against the
flies."

The Foxes were driven back and forced to throw
up entrenchments and were reduced to the last
extremity. Availing themselves of a stormy night
they crept away under the friendly shelter of the
darkness, and fortified themselves at Presque Isle,
near Windmill Point, eight miles distant from
Detroit, and at the entrance of Lake Ste. Claire.
When the Hurons and other French allies discovered their flight they were soon in pursuit. For some
days the Foxes held their fort but at last fell beneath the tomahawk of the besieger.† In vain Du
Buisson endeavored to stop the fearful massacre,
but his voice fell on ears open only to catch the

---

*Pronounced Sauks.
†More than a thousand Indians were killed in this battle.

agonizing wails of the victims, the sweetest music to the Indian warrior. The ground was saturated with blood, and the dead as numerous as the leaves of the forest; the blood-curdling yells of the conquerers, mingled with the groans of the dying, made so fearful a picture that the French soldiers, accustomed to war and carnage, turned away with sickened hearts. The allies carried away their dead and wounded, but left the remains of the conquered to the mercy of the elements and to become the prey of the birds. Shortly afterwards the last remnants of the Fox nation came to Presque Isle to "hold the feast of the dead" and to cover the bones of their warriors that they would no longer be excluded from the happy hunting ground of their ancestors. To-day their bleached bones are exposed by the ruthless plow, and any one interested in Indian antiquities can have that interest gratified by a visit to Presque Isle.

Years after the dreadful massacre which converted the beautiful spot called Presque Isle into the grave of the Fox nation, a stone mill was built there by a French settler, who came to reside with his sister Josette, undaunted by the current traditions which peopled it with the spirits of the departed warriors. Jean was a quiet, morose man, different from the laughing, careless, pleasure-loving Canadian,—for rare were his visits to the fort, and it was noticed that he never lingered over his *cidre*, nor spoke to the smiling, piquante daughters of the habitants. Men shrugged their shoulders, and the fair damsels pouting their pretty lips would cluster around the coureur des bois, who, going everywhere, was the recognized gossip of the day, and ask him why Jean was so different from others, while with a wise look on his face, the coureur would reply that Jean had met with a disappointment in his early youth, and had since kept shy of the fair sex, by a vow which was then customary, for when a man's addresses were once refused he seldom tried a second time.

Josette was much older than her brother, and by dint of thrift and economy had saved enough to become a half owner in the mill. The favored few who had tasted her "croquecignoles"* and "galette au beurre," spoke of it as an era in their existence. Naught disturbed the monotony of their lives; each day was but a repetition. The river flowed calmly on, the birds sang their songs—for nature has no moods, they belong to man alone. At last Josette fell sick. Jean attended her as

---

*Croquecignoles. A sort of doughnut. Galette au beurre. A kind of bread, to which is added milk and butter.

carefully as he could, and like a prudent man, would frequently ask her to whom she would leave her interest in the mill. Irritable from suffering, she became annoyed at his importunities, accused him of taking care of her for the sake of obtaining her money, and told him "she would leave it to the devil." Jean tried in his clumsy fashion, to soothe her. He sent for some of his kindred to reason with her, but they only infuriated her the more, and she solemnly declared that not one of them should have her share in the mill, but "she would sooner leave it to the devil."

Josette recovered, however, and with that perversity born of stubbornness, would not relent. A few months afterwards she was found dead in her bed, having died suddenly. That same night, whilst the candles threw their dim shadowy light in the room of the dead, a furious storm arose, lashing the waves against the shore, the winds howling fiercely around the point, the black clouds chasing each other across the lowering skies, as lurid gleams of lightning and deafening reverberations of thunder, made all the habitants shudder while they crossed themselves and told their beads. All at once there came so tremenduous a shock that it seemed to swallow the island. The old stone mill was rent in twain. A pungent smell of sulphur filled the air, and a fiendish laugh was heard loud above the raging storm from the shattered ruins. The arch fiend had come to claim his share.

For years afterwards when a northeast storm blew from the lake, making night hideous by its echoing peals of thunder, it was said that a hairy figure, with a horned head and forked tail tipped with fire, his mouth and eyes darting forth ruddy flame, could be seen in the mill, trying to put together the ruined machinery to grind the devil's grist. And the lonely wayfarer to Grosse Pointe would see the marshes around Presque Isle all illuminated by flames, called by the habitants feu-follet,* which would try to inveigle the unhappy traveler and bring him to help grind the devil's grist.

---

*Feu-follet. Will-o'-the-Wisp, Jack-o'-Lantern.

IX

JEAN CHIQUOT.

A Legend of Charlevoix's Visit.

A GRAND council of all the neighboring tribes of Le Détroit had been convened early in the spring of 1721. Thither came the witty, brave, but deceitful Huron, the Athenian of the American forest; the stern, Spartan-like Iroquois, the gaudy Ottawa, and eloquent Pottawatomie resplendent in swaying feathers and brilliant in dashes of vermillion.

Alphonse de Tonty, Baron de Palude, Commandant of Fort Pontchartrain, explained to the red warriors the object of the assembly. By his side stood a man of fine, imposing appearance whose dress revealed his priestly character, and whose eager, observant eye glanced from object to object with that lightning flash of mental photography which transmits to the pen with wonderful faithfulness its impressions. He was introduced as the bearer of messages and presents from Onontio to his forest children. It was the distinguished traveler and priest, Charlevoix, whose writings are our chief authority as to the condition of the West in those early days.

One edict in an instant electrified the statue-like audience, causing the mask of immobility to drop before the sweeping blast of kindled passion which broke forth in a sullen roar like a mighty cataract. It was the prohibition of selling liquor to them,—a custom introduced by Cadillac and continued by his successors, notwithstanding the earnest protestations of the Jesuits, who saw in the dim future the fatal calamities which would befall the colony engendered by this disastrous traffic.

Amidst the deep grunts and murmurs of dissent, Onanguice, the great Pottawatomie orator rose, and in an impassioned voice with torrents of burning eloquence, poured out his indignant protest. "We know that firewater does us no good, it steals our tongues and our hands. You have made us taste it, and now we cannot do without it. If you refuse to give it to us, we shall get it from your enemies, the English." Drawing his blanket around him he haughtily stepped out of the council, followed by all the warriors, who filed along the narrow trail in silence to the Pottawatomie village, two miles below the fort.

De Tonty was annoyed and thought the measure unwise, and still more for personal reasons, as, if tradition be true, he was not averse to exchange a gill of brandy for a pound of beaver skins, for then every white man's hand weighed a pound.* De Tonty called one of the traders and told him in confidence to take a cask of brandy to the Pottawatomie village, to secure thus the valuable furs which the Indians were known to have taken during their winter hunting, and which owing to the edict would pass into the hands of the English; that he (De Tonty) would protect the trader (Jean Chiquot) from all harm—the proceeds to be divided between them. Jean started off. Arriving at the village he found the old sachems in council, and the younger ones roaming about idle. To these he proposed the game of bowl, the stakes being measures of brandy which he exchanged for their furs. The offer was eagerly accepted, and

---

*It was a custom then among traders to put their hands on the scale in weighing furs, thus pressing it down, unbeknown to the Indian. Consequently the term, "Each white man's hand weighed a pound."

each Indian rushed to his wigwam to bring his pelletries, until there rose a pile which made Jean's eyes glisten and his imagination swim over with the probabilities which the sale of these suggested.

The Indians are inveterate gamblers and will stake anything they possess with the most sublime recklessness. Human nature is in every age the same where traffic is concerned, though culture and education apparently refine the method and soften the terms—but the underlying principle remains. The shrewd trader of those days understood as well as the present one, the art of playing skillfully on the foibles of others and making of them a source of revenue.

Sides were chosen and the air rang with the wild, guttural sounds of the savages as the bowl touched the ground and the little, painted pieces of bone were tossed in the air. The seductiveness of the game penetrated into the grave council of the sachems and drew them into its fascinating vortex.

Jean's gains in furs steadily increased, and so did the Indians' desire to obtain the coveted liquor, which was drank as fast as won. Towards night the pandemonium of giddy excitement subsided, and the players lay strewn about in helpless intoxication. Jean strapped his heavy pile of skins to his back and slowly wended his way towards the fort. It was a glorious evening. Drops of moonlight fell through the budding foliage of the trees and glistened like scattered gems in the grass. Jean was in that happy frame of mind which a good bargain concluded by a generous draught of eau de vie is apt to produce, and thought how bright and attractive the world looked to him in contrast with the morning, when he first heard the edict. Whether he looked different to the world was a question Jean did not ask himself.

Suddenly his meditations were rudely broken by a number of "Dames Blanches,"* who were dancing around an oak tree, and who, as soon as they saw Jean, caught hold of him and made him dance until he was ready to drop with exhaustion. He who a few moments before felt as if he trod on air and walked like a god on the clouds, now thought his feet imprisoned in irons. In vain he pleaded to be let alone; wild laughter was his only answer. His pack fell off, and with swift hands the fairies had each secured one of his valuable furs. The physical fatigues of the man were forgotten in the natural instincts of

---

*Literally "White Ladies," a term used to designate the little fairies which were then implicitly believed in by many of the superstitious habitants.

the trader, and jumping up Jean pursued the "Dames Blanches." Round and round they flew until Jean grew dizzy, and then just as he would think he had secured his prize the fairy would vanish in the earth, leaving a spring of clear water in which he could hear the mocking laughter of his tormentor. Almost distracted and aching in every bone, he picked up the few remaining furs which had escaped the clutches of the fairy robbers and again started on his homeward journey.

He was obliged to pass near the Sand Hills,* which were used by the Indians as a burying-ground. On several mounds he noticed a number of caged birds,† which fluttering against their bars, made a weird sound that sent a doleful message to Jean's heart and a cold chill down his back, for he was not as brave as an hour before. Just as he was urging his weary, battered feet to the utmost, he heard a wild, demoniacal shriek, and looking up cautiously saw on a branch of a tree a Loup Garou who

---

*This property was afterwards deeded by the Pottawatomie chiefs to Robert Navarre, Jr.

†When an Indian maiden died the Indians imprisoned a young bird until it first began to sing, then loading it with kisses and caresses they loosed its bonds over the grave, in the belief that it would not fold its wings until it flew to the spirit land and delivered its precious burden.

gave him a malicious leer and jumped so suddenly on Jean's back that both rolled down the sand hill. Jean's blouse flew open and out came his beads which he always carried "*en cas.*"

When the trader got up and rubbed his eyes and straightened his bruised limbs he looked about in vain for his foe, then ran breathlessly to the fort where he related his strange adventures, but was met with smiles of incredulity.

Early next morning he started with several skeptical companions for the scenes of the night before. To their amazement the grass seemed scorched around the oak tree and everywhere little fountains were bubbling forth their strange tale. Where the Loup Garou had disappeared a sulphur spring had sprung up. The place was ever afterwards called by the French "La Belle Fontaine," by the English, *Springwells*, and according to the tradition of an old habitant, "La Belle Fontaine water gives complexion brillante, wile ze sulphur spring cure ze internal complaint."

X

THE WIDOW'S CURSE.

A Legend of the old Pear Trees.

IT WAS Mardi Gras evening in 1735. A furious storm raged outside, the wind howled through the leafless trees, and the restless waters of Lake Ste. Claire were fast imprisoned in ice.

But there were sounds of merriment in the house of Charles Chauvin. It was built of hewn logs and fronted the lake, where the new water works now stand. The lights from the windows were like bright beams of promise in that waste of darkness. A party was gathered in la salle à manger (dining-room) to celebrate Shrove Tuesday. The floor was partly covered with a rag carpet, whose bright tints lent a glow of warmth to the room. The furniture was covered in chintz and the legs carved in grotesque effigies of birds, the classifying of which would have driven Cuvier to despair. A cupboard reaching to the ceiling displayed rows of blue china, of a thickness which would now alleviate the fear of many house-keepers and defy the rough handling of the modern servant.

Before an open fireplace with its crackling, hickory log, stood three girls, each armed with a long-handled frying pan and trying to toss pancakes—"virez les crêpes"—a custom still preserved in many of the old French families. Near by were several who poured in the batter as fast as the pans were emptied, whilst la dame Chauvin placed powdered maple sugar between the cakes and piled them up in pyramid form. The art consisted in tossing the light cake as high as possible while turning it. It was accomplished by a dexterous motion of the hand, and merry were the peals of laughter which greeted the unfortunate one whose cake fell on the glowing coals.

The table was set with savory meats, and all ate with a relish inspired by the morrow which would be Ash Wednesday, for Lent then was rigidly kept. The forfeits were redeemed all save la dame Chauvin's, who only was released when she promised to tell them a conte (story). "What shall it be?" she said. "Oh tell us, grandmère, about the old mill on Connor's Creek and the twelve pear trees in our orchard," answered the bright-eyed Susanne, a little thing of twelve.

Caressing gently the dark hair of the girl, the old dame began :

Just such a night as this, many years ago, Felix Robert brought his young wife to live in the mill he had just built near Pont Rouge (Red Bridge) on Connor's Creek. His brother Louis accompanied them. It was impossible to find a greater contrast. Felix was short, with laughing eyes and a pleasant word for everyone. He loved a ball or a race on the ice with that true zest of enjoyment which the old habitants possessed in so eminent a degree. Louis was tall and spare, with a yellow, lean face, silent and reserved in manner. Seldom did he enter in the simple pleasures of those days. His presence seemed like a pall, and the old habitant would say : "C'est un oiseau d'une mauvaise augure" (he is a bird of ill omen). The mill prospered,—they appeared to live in harmony ; children gathered around the hearth, but the morose Louis paid little heed to them, for his two cows seemed to be the only things for which he entertained affection.

Felix was fatally injured by a falling tree and expired soon after, though not before he had made Louis promise to watch over his wife and children, and to set aside for them a half of the proceeds of the mill.

After his brother's death Louis grew more and more absorbed in himself; the children kept out of his way as if by instinct, hushing their infantile prattle when his shadow fell across the threshold; and he developed the true traits of a miser. Food was measured for the home consumption, and he looked scrupulously after every detail of the simple menage. In vain the widow pleaded she was starving. The inflexible man would not listen. He would not allow them out of his sight, and no complaint could she make, for he gave her no opportunity of conversing with any one, and few came to the mill except on business, and none cared to loiter.

One by one the children drooped and were laid to rest. The mother implored in vain more food and warmer clothing, and soon her frail form told that her days were numbered. One day, escaping the severe vigilance of her stern guardian, she wandered off towards the pear trees, the stately survivors of the age of Louis XIV., which, proud in their decay, leave no successors, as if unwilling to allow their race to be perpetuated in new soil. Her absence was discovered, and fearing she might betray his miserly habits to the neighbors, Louis came to lead her back quickly to the house, saying he could not afford to feed lazy people; he had supported her long enough. It was time to work.

Raising her hands to Heaven she cried out: "Woe, woe is my lot. I call these twelve trees, which are named after the Apostles, to witness my wrongs. May your property be swept away, your cows refuse to give milk, and you yourself be haunted by me and by my children. You have defrauded the widow and the orphan; you have starved them to death and broken a solemn promise to the dead. The pear tree under which you stand will be shunned by its comrades, and like Judas, stand alone, for the curse of the widow rested on an object beneath it."

Shortly afterwards she died. The habitants were indignant, and avoided Louis more than ever. It was soon rumored that strange things were going on at the mill. Weird sounds were heard on Sunday nights especially, and one with more courage or curiosity than the others peeped through the cracks of the mill and saw a great number of black cats, "all dancing like Christians," he said, whilst the time was beaten by phantom hands which seem to float about in the air. The people shook their heads mysteriously, saying that it was "le-Sabbat des chats"* (the

---

*Cats were believed to be in league with the devil, who fre-

cat's Sabbat) and hinted at secret dealings with the evil one. The cows sickened and died, the habitants refused to bring their corn to the grist for they heard such piteous wails and saw there cadaverous, ghostly hands as if imploring for food. The old pear tree was found one morning mysteriously separated from its companions on the north side and its withered leaves and drooping boughs spoke of some blight which had robbed it of its proud and stately beauty.

Lewis saw all this and his land passed into the hands of strangers. He left, no one ever hearing again of him, and with him died the Widow's Curse.

---

quently borrowed the form of a black cat. Some believe that the male cat has the power of assisting at the "Sabbat," to prevent which they frequently cut a piece off the tail or ear (C. Vaugeórs, Histoire des Antiquities de la Ville de l'Aigle, p. 586).

XI

LE LUTIN.

A Legend of the Goblin Horseman.

IN 1796, when the Stars and Stripes first waved in proud exaltation over the haughty standard of England, there lived on the banks of the beautiful Lake Sainte Claire, at Grosse Pointe, an old French habitant named Jean Marie Tetit, *dit le merveilleux.*

It was a noticeable custom in those early days to give each other soubriquets, and with that wonderful perceptiveness of the French which almost amounts to a sixth sense, the nickname would be a happy hit at some marked characteristic. To-day some of the descendants of these old families are known only by the soubriquet; other branches still bear the original name, but in several cases the old name has entirely disappeared.

Jean Marie was a famous raconteur, equaling Vernon, of the Long Bow. On autumn afternoons the habitants would congregate at his house, and only when the shadows had lengthened into twilight and the church bell pealed the evening hour, would the spell-bound listeners slowly come back to the realities of life and give a thought to the impatient housewife and waiting meal. Perhaps it was the soft beauty of the scene, lit up by the hazy, luminous atmosphere peculiar to Indian summer which gave a more brilliant hue to the glowing forest trees, a rosy tint to the placid waters of the lake, a touch of picturesqueness to the group of habitants, with their eager, expectant faces, which lent its seductive charm to Jean Marie's imagination. Quietly taking a few whiffs from his loved pipe filled with killikanick (a weed used by the Indians in the absence of tobacco, and from which a fancy brand of Virginia tobacco takes its name), and in the midst of that hushed silence which is in itself an eloquent tribute to the raconteur's powers, he would relate the wonderful stories of

"Le Lutin," and "Le Loup Garou" (wehr-wolf); the first of which is as follows:

Jacques L'Esperance, or Jaco, as he was familiarly called "for short," on the death of his father found himself sole proprietor of a fine "concession" at Grosse Pointe. The soil was rich, the arpents numerous, and all bespoke goodly promise to the industrious farmer. Jaco was not lazy, but somehow his efforts did not meet with the success which crowned his neighbors. His taste ran towards horses, and he became one of the most celebrated horse breeders in that section of the country, and was referred to as an oracle on the subject. He was in fact the Tom Ochiltree of his day. It was in the winter races on the ice along the lake shore and Grand Marais that Jaco gained his greatest triumph. Perched on the high seat of his cariole, well protected from the rude blasts by his Indian-blanket coat with its deep black stripe, the hood of which was drawn tightly over his head, a wide red sash encircling his waist, his hands covered with mole-skin gloves, his ringing voice could be heard loud above the others as he urged his little Canadian pony on: "Avance donc Caribou! avance Lambreur!" With lightning speed he flew, and ere the sound of his voice had died away only a tiny speck on the ice marked the steed and its driver. Arriving at the Hotel of the Grand Marais, under the genial influence of the "liqueur de pêche" (peach brandy) and the subtle incense of flattery, in his enthusiasm he would claim for his pony a speed which even in these days of St. Julien and Maud S., with their unprecedented records, would be considered marvelous, "clearing at a bound," he said, "cracks in the ice twenty feet wide."

We must acknowledge that the present Canadian pony is a degenerate scion of a fine stock, for they are mostly descended from a cross between a noble stallion, caught wild on the prairies of Mexico, the breed half Arabian and Spanish, (having been introduced there by Hernando Cortes in his conquest of that country in 1520 and brought here by the Indians in 1750,) and a splendid Norman mare, brought to this country by Gen. Braddock and taken from him at his defeat near Fort Duquesne (Pittsburgh). Ten years later Capt. Morris, of His Majesty's Seventeenth Regiment of Infantry, who visited the country of the Illinois under the guidance of Jacques Godfroy in 1764, mentions in his journal seeing this handsome milk-white horse still in possession of the Indians.

Jaco could be seen every day driving his favorite along the lake shore, and L'Éclair (lightning), as he called her, carried herself as if conscious of the admiration which she created.

One night, with the rest of the habitants, Jaco went to Antoine Griffard's, whose magic violin could compel the most unwilling feet to chase the flying hours. At dawn, going to the stable to harness L'Éclair, for he had a long drive, he found her all covered with foam, her mane all tangled with burrs. Annoyed that anyone should have played him such a trick, but not wishing to express any suspicion for fear of making a disturbance, Jaco like a prudent man held his tongue, but determined that when he came to another ball, a less valuable horse would be his companion. But the next morning, and the next, he found his favorite with dejected head, tired and wearied as if she had been driven hard all night. He put a padlock on his barn door, strewed ashes about to discover the footsteps, yet to his great amazement he found L'Éclair in the same lamentable plight, the padlock intact and no impress on the ashes.

At length Jaco, much perplexed, went to consult one of his great cronies who listened attentively to his story, and at its conclusion, gazing around cautiously as if afraid of being overheard, whispered hurriedly, "C'est Le Lutin qui la soigne," (it is the goblin who takes care of her).

Le Lutin was a dreaded monster which had

haunted the Pointe many years before, and was supposed, when for some reason he took a dislike to an habitant, to tantalize him by riding his finest horses by night. Jaco was not credulous. He shook his head smilingly and said it was the work of some enemy jealous of L'Éclair. He had heard of "La bête a Cornes," or horned beast, as some called Le Lutin, but only thought of it as one of the stories his mother would relate to him in his infancy as she rocked him to sleep. His friend told him he should brand his horses with a cross, or put an amulet or charm about their necks. Jaco returned home sad and dejected. He had not met with the counsel he wished, and determined to find out for himself who this enemy was.

One bright moonlight night he stationed himself at his window where he could command a good view of his barn without being seen himself, and armed with his trusty rifle, waited for his foe. Not a sound disturbed the night air save the low murmuring of the waters against the beach, the lone cry of the whip-poor-will, or the occasional plash of some restless bullfrog. All nature seemed to slumber. Suddenly a sound like the troubled neighing of a horse fell on his strained ear, and keeping his eyes on the barn doors, he saw them noiselessly open and his favorite L'Éclair, trembling like a leaf, fly out. On her back was a fearful apparition. Jaco was no coward, but he felt his courage oozing out at his knees, cold chills chasing each other down his back, and great beads of perspiration standing on his forehead. The monster resembled a baboon, with a horned head, a skin of bristling black hair, brilliant, restless eyes, and a devilish leer on its face. It clutched with one hand L'Éclair's mane, and with the other belabored her with a stick of the thorn bush, for the fiend rode without saddle or bridle.

Jaco recognized in an instant that his rifle was powerless against such a foe, and like a bright inspiration came to him the old mode used to exorcise a demon; he seized the holy water font, one of which hung at the head of every good habitant's bed, and threw it and its contents down upon the monster as he passed beneath the window. A demoniacal shriek rent the air, the horse snorted, reared, and notwithstanding the efforts of the fiend, plunged into the chilly waters of the lake. Jaco rushed in pursuit, but when he arrived at the beach, only the circling eddies marked the spot where the affrighted animal and its fiendish rider had disappeared. Firing his rifle to awaken his neighbors, who, unaccustomed to such signals, rushed to find out what was the matter,

Jaco related his adventure. His disordered appearance, the absence of the horse, the broken fragments of the holy water font, and the thornbush stick dropped by the goblin, confirmed his tale. Like a judicious man he marked all his horses thereafter with a cross fearing the return of Le Lutin.* And to this day the Grosse Pointe habitants retain this custom, and whenever in the early morn on going to the barn they find a favorite horse reeking with sweat and foam, and with mane all tangled as if by the claws of a beast, they shake their heads mysteriously and say that it is Le Lutin come again.

---

*Aubrey in his "Miscellanies" mentions the practice for preventing nightmare in horses, "to hang in a string a flint with a hole in it, by the manger; but best of all they say hung about their necks, and a flint will do it that hath not a hole in it. It is to prevent the nightmare, viz: the hag from riding their horses that will sometimes sweat all night. The flint thus hung does hinder it." Herrick says:

"Hang up hooks and shears to scare
Hence the hag that rides the mare
Till they be all over wet
With the mire and the sweat,
This observed, the manes shall be
Of your horses, all knot free."

XII

THE WARRIOR'S LOVE.

A Legend of Bois Blanc.

THE admirable site of Bois Blanc on the Canadian side of the mouth of the Detroit River, commanding the main channel, attracted in the early days of the colony, the eye of the experienced soldier. It was for a long time a mooted question whether Fort Pontchartrain would remain at Detroit or be removed to this island. It received its name from a superb forest of white wood, but it was shorn of its crown of glory by an act of vandalism during that brief panic of patriotism in 1837, called by the self-styled "patriots" The Patriot War. They felled these glorious giant trees for purposes of military observation. Here Tecumseh and his warriors in 1813 awaited the issue of the Battle of Lake

Erie, and as soon as the fatal import to the English was known, the chief crossed over to Malden, then garrisoned by Proctor. To his amazement he found the British commander making hurried preparations to evacuate without the faintest show of resistance. Forced to passive obedience by circumstances he could not crush and despising the cowardice of the act, Tecumseh begged Proctor to leave him arms and ammunition, that he and his braves might defend the fort against the victorious Americans. The British general's refusal to do so called forth the stinging and contemptuous remark from the outraged savage, "that he (Proctor) was like a fat cur sneaking away with his tail between his legs, after making a great show of courage."

After Charlevoix's visit in 1722 to these regions, a Huron mission was established on this island under the direction of Fathers Potier and de la Richardie. Several hundred of the tribe came, and soon their tents blossomed like wild flowers through the woods. The joyous laughter of children sent its warm, exhilarating tones over the waters. The sweet sound of the bell from the rude, birchen chapel bade the echoes of the forest awake and respond gladly to the message of redemption. But the English with their eager desire to extend their trade to the West, sowed seeds of dissension among the Indians and poisoned their hearts against the French. In 1747 a general uprising of all the tribes took place, and Bois Blanc became the theatre of a conspiracy to massacre the French at Fort Pontchartrain. It was betrayed to De Longueil, the Commandant, who used wise and precautionary measures which not only stemmed the tide of savage mutiny, but restored peace and order. Still it was considered more prudent to remove the Huron mission nearer the fort. Bois Blanc was abandoned, and the settlement located at Sandwich, the present church there being the successor of the one built by Father Potier.

One incident of early days invests this island with romantic interest, where the noble heart of a Huron chief became the sacrifice of a glorious self-devotion. Many years have passed since that act, but it is still handed down from generation to generation. White Fawn was the daughter of a celebrated Huron brave who had accompanied DeBellestre to Montreal to see the Governor, and whilst there had died. Her mother who belonged to the pale-face, had faded away many years before. The maiden was the pride of the tribe, and her admirers, as numerous as the leaves of the forest, endeavored to woo her by their peculiar mode of courtship. They would whittle tiny sticks and throw them at her. If the girl picked them up the Indian's suit was favored, but if she heeded them not he carefully collected and buried them with his unrequited affection. White Fawn had shyly hesitated over the love tokens of a distinguished warrior, thereby conveying that she needed more time.

One day he returned from the forest, bringing a wounded hunter, whom he had accidentally shot. The medicine men worked their charms over the stranger, and the maiden nursed him tenderly, for she knew that if the pale-face died there would be a shadow on the heart of the warrior. But soon a mist came over her eyes, and the voice of the brave which had been as the summer wind, to which she bent like the reed, no longer whispered its sweet song. The traditions of her mother's race found their way to her heart; the words of the pale-face became stars and the heart of the maiden the lake whereon they rested, and as he looked down he saw no other light reflected there. The warrior soon noticing the change, upbraided the maiden, who bowed her head in silence. The bright knife of the Indian gleamed a second in his uplifted hand, but the next instant it was whirled far out into the river and burying its keen edge in the peaceful waters. "No," said the Indian, "the arm of Kenen is stronger than his voice and his anger like the mighty tempest that sweeps over the forest, but he is not strong enough to strike the heart of the White Fawn."

Shortly afterward the tribe removed to their winter hunting grounds, and the Iroquois, the hereditary foes of the Hurons, becoming annoyed at some act, warred against them. Among the prisoners that they captured was the paleface, whom they brought to Bois Blanc. Here, where everything spoke to him of his former happiness, was he to take his last farewell of life, with no friendly voices, or kind, comforting words to soothe his agony. A hush fell on the assembled Indians gathered around to see the pale-face die. A haughty warrior advanced, and despite the usual decorum of the council, the name of *Kenen* ran in sounding tones around the circle. "Have the Iroquois heard the name of Kenen?" he asked. "There is no greater in his nation," was the reply. The dark eye of the Huron flashed proudly. "Let the pale-face be free," he said, "a Huron chief will take his place." The cords were severed which bound the white man, and the Huron whispered to him: "There is sorrow in the heart of the White Fawn, and the eyes of Kenen cannot look upon it. When he is gone the White Fawn will be happy in the shelter she loves." So quickly was all done that the pale-face had not time to remonstrate. He was borne along to a canoe, and soon swift oars wafted him from the fatal spot. When the bright moon rose, the spirit of the warrior rested on the bosom of his fathers.

XIII

THE MIAMI SEER'S PROPHECY.

A Legend of Braddock's Defeat.

DE CELERON, whilst commander of Fort Pontchartrain, had received orders to reassert the French claim to all the country west of the Alleghanies. He did so by ordering the English traders away and placing at the junction of the Alleghany and Monongahela Rivers a silver plate, upon which was this inscription: "In the year 1749 during the reign of Louis XV., King of France, we, Celeron, commander of a detachment sent by the Marquis de la Galissonnière, commander-in-chief of New France, for the restoration of tranquility in some villages of Indians in this district, have buried this plate at the confluence of the Ohio and Tchadakoin this 29th day of July, near the River Ohio, otherwise

Beautiful River, as a monument of the renewal of possession which we have taken of the said River Ohio and of all those that therein fall and of all the said lands on both sides as far as the sources of said rivers, as enjoyed, or ought to be enjoyed, by the preceding King of France, and as they therein maintained themselves by arms and by treaties, especially by those of Ryswick, of Utrecht, and of Aix-la-Chapelle."

Petty hostilities between France and England had been growing warmer for years, until in 1755 they had reached a degree when open warfare seemed inevitable. England determined to stop the so-called encroachments of the French by sending a vast army to join the recruits raised by the Colonists along the Atlantic. The latter were to light the torch of war by attacking the French posts between Fort Duquesne (Pittsburg) and Niagara.

In the early spring of 1755 DeBellestre, the commander of Fort Pontchartrain, received orders from the Governor General of New France to summon every able-bodied man to arms and to rouse the Indian tribes even as far as the Mississippi. For many days the little fort was the scene of unusual commotion. Scouts had been sent to the Indian tribes of the North and West, detachments of which were constantly arriving

in answer to the summons. DeBellestre was to
remain at the fort; his uncle, Alexis des Ruis-
seaux, was to command the outgoing regulars.
The militia were awaiting orders for an immediate
march to the Ohio, with detachments of Indians
and coureurs des bois, commanded by Jon-
caire, Isidore Chesne, Godefroy, Campeau, Medor
Gamelin, La Butte and Jadot. Pontiac with the
Ottawas, Sauteurs, Poux, and all the tribes of the
North, Takay of the wicked bands of Hurons,
Baby and Peatan of the Christian band, and Gros
Oreilles (Big Ears) and Kenouchamek of the
Loups and Shawnees, hastened to obey the summons. They encamped two miles above the
Huron mission (now Windsor, opposite Detroit).
As the time approached for the departure of the
expedition, DeBellestre, well versed, like all the
French officers, in Indian customs, called a gen-
eral council of all the tribes, to be held on the
site of their encampment. Belts of wampum
were prepared, barrels of eau de vie opened,
cloths, blankets, ornaments of silver, guns, balls,
powder and knives were lavishly distributed
as presents from Onontio to his dusky children.
Rumors of the extraordinary strength of the
English marching force had reached the savages.
Some of the wiser and cooler of the chieftains
wished to obtain further information as to the

risk to be incurred. Bellestre was compelled to harangue his savage allies. "My children," he said, "are you ungrateful for all the kindness Onontio has shown you? His enemies have come upon him like a band of wolves at night, and he depends upon his children to run to his aid. New presents will be distributed to you on your return, and to the families of those who fall a double supply shall be given."

A noted chief of the Miamis, and a renowned seer and dreamer, rose to reply. "What my father says is true, and my heart sorrows that any warrior should refuse to obey Onontio's call. Last night in my sleep I saw a lofty mountain, along whose sides marched countless numbers of pale-face warriors. Their brilliant scarlet blankets glowed like the leaves of the sumach in the sun. Their polished knives glistened like the sleeping waters of the lake under the light of the full moon. On a snow-white horse sat their proud leader, and his eagle eye seemed to pierce the cowardly heart. Great guns on wheels, drawn by stout horses, followed in the line which trailed like a serpent through the valley. Last came countless 'long-knife' warriors clad in coats the color of the sky. On a black horse at their head rode a young chieftain whose stern, majestic face and pale blue eye made me shrink. At last, I thought, the tribes are to be driven from their hunting grounds. Desolation will encompass every wigwam of the West. As I was about to flee I heard a shout, and one of our French brothers, clad in an Indian hunting dress with a silver gorget on his breast, leaped from the woods and sprang down the hill-side. As he waved his sword above his head I saw the warriors of our tribes, the Miamis, the Ottawas, the Loups, the Hurons, the Shawnees and others dart from behind every tree, and pour in a fire which fell like hail upon the proud foe, and as the leaves before a hurricane the red-coats went down. In vain their brave chief tried to rally them; they fled, and their leader was slain. Had it not been for the pale blue-eyed chief of the 'long-knives,' every scalp would have hung at the belts of our warriors. Though bullet after bullet was sent after him, and all around him fell, he was untouched, for he bore a charmed life. The great Manitou had taken him under his wing. Many of our braves returned to their camps loaded down with plunder, and one brought the beautiful snow-white steed of the red-coat leader. Years hence I see her colts, swifter than the wind and numerous as the blades of grass scattered over the boundless plains of the West. Brothers, I have done."

The warriors who had clustered around listening eagerly to their-inspired seer gave utterance to many ughs! ughs! expressive of their delight and full faith in coming victory.

The expedition started out. How the brave Beaujeu and his Indian followers brought about Braddock's defeat, and how the savages came to regard Washington, the leader of the "long-knives," with superstitious awe are matters of history. It is not so well known that from Braddock's white mare and a spirited stallion of the West, left by Cortes, the hardy, swift Canadian and Indian ponies so famous along the lakes, are descended.

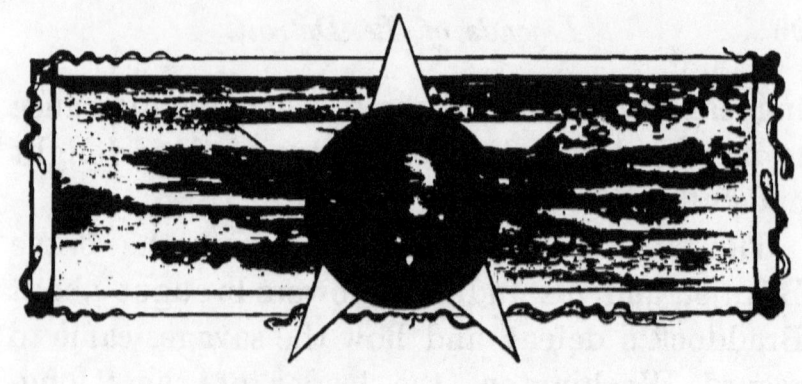

THE BONES OF THE PROPHET.

A Legend of Isle au Peche.

SAILING along the Detroit and Lake Ste. Claire, the eye is charmed by the beautiful islands which nestle on the bosom of the bright waters. The Indian legend regarding their origin is a pretty and poetical conception. One little one just above Belle Isle—"Peach Island,"* as it is called—is a bit of wandering fairyland, around which romance has

---

* On account of a misnomer Isle au Pêche has been Anglicised into "Peach Island," whereas it should have been translated Fishing Island, on account of an old fishery established there as early as 1722.—(Charlevoix.)

woven its gossamer web and which history has gilded with its magic pencil.

The spirit who inhabited the Sand Mountains, called the "Sleeping Bear,"* had a daughter who was endowed with such seductive beauty and matchless perfection that the mother feared she would be stolen. The spirit hid her in a box, tying it by a long string to a stake on the beach, and every day would draw the box in to feed the fair maiden and comb her yellow tresses.

The South Wind passed once at this hour, and saw her. He murmured caressingly his soft and balmy sighs through the golden meshes of her flowing hair. This gentle wooing gave birth to that beautiful, but too brief, Indian summer. The North and West Winds heard of the mysterious beauty through their zephyr couriers. A fierce rivalry ensued and the elements were at war. A violent storm arose, snapped the frail thread which held the box to its moorings, and it drifted along borne by the waves to the lodge of the Prophet, the Keeper of the Gates of the Lakes, who resided at the outlet of Lake Huron. Joyfully he received as his bride this beautiful waif of the foamy billows.

---

*Sleeping Bear. A point of land on the eastern coast of Lake Michigan, noted for the prevalence of storms in its vicinity.

The dusky Pandora brought evil in her train. The storm revived in all its fury, sweeping away the lodge and portions of the land of the old Magician. These floated down and formed the islands in the Detroit River. The old Prophet was buried beneath Isle au Pêche which became the Mecca of the Ottawa warriors.

The fragments of the box formed Belle Isle, and the great Manitou, in order to prevent any more contentions, girded the island with rattle-snakes. No other sentinels were required to guard the imprisoned beauty than these reptiles with their bewitching craft of eyes and forked tongues, and which were held in superstitious veneration by the Indians.

It was in October of 1762 that the wonderful "pluie de suie" or "Black Rain"* occurred; this day is known in history as the "Black Day of Canada." Clouds of inky blackness hung over Detroit. Water, land, everything was enveloped in this sombre drapery of darkness. The howling of wolves and the despairing moans of animals, combining all that is savage in beast and fearful in man, prophesying and deploring the approaching misfortune, lent terror to this weird carnival of Tenebrae. When the rain fell, the drops emitted a strong sulphurous odor, and

---

*Literally, "rain of soot."

were so deeply colored that they could be used as ink. Philosophy and science gave their solution of this strange phenomenon, but the learned explanation fell on deaf ears, for the Canadians and Indians read for themselves the mystic language foreboding disaster.

Pontiac, the wily diplomat of the forest, whose eloquence, subtlety and consummate ambition, commanded the admiration of his civilized foes and gained for him the title of the Mithridates of the West, viewed these signs as prophetic warnings. Following the ancient customs of the Indians who prepared themselves for great undertakings by fasting,* he dismissed his squaws and retinue to the Ottawa village on the eastern shore of Le Détroit, and went alone to Isle au Pêche to consult the Prophet whose bones lay beneath. There, amid the calm and picturesque scenes of nature, and in that harmonious silence so eloquent in its muteness, he conceived the plan of that wonderful coup d'etat which has blazoned his name on history's page, by which he aimed to destroy all the English forts on the

---

* The Indians believed in fasting, and thought that by weakening the body, they entered into closer communion with the spirit. The dreams or visions which came to them whilst in this condition were carefully treasured, and frequently guided and influenced them in all their undertakings during their lifetimes.

same day, and to drive the invaders from the country. Brought up in the solemn grandeur of the primitive forests where no passing mood or fancy of the mind but had its image or echo in the wild world around, the autumn blast as it shrieked its discordant symphonies through the forest poured its fierce energy into his heart. The sullen roar of the waves as they dashed against the beach in foaming rage inflamed his resentment; his fevered imagination saw the phantoms of his race urging him on to defend their resting-place from the despoiling hand of the invader. In the moaning reeds the voice of the Prophet bade him gather his tribe, to rise up, to be strong as the whirlwind and to go forth like the lightning and scatter the English like leaves before the autumn wind.

The evening of the seventh day he returned to his tribe, emaciated from his long vigils and fasting. He sent his messengers with the war-belt of wampum* and the tomahawk stained red in token of war, from tribe to tribe, from village to village.

---

*The Indians among themselves had no written contracts, the belt of wampum supplying the place, as a reminder of a bond or promise given. It was painted different colors to suit the occasion ; *red*, for instance, signifying war, etc. The belts were carefully preserved and handed down in the tribe from generation to generation.

Pontiac, as chief of the Metai, a magical association among the warriors of the lakes, obtained great influence over all the tribes which enabled him to play on the superstition of his followers. He called them to a great council, and in burning words of eloquence spoke of the wrongs and injuries they had received from the English, and revealed to them the command he had received from the Prophet of Isle au Pêche. The plan gave satisfaction to the grave and silent warriors, who, drawing their blankets over their heads, retired to their villages to await the signal which was to return to them the hunting-grounds of their forefathers.

XV

THE BLOODY RUN.

A Legend of Pontiac's Siege.

ONE bright May morning in 1763, whilst Pontiac and his savage hordes lay before Detroit, two men were engaged in earnest conversation in front of the council house within the besieged place. The more conspicuous was a tall, determined looking man, clad in the uniform of an English officer, whose features were almost picturesque in their ruggedness. This was Maj. Gladwyn, commander of the post. His abrupt and impatient gestures were in striking contrast with the easy, graceful manners of his companion, Maj. Jean Chapoton, the first surgeon of Fort Pontchartrain, who, several years previous to the English conquest, had resigned from the French army and settled in Detroit.

It was evident from the eager, anxious glances they cast along the street every now and then, that they expected some one. Presently they were joined by a younger man of medium height, but of powerful physique, and whose dress bespoke preparations for a long and tedious journey. The new-comer was Jacques Godefroy de Marbœuf, whose kindred, Godefroy de Linctot, and Godefroy de Tonnancour, had come to Canada in 1636. Left an orphan at a tender age, he had been brought up by his eldest sister, the wife of Trotier des Ruisseaux, the sister-in-law of De Tonty and DeBellestre, two French Commandants of Fort Pontchartrain. It was the English policy to conciliate the French element who were placed in a strange and trying position, like prisoners on capitulation, and who preserved neutral ground in the quarrel between the English and Indians. Godefroy's thorough knowledge of the Indian habits and customs, his love of adventure and his family connection, had made him an invaluable acquisition to Gladwyn. He and Maj. Chapoton had been sent to try their influence on Pontiac, but in vain, and it was at the request of the chief (Pontiac) himself that Godefroy was now going to the country of the Illinois, where a French soldier, Monsieur de Leon, still retained command, the object being to bring the officer or another influential one to convince the Indians that France had no longer claims on Detroit—a delusion they fondly cherished and in which they were encouraged by many of the French habitants.

Gladwyn seemed to approve of the project, and had been waiting to give Godefroy a few instructions before he started out with Mesnil Chesne. Godefroy commended to the officer's care his infant son and his young relative, Madeleine de Tonnancour, and started on his hazardous journey.*

Madeleine de Tonnancour was an orphan and had been educated at the Ursuline Convent at Quebec. Endowed with great personal beauty, and possessing more than the usual accomplishments of the Canadian girl, she became the belle of the gay capital of New France. At a ball she met the dashing officer, Capt. Dalzell, then attached to Sir Jeffrey Amherst's staff; it was a case of love at first sight. Madeleine's friends who bitterly resented the invasion of the English, opposed the idea of her marriage with an English officer, and being a minor and therefore subject to the control of her relatives she was obliged to succumb to her fate. She entered

---

*Infant son was afterwards Col. Gabriel Godefroy, for forty years in the American service as Indian Agent and interpreter.

a convent, but having no vocation conceived the romantic plan of burying herself with relatives who resided in the far off frontier post, the Detroit of Erie. Here she arrived just as the Indian troubles were commencing. The society of the little colony was far different from that of the gay capital, and no doubt moments of regret came for her hasty act of self-exile.

Gladwyn would occasionally call at Madame des Ruisseaux's, at whose house on Ste. Anne's street Madeleine resided, and he would try and soothe the ladies' apprehensions. For the times were critical, and it required a brave and courageous heart to witness the fearful sights of which they were powerless spectators. Ghostly processions of massacred captives would float down on the river past the fort during the day, while night was robbed of its darkness by the fire-rafts sent by the wily Indian to destroy the two small vessels, the only hope of the beleagured garrison. Gradually Gladwyn's visits became more frequent, and it was soon evident that the English officer found his chief pleasure and forgot his precarious position in the smiles of the beautiful Madeleine. She was flattered by his attentions, and his society beguiled many an anxious hour. But when he laid his heart at her disposal she turned a deaf ear to his entreaties, becoming more distant in her intercourse with him. Possessing a nature not easily balked in its purpose, he determined to find the cause of his rejection, and leave no means unturned to secure her.

Matters stood thus when one sultry July day, Godefroy returning, reported himself to Gladwyn. He was well received by the officer, though he brought news of the ill success of his mission. Gladwyn then spoke of his affection for Mlle. de Tonnancour, and tried to enlist the sympathy of Godefroy and his influence with his beautiful relative, holding forth promises of interest, etc. Godefroy, much surprised, refused, but couched his reply in terms as courteous as possible, Gladwyn's habits of life being well known. He spoke also of the enmity which he would incur from Madeleine's relatives, who might think he had thus purchased advancement. Gladwyn turned haughtily away, saying something which roused the blood of the Frenchman, who, forgetting the habitual prudence and policy used by the habitants in their intercourse with the English, made a bitter retort and left the officer's quarters. That same evening Gladwyn penned an epistle to Sir William Johnson in which he made a most sweeping assertion, imputing to the French, and particularly to Godefroy and his friends, the blame for the Indian outbreak.

On Godefroy's return to his sister's, he remarked that he would have to be cautious and be ready to leave the fort at a moment's warning, for, said he, "I noticed from the glitter of the Major's steel gray eyes that mischief is in store for me," and related the interview with Gladwyn.

Poor Madeleine was in despair feeling as if she was born under an unlucky star to bring misfortune upon all, and kept secluded for several days. One evening at twilight tired of the house she determined to stroll out. Passing the water-gate she sauntered towards the Rigolet des Hurons (Savoyard) that flowed back of the pickets. On its sloping banks was a stately oak, within whose hollow trunk a pious hand had placed an image of the Virgin, for the spot was pointed out by tradition as the place where the saintly Father Constantin had been murdered many years before. As she walked along she noticed the new moon over her right shoulder—a lucky omen, she thought—and remembered that in the morning whilst sadly musing on her misfortunes a little wren,* the bird "au Bon Dieu,"

---

*This bird was fabled to have brought fire from Heaven to earth. He brings good fortune, and he who tears down his nest brings the fire of Heaven on his own household.

had come to build its nest under her dormer window.

We are prismatic in our nature and reflect every varying mood of our surroundings. Can it be wondered at, that those brought up in the wild, half savage life of the frontier, caught that tinge of the supernatural which hides in the heart of primeval forests, blends itself in the myths of the Indians, and appeals to that superstition which lurks in every heart, investing each freak of nature, every unusual occurrence, with an occult and mystic meaning? Thus, to one of Madeleine's temperament, nature could never be mute. Should a little flake of snow suddenly dart across her path, it was the soul of an unbaptized infant, she thought, condemned to wander. If a white pigeon flew near and was exceptionally tame, it was the soul of some departed friend for whose repose she had forgotten to pray. The cheerful cricket on the hearth must be welcomed, for he brought joy and peace; the little swallow could always bring you a stone that would restore sight to the blind, and any young girl whose heart was pure could, by touching the flower marigold with her bare, dimpled foot on a certain night, understand the language of birds. Nor did the fair maiden shriek out when the industrious spider, whose web extended across the ancient rafters, dropped on her plump neck, for it was a sign of money coming. And whosoever heard the first cuckoo of spring singing was sure to keep safe what money he possessed the rest of the year. Madeleine knelt before the humble shrine and besought her Heavenly Mother to obtain from her Divine Son guidance out of her troubles.

With a lighter heart she rose from her devotions and turned her steps homeward. Suddenly a hooting owl flew past her, muttering its dismal sound, and the distant mournful notes of a tolling bell fell on her ear. A prophetic feeling of impending woe seized her. Ere she had time to analyze the sensation the cannon of the fort thundered forth and was instantly answered by a salute from the water.

Hastening her steps she saw coming up the river a long line of batteaux crowded with men, proclaiming that at last the expected relief had come. The troops landed and were warmly welcomed by the garrison, and she heard the name of Dalzell,* which fell like a bright ray on the dark drapery of her forebodings. As soon as Dalzell learnt that Madeleine was in the fort, accompanied by Gladwyn he sought her presence. The blushing cheek and gladsome light which

---

*Dalzell is pronounced Dalyell.

lighted up the dark eye revealed to the Commandant why he had pleaded in vain. He soon took his leave, and Madeleine laid her troubles before her lover. "We shall now put an end to all this," he answered. "I have three hundred veterans, and with the Major's permission will soon demonstrate the folly of remaining here pent up at the behest of the savages." "Alas!" replied she, "you know not the craft nor the power of this Indian chieftain. Besides, I have a strange presentiment that if you undertake so hazardous a project we shall never meet again." In vain he tried with all a soldier's ardor added to a lover's tenderness, to lull her fears; but a vague, inexplicable something seemed to warn her that this was their last meeting on earth.

The graphic pen of history has chronicled the result and verified the girl's apprehensions—how the consent of Gladwyn was apparently reluctantly given; the early march at dawn of Dalzell and his men to Pontiac's camp; the ambuscade that he fell into, and how the waters of Bloody Run were crimsoned by the blood of his brave soldiers; and finally the heroic death of the gallant Dalzell in trying to save a wounded comrade. When the terrible news was brought to Madeleine she nobly dried her tears while trying to alleviate the sufferings of the wounded which each boat brought to the fort. Overhearing some one say that Dalzell's head was placed on a picket, she lost consciousness, and ere many days had passed had joined her lover in a better land. Gladwyn seemed ever after like one on whose mind some great burden of sorrow was resting. His bitterness towards the French increased, and on Bradstreet's arrival Godefroy was found under arrest and condemned to death by a court martial on the grounds of having incited the Indians to revolt. He was released on condition of acting as interpreter to an English officer, whose expedition to the Illinois country probably saved the British army from destruction.

The stately tree on Jefferson avenue known as the Pontiac Oak, is all that is left to remind one of that bloody romance; the stream itself has disappeared.

XVI

LE LOUP GAROU.

A Legend of Grosse Pointe.

ANY years before Commodore Grant, formerly in command of a British vessel on Lake Erie* built his great castle at Grosse Pointe, a trapper named Simonet had settled near there on the margin of the lake.

His young wife had faded away in the early years of their married life, but as if in compensation, had left the little prattler Archange to wean him from his grief and to cheer his loneliness. And the strong, hardy man, with his

---

*Erie in the Huron language signifies *cat*.

sunburnt face and brawny arms hardened by toil and exposure, in his yearning love for his child, learned to soften his rough manners and soothe her with the gentle ways of a woman. Anxiously he watched the unfolding of his "pretty flower," as he called her, and with a solicitude touching in its simple pathos, he would select the softest skin of the bear to keep her feet warm, search for the brightest wings of the bird to adorn her hat. When she grew up he taught her to skin the beaver, muskrat and deer which he brought home, and to stretch them out on the drying frame near the house. He was wont to boast that no one could excel Archange preparing the poisson blanc (whitefish), poisson doré (pickerel), or give that peculiar shade of brown which is in itself an art, to the savory cochon au lait (sucking pig).

She was as light-hearted as the cricket that chirped on the hearth, and her cheery voice could be heard caroling away to the music of her spinning wheel. In the long winter evenings her deft fingers would plait the straw into hats which found a ready sale, and which, added to the sum she gained by her knitted socks and dried corn, enabled her to secure many little articles that her vanity suggested to enhance her charms. For the Canadian girl, in the rude surroundings of her forest home, was as anxious to please and bewitch by her toilet as her more favored Parisian sister; the instincts of the sex still lived in the wilderness. At the corn-huskings and dances on the greensward Archange was the reigning belle, and held her little court of homespun dressed youths fascinated by the magic of her dark eyes, her brunette complexion with its warm glow, her raven tresses and piquante tongue. Many admiring eyes followed her lithe form as she tripped in marvelous rapidity "la jig a deux," or as she changed into the more graceful, swaying motion of "la dance ronde."

Pierre La Fontaine, a young farmer, wooed the fair Archange, and the light of happiness which crept into the dark, winsome eyes shyly raised to his in answer, told him he had not pleaded in vain. Simonet gave his consent and blessed them, rejoicing in the happiness of his child. On bright moonlight nights Pierre would come to take his fair fiancée out for a row. Impelled by his sinewy arm, merrily would the fragile canoe dance along on the rippling waters lit up by elfish moonbeams, and the lovers would talk about the wedding, which was soon to take place, for Pierre's new cabin that he was building for his "bonnie bride" was nearly completed, almost a mile distant from his father's, where the willows stooped so low that their graceful tresses touched the water. Archange would tell him of the red cow her god-father had promised her, and the additions to their humble menage her god-mother had made.*

One evening as Pierre placed Archange on the beach near her home and she lingered, following him with her loving eyes as he swiftly rowed away until he had disappeared and only the faint echo of his Canadian boat song floated towards her, she was startled by a rustling sound near by. Looking up a wild shriek escaped her, for a monster with a wolf's head and an enormous tail, walking erect as a human being, crossed her path. Quickly the cabin door was thrown open by Simonet, who had been roused by his daughter's scream. Archange flew into her father's arms and pointed to the spot where she had seen the monster, but the animal surprised by the light, had fled into the woods. Simonet's face grew pale as Archange described, as accurately as her fears had allowed her to see, the apparition, and he recognized the dreaded Loup Garou.† He quieted her,

---

*It was customary for the god-mother to give the bride the necessary articles for a bedroom, hence the term "la chambre garne" (the furnished room), "le lit garni" (the furnished bed).

†The term Loup Garou. Its Latin equivalent in the Middle Age was gerulphus. The German wer-wolf and English were-

and soon with the happy faculty youth has of
forgetting disagreeable things she was dreaming
of Pierre and her wedding. Long after the girl
slept Simonet sat musing. He lit his pipe seeking companionship in his thoughts. That it was
the Loup Garou or wehr-wolf Archange had seen
he did not doubt, and he recalled all the traditions of his youth, how the dreaded monster had
stolen young children; sometimes a young man
would be inveigled away into the forest and
never heard of afterwards, and his fate conjec-
tured by some, having seen the wolf dressed in
his clothes. It was for young maidens he

---

wolf have the same meaning. Oservais de Tilbury in his Oisior-
tés Imperiales gives the following explanation: "We have
frequently seen in England," says he, "under the influence of
certain conditions, men transformed into wolves, species of men
called by the French garous (gerulphus), and the English, were-
wolf." Were in English signifies man, and wolf, loup—man-wolf.
In Longfellow's Evangeline the following relative to the Loup
Garou and other old Norman superstitions is found:
"He was beloved by all, and most of all by the children,
 For he told them tales of the Loup Garou in the forest,
 And of the goblin that came in the night to water the horses,
 And of the White Létiche, the ghost of a child who unchris-
   tened
 Died, and was doomed to haunt unseen the chambers of chil-
   dren,
 And how on Christmas Eve the oxen talked in the stable,
 And how the fever was cured by a spider shut up in a nut-
   shell,
 And of the marvelous powers of four-leaved clovers and
   horse-shoes,
 With whatever else was writ in the lore of the village."

showed the greatest fondness, and "it boded no good to her whose path he crossed." Several attempts had been made to kill the beast, yet all failed and it was thought he bore a charmed life. But one adventurous hunter determined to try his skill, so he molded a bullet from silver coin and patiently waited for his victim "to cross his path." The charmed missile sped towards its destination and instead of killing the monster only *severed his tail*, which was secured, dried and stuffed. It was the wonder of the whole country, and was worshiped for years by the Indians as a powerful fetich. Simonet hoped all would be well, still a strange feeling came over him like a presentiment, which in vain he tried to shake off.

The wedding day at last dawned, the sun shone brightly and all nature seemed to smile on the fair bride of that day. Archange, arrayed in her simple dress of white batiste, was a charming picture of innocence and beauty. Going into the woods to gather her bouquet of wild flowers, "the Garou again crossed her path." but this time she forgot her fears in her sense of the ludicrous at the figure of the beast, which had robbed some habitant of his coat and hat, and had carefully tucked his tail away. In his hand he held a cane, which he twisted in a nonchalant manner; he was a fair caricature of a Parisian dandy. Seeing she did not fly in terror, he was encouraged to give her a lovesick leer displaying his wolfish tongue and teeth. Scattering her flowers, Archange fled and arrived breathlessly home just in time to slam the door on the wolf, which had pursued her there.

Soon after she joined Pierre and hand in hand, followed by all the habitants in their holiday attire, they entered the little church of logs hewn square, the interstices chinked in with clay, the roof of overlapping strips of bark. In front of the altar, decorated with flowers arranged by loving hands, they knelt. Father Freshet, who had baptized Pierre and Archange and prepared them for their first communion, now came to unite them in the holy bonds of matrimony. After the ceremony they went to the sacristy and inscribed their names in the registry, then hurried off to Pierre's new house, where the festivities were to take place. On the green lawn in front of her new cabin the blushing Archange greeted all her friends. The Seigneur of the neighborhood came to claim the right of premier baiser (first kiss). The refreshments were in abundance and all gave themselves up to the enjoyment of the moment, for the Canadians dearly loved a wedding and kept up its festivities for days.

Whilst the merry making was at its height the dreaded Garou with a rush like the wind sprang into their midst, seized Archange and escaped with her into the forest. All were paralyzed by the sudden, daring deed. But Pierre recovering, started in quick pursuit guided by the despairing cry of Archange, followed by all the men, whilst the women and children said their prayers and gave vent to loud lamentations. Long after the shadows had fallen they returned to report to the anxious, trembling crowd, and their sad, dejected faces spoke of the fruitlessness of their search. The monster had baffled them. But Pierre returned not. He was shortly after found by his friends wandering around and around a swamp, and clutching a piece of white batiste. When questioned as to how he had obtained this clue to Archange, he returned a maniacal stare and with a blood-curdling shriek, would have jumped into the swamp if he had not been held back by his companions, who with sorrowful accents said "La folie du bois." He would always return to the same swamp, remaining there for hours gazing vacantly in the weird reflections in its slimy, stagnant waters, until some friend led him home.

At the marriage of his sister, which occurred about a year afterwards, Pierre, always dead to the outside world, seemed to be roused by the preparations. After the ceremony he rushed into the woods as if in pursuit of something. He did not return until nearly sunset when he was seen, with wild eyes, flying hair, his clothes torn as if by briers, chasing a Loup Garou to the very edge of the lake. All stood petrified by the strange apparition and feared a repetition of Archange's fate. But the animal, seeing no escape, stood on one of the boulders strewn along the shore and stretched out his arms as if beckoning to some mysterious one. A large cat-fish was seen to rise on the surface of the water and opening its mouth the Loup Garou vanished; and to this day no Canadian will eat catfish. The footprint of the wolf is still shown at Grosse Pointe indelibly impressed on one of the boulders.

THE OLD RED MILL.

A Legend of the English Rule.

IN THE former district of Springwells (at the foot of 24th street), the present city of Detroit, in 1795, stood an old red mill. It was circular in form, and had a stone foundation supporting an upright wooden body, with a conical roof.

It was a weird sight on a moonlight night with its long arms stretched out as if beseeching aid, and its tattered sails drooping mournfully telling its melancholy story like a flag at half-mast. The beholder involuntarily felt that creeping shudder of awe which contact with the mysterious calls forth. There are buildings like human beings upon which nature places her signet,—a history.

The Indian, as he returned from his day's hunting, ladened with the trophies of his skill, pushed his canoe out into the stream far from its shadow. The gay, joyous voices in the pleasure boats of the officers of Fort Lenoult were hushed as they silently glided by, and the coureur des bois who had faced untold dangers, devoutly crossed himself as the old red mill rose in view on his return from his distant and perilous expeditions. On winter evenings, under the genial warmth of a hickory log and the soothing influence of his *cidre au charbon*, the old habitant would tell to his children, who listened with bated breath, the legend of the old red mill.

Many years before, when the English under Col. Rogers, had taken possession of Detroit, there lived at the mill a Canadian family who had adopted a daughter of the tribe of Pontiac. She was beloved by a British officer, but belonging to the Ottawas whose haughty chief was disposed to resist the new comers, and residing among the French who looked suspiciously at the invaders, waiting to see if the promises made in the treaty would be ratified (a suspicion which subsequent events proved not without cause), it is not to be supposed that the course of true love could run smoothly. Yet love, which laughs in the face of all danger and is prolific in resources, soon found a means by which the lovers could meet. It was agreed upon by them that a signal should be given when there was no danger of a surprise,—a lighted candle to be placed in her window; quickly then would the officer obey the summons of his lady love.

Wasson,* a warrior of the Saginaws, allies of Pontiac, had long loved the fair maiden and had laid at her feet the trophies of the chase, but the Indian girl saw them not, nor heard his pleadings, for her ears yearned for the sound of another voice whose soft accents had nestled in her heart like hushed music. Wounded by his rejection, the brave sought the cause, found it, and courted revenge as his companion. Watching his opportunity when the girl was alone, he upbraided her for having forgotten her duties as an Indian maiden and for deserting the traditions of her race, and raising his tomahawk told her that she should pay the penalty of her treason with her life. As the savage's arm descended the girl sank deluged in her blood. The Indian had not completed the sacrifice; one more victim his revenge demanded. He lighted the candle, the secret of which he had

---

*A noted warrior, Wasson or Warsong.

learned, and patiently waited. Splashing oars and
a low cautious call soon told him that the lover
had obeyed the beacon of love. The savage glut-
ted over his success and waited breathlessly with
weapon poised to hurl at his intended victim as he
opened the door, when suddenly other footsteps
were heard proclaiming the return of the family.
In the general confusion which ensued on the dis-
covery of the murder the Indian slipped away
unnoticed, balked for the time of half of his revenge. The lifeless remains of the lovely victim
were tenderly laid to rest. The officer sought in
the busy strife of the period to forget his grief,
but the Indian's revenge only slumbered, and
shortly afterwards the officer was basely murdered
by him while he was detained as a hostage at Pontiac's camp at Bloody Run.*

The mill was afterwards deserted, but the lonely
wayfarer who passed there at night whispered
strange stories of its being haunted by an Indian
maiden who stood at a window with a lighted
candle.

---

* Col. Campbell, who had gone with Lt. George McDougall to
Pontiac's camp; McDougall escaped.

LA CHASSE GALERIE.

A Legend of the Canadian Shore.

THERE is a strange resemblance in the legends of the different countries which leads one to believe that they derive their source from the same fountain. History places its signet on some, mythology throws its classic veil over others, while the rest, like floating islands which ever and anon appear as bits of stray fairy-land in our large bodies of water, dazzle us by their beauty, charm us by their uniqueness, and glide away as magically as they came to seek a sheltered nook in some picturesque haven. So with regard to many of these legends once current along "La Cote du Nord"* history is silent.

---

* "La Cote du Nord." The name by which that section lying east of what is now Woodward avenue was called.

The charming ideas conveyed in them seem akin to the classic, but it is only in the memory of some old habitante who has outlived her age and generation that they find a revered niche. Seated by the side of one of these, whose hair the frosts of ninety years have bleached, and who has never left the banks of the beautiful lake where she first drew the breath of life, one can pick up many of these legends, carelessly thrown aside by this progressive age.

Among the traditions related by this survivor of a past generation, the best known and oldest is that of "La Chasse Galerie," or "The Spectral Aerial Hunt." Many honest, upright people still living will testify to having seen this phenomenon at some period of their lives. It does not always appear under the same form. Sometimes a canoe is visible, manned by twelve men, and in its prow is a dog whose incessant barking attracts the attention of the person who is to see the vision. Always to the north flies the phantom boat. At other times dogs of a shaggy black, with drooping ears, are constantly seen running on the water, barking as if in the scent of game. Once in seven years a solitary horseman, with gaunt, bronzed face, rifle in hand, followed by his pack of dogs, is seen in the sky after sunset. He who sees the "chasse galerie*" knows that it betokens death either to himself or to others dear to him.

There once dwelt at Askin Pointe, on the Canadian shore, a Nimrod of the forest called Sebastien Lacelle. So devoted to the chase was he that his friends said that he was born with a gun in his hand, and no persuasion of theirs could induce him to join them in other sports. For weeks at a time he would be gone, and then return laden with game. After one of these excursions it was noticed that Sebastien was more silent than usual, had little to say of his hair-breadth escapes, nor did he boast, as was his wont, of the fruits of his trusty rifle.

The mystery was soon solved. One day, tired and weary, baffled by a deer he was pursuing, Sebastien came to a cabin in the woods. A young girl was caressing a deer and deftly dressing a wound in its side. Sebastien recognized it as the one at which he had shot. She was Zoé de Mersac, who had accompanied her father to help him extract the maple syrup from the trees. In the magic witchcraft of her smile Sebastien buried his heart. Zoé admired the strong arm and the vigorous manhood which could shield her from the rough blasts of the world.

---

*Galerie is a corruption of galere, a low, flat built vessel with one deck, and propelled by sails or oars.

It was on a glorious September day that Sebastien and Zoé were strolling along the beach, discussing the morrow, which was to be their wedding day. Zoé was possessed of a highly nervous organization which, like the Æolian harp, is played upon by each passing zephyr, and is peculiarly susceptible to superstition. She was telling her lover how she feared her happiness could not last and spoke of that *serrement du cœur* which seemed prophetic of evil. Sebastien, in the superb enjoyment of his healthy physique, could not sympathize with her, and only laughed at her fears.

What had presentiments to do with him, he thought; would he not be obliged to relinquish his bachelor habits and become a serious, home-staying man? An unconscious sigh escaped him. Raising his eyes, he abruptly left Zoé. He returned shortly afterwards accompanied by several men, guns in hand, whom he had called from the "seines" near by, and followed by Sebastien's dog, Chasseur. Whilst his friends were loosening the boat from its moorings Sebastien joined his fiancée who asked him to explain the cause of his sudden departure. He pointed to a flock of ducks flying towards the flats (an unusual occurrence at that season) and said he was going for a farewell hunt. As soon as she heard this she hid her face in her hands, and the slender, girlish figure was convulsed. In accents tremulous with unshed tears she besought him not to leave her, for if he did he would never return. Sebastien tried to reason with her, but it was of no avail. He petted her and tried those arts in which the lover is so proficient. She told him that she had heard the past night the screech-owl in the willow tree near her window, at the same time the barking of dogs and ringing of bells in the air—doleful foreshadowings of approaching disaster.

Sebastien gazed tenderly into the upturned face, so pathetic in its tearful appeal, and felt his resolve melting away. But the impatient call of his friends and a shy feeling of being laughed at prompted him to hastily say good-bye to his promised bride. "When shall you return?" asked Zoé. "To-morrow at dawn, dead or alive, sure," he jestingly added, to quiet her fears. Soon the hunters were off. Sebastien waved the end of his red sash and Chasseur barked a jubilant farewell, for he seemed to share his master's love of the chase.

At early dawn Zoé came to the shore to welcome the returning hunters. She seated herself on one of the great boulders which are strewn upon the shores of the lake, thrown there by the Indian spirit Manabozbo, who cast them at his father in his memorable combat. Seldom had so glorious a scene burst on her view and all was in harmony with her nature. The dark forests melted with azure softness the magical veil of misty, golden haziness hung over everything, transforming the scene into a sea of gold dissolved in rainbow tints. Lake, sky, land, all seemed flooded and transfigured. The indescribable shades flowed into each other with a beauty which, while enchanting, was the despair of the artist. The girl drank in the delicious draught of loveliness, and thought if this was the dawn of a perfect earthly day which must die in all its splendor, what must be that of the eternal one in its undying beauty. To-day was her wedding day! Why did Sebastien tarry? Had he not a loving impatience to meet his bride? Hour after hour she waited, sending forth her petitions to Ste. Anne, the patroness of mariners, to guide her Sebastien back. Others whose husbands and brothers had gone with Sebastien joined her in her weary watchings. Night came but brought no returning hunters. Day after day Zoé still came to the beach, questioning the vast waters and the horizon for Sebastien. Winter passed, spring again hung her bright blossoms on the trees, but Sebastien came not to gladden the the sorrow-haunted heart of the girl. Yet she seemed cheerful, as if buoyed up by some inward hope. She constantly said that her lover would return to claim her,—he had promised and he had never deceived any one. Once, shortly after he left, she had heard Sebastien's voice, and looking up saw him in a boat in the clouds. Chasseur was with him, and Sebastien said: "I will come for you in a year and a day." Then towards the north the mystic apparition glided and the voice died away in the moaning wind.

It was a year and a day. The pale cheek with its hectic flush, the fragile figure, the transparent hand told that this was a blossom for the grave.

Zoé desired that she should be dressed as a bride and carried to the beach to watch for her bridegroom. Her chair was brought to the place she designated. The scene was by a strange coincidence of nature, nearly the same as on the bright day she waited Sebastien's return. Nature seemed anxious that the dying girl should take the sweetest and most beautiful memories of earth with her. The wakening waves chanted their low matins as they broke at her feet, the birds greeted her with jubilant notes and the soft, balmy air played hide and seek through the meshes of her hair.

The maiden heeded not the beauty of the scene; her eyes were intently fixed on a spot in the skies. Suddenly an ecstatic expression crept over her face, and raising herself up she exclaimed, "See! see! there is Sebastien in the boat; he beckons to me, and Chasseur is barking so joyously! Did I not tell you he would come for me? Sebastien, I come, I come." And the pure spirit of the girl leaped from its mortal tenement to rejoin that of her spirit bridegroom. Her awe-stricken friends looked where she pointed and saw a phantom boat drifting on a billow of clouds, and distinctly heard the echo of a barking dog as the vision melted into the boundless blue.

XIX

LE FEU FOLLET.

A Legend of Grosse Isle.

BOUT fifteen miles below Detroit lies the beautiful island called Grosse Isle, it being the largest of the group between Lakes Erie and Sainte Claire.
Its wonderful fertility, the luxuriant growth of its forest trees and the beauty of its situation so wove the spell of its seductive charm around the heart of an English officer, that he resolved to resign and spend the remainder of his days in this enchanting retreat.* His name was William Macomb. He was of Scottish extraction, and he had come to Detroit with the English troops in 1760. Macomb obtained an Indian grant for his coveted

treasure, and soon improvements arose, testifying his earnest desire to make himself comfortable in his island home. In 1808 his heirs, John, William and David, through their attorney, Solomon Sibley, and their agent, Angus McIntosh, received full acknowledgment from the American Government. Energy, enterprise and administrative ability were inseparable from the name of Macomb, one of its members, Alexander, becoming general-in-chief of the army of the United States. Grosse Isle, Belle Isle,* and large tracts of land in Detroit, belonged to this family, and if retained until the present time would have made them immensely wealthy. The lavish hospitality and unbounded extravagance which characterized all the old families during the military epoch, compelled a gradual transfer of property. But some of the descendants, though no longer bearing the family name, still preserve homesteads on Grosse Isle.

---

*See page 273 and page 479 Land Titles in the Michigan Territory American State Papers xvi., vol. 1, Public Lands.

Monday, December 2, 1805.

John, William and David Macomb claimed an island situated in the Strait, three miles above Detroit, called Hog Island. It contains 704 acres, was surveyed by Mr. Boyd in 1771, and purchased from the Indians of the Ottawa and Chippewa nations in council, under direction of his Majesty's commander-in-chief, and conveyed to Lt. George McDougall, whose heirs sold it to Wm. Macomb in 1793.

Cotemporary with the Macombs was the family of the Navarres. Robert 1st of the name was fifth in descent from Antoine, Duke of Vendôme, half-brother of Henry 4th of Navarre. He came to Detroit in 1730 as sub-intendant of Louis XIV, having entire control of all the affairs of the French Government outside of the military authority, in this part of la Nouvelle France. His children and grandchildren became an honor to him, and proverbial for their great beauty and Bourbon faces. They so married and intermarried with the Macombs, that it was difficult to say where one family ended and the other began.

William Macomb, Jr., had become the humble captive of the beautiful Monique Navarre, a granddaughter of "Robert the Writer," as he was called. He had invited her with her brother Robert, to visit the island during the sultry August weather, and one morning they embarked in their little sailboat to drink in the refreshing breezes from Lake Erie. On landing before the Macomb mansion they were disappointed to learn that the family had been called to Elba Island, just below, by the death of a friend, but the "pani"* slave left in attendance assured them

---

* At the time referred to slavery was universal, and originally all prisoners taken in Indian wars, who were not whites, were called by the French "pani"—spelled by the English to conform with the

they must come in and make themselves comfortable, as Master William had left word, thinking it possible that the visitors would come, that he would reach home by sunset. The aspect of the sky silenced all hesitancy, as one of those sudden storms born only on a sultry, tropical day, swept over the island.

As the vivid flashes darted across the water, Monique, who was of a nervous temperament, begged the pani slave to split off fragments of the Christmas log (usually preserved half-burnt from year to year) and to throw them on the fire, "to prevent the thunder from falling;" then, glancing at the door and seeing a branch of white thorn suspended there she became tranquil. This bush was considered a divine lightning rod, the superstition probably arising from the fact that its thorny branches crowned the Saviour's head. An old legend says that wherever drops of His precious blood fell, flowers sprang forth. A portion of this crown is still seen in the relics of the Holy Roman Empire in the government collection at Vienna.*

pronunciation, "pawnee." The word gradually came to mean a person of mixed Indian and negro blood, and is so used in this narrative.

*Another superstition was that a piece of bread which had been blessed at three Christmas masses would preserve a house from harm.

Gradually the storm subsided, but the shadows of night crept swiftly on and still the family returned not. Suddenly a sharp, shrill whistle fell on the expectant ears, startling all to their feet. Monique, who had been gazing vaguely into the twilight, slammed the blinds together hurriedly exclaiming, "It is the feu follet dancing over the fields, and if I had not shut it out, it would have entered and strangled us. Le Bon Dieu preserve William and the others."

"A truce to your fears, ma sœur," answered Robert. "They can take care of themselves, but as it is clearing up we will soon go in search of them." Thus did he soothe the nervous girl; for himself he had no fears, and being a student at the bar, naturally felt little respect for the higher powers or the devil.

Like other scoffers of the period he thought the feu follet merely inflammable gases arising from miasmatic exhalations of swampy lands. Monique and many others thought this "an easy way of explaining it." Had they lived in our days they would have found a great number who attribute to electricity things which they can not explain.

"Tell me all about the feu follet, chère sœur," said Robert, anxious to divert her and lull her apprehensions. A glad light of pleasure stole into her eyes, and a tender blush suffused her face, battling with that triumphant expression which every woman wears when she thinks she has won a convert to her opinions.

"Mon frère, the feu follet are not always considered dangerous. When twin lights are seen stealing along in the soft twilight they are called 'Castor and Pollux,' and this is a happy omen. But when a single intense light appears it is named 'Helene,' and he who sees it must at once throw himself on the ground covering his face, for so seductive is its fascination that it allures him to deserted bogs and steep ravines, and leaves him to die. There is a Norman tradition which exists among the habitants coming from Caen, in Normandy, that the feu follet are divided into two species, the male and female, and are supposed to be the souls of those who have sinned against purity. These people of the Norman race also call maidens who have fallen from grace 'fourolle,' as fourolle Jeanne, fourolle Katishe, and believe that the evil one gives them the power of divesting themselves of their body, and transforming into a bright light which runs 'en fourolle,' leading many to destruction who mistake it for some friendly signal when astray in swampy places."

As Monique finished her explanation she rose

and insisted that they should go in search of the host and family. They started out followed by the pani, who held his blazing pine knot which threw its uncertain light on the pathway and made a weird tableau as its flickering rays alternately bathed the little procession in light, then in shadow. They made the woods resound with their shouts, but no answering call greeted their anxious ears, and the pani expressed his anxiety, as "Master William had surely promised to return, and he never knew him to fail in spite of rain or sunshine." At last, as they proceeded on their doleful journey, the ground grew miry and swampy, while the dismal croaking of frogs and the sickly miasmatic odors added to their dread forebodings. Just then, when the saddest presentiments were invading the hearts of the courageous searchers, Monique uttered one last despairing cry in which all the energy of her nature seemed centered, so anxious was she it should reach the lost one. Instantaneously the sharp report of a pistol startled from their nests the little birds which fluttered around chirping plaintively, as if seeking companionship from the invaders of their solitary and mournful abode. Following the sound of the pistol, the searchers saw in the swamp an object in the water, and soon their willing hands had made a sort of bridge which enabled them to approach it. It proved to be the lost wanderer, hopelessly struggling in the miry embrace. He was extricated from his perilous position and the little procession went back rejoicing.

On arriving at home, seated at the hospitable table, William related his adventure. As soon as the storm subsided he had started homeward ; the remainder of the family were to stay at Elba until the morning. In the darkness he had lost his way, and seeing a bright light had followed it. As he drew nearer it appeared to recede until he found himself plunged into the swamp. He cried out for help until exhausted, and his only answer was the mocking laughter of goblins. Realizing the hopelessness of his position, he commended his spirit to his Maker and calmly awaited the result. Suddenly it seemed to him as if the voice of his loved one was borne to his ears to soften the anguish of his last moments. Then other voices came so distinctly that he awoke from his lethargy, and thinking it possible that friends had heard his former cries for help, fired his pistol.

"It was the feu follet, mon ami, which led you astray. You cannot say you do not believe in it now," said Monique, as she glanced archly at her lover.

"Anything you believe in will suit me now and for all time," said the gallant William.

So on the next feast day they stood before the altar of Ste. Anne's in Detroit, and were made one forever.

XX

THE FEAST OF ST. JEAN.

A Legend of Sandwich.

IT WAS the eve of Pentecost which fell amid the roses of June in 1790.

There was a great commotion in the spacious kitchen of Dominique Gaudet, who lived near the church on the banks of the Detroit. The hurrying to and fro of busy feet, the gleeful voices of merriment, mingled with the clatter of dishes, fragments of song and the deeper bass tones of the men, formed an admirable orchestra of babel and confusion; for on the morrow it was Dominique who was to present the *pain bénit* (blessed bread) and its accessory *cousins* (a kind of cake) to be distributed at high mass. Each family along *la cote* in turn furnished them, save at the Assumption (15th of August) when a portion of the Huron tribe came to camp in the grove near the church and claimed the privilege, as they had donated the ground. Josephte and Lizette, the pani slaves, were industriously kneading the huge mass of dough in the wooden *huche* (trough) whilst Soulange Gaudet, with her sleeves rolled up displaying the dimpled arms, and her mignonne face and hair all powdered with flour, was trying to plait the refractory dough into the semblance of a large wreath. This "couronne" was the ornament on the top loaf, and was always detached after mass and sent as a token to the person whose turn it would be to prepare the *pain bénit* for the next feast. At a table was a gay bevy of girls who were cutting the *cousins* into palm shapes, and with a feather brushing the top of them with egg and sugar. La dame Gaudet received them and placed them in the big *four* (oven). The light from the open chimney threw its flickering gleams around, lighting up the joyous faces and producing a Rembrandt effect of light and shade. It was a charming study for an artist's pencil. Soulange with two or three of her companions having completed their task, brushed the flour from their hair and dresses and strolled along the banks to cool their heated cheeks. The twilight shades were deepening and the rosy reflection in the sky left its promise of a beautiful morrow. They were presently joined by several young men who had come to help them carry the *pain bénit* and *cousins* to the church. Whilst they were gayly chatting Soulange, who seemed distrait and anxiously waiting for somebody, suddenly called attention to an object in the water. They could distinguish the figure of a man who was apparently seated on the water. No canoe was visible, and yet he seemed to glide along by the aid of a paddle. Whilst speculating on the strange phenomenon, the increasing darkness having prevented close inspection, the sound of something grating on the sand near them and a merry laugh, caused all to hurry down to the beach. They were greeted by David Fisher, who resided in Detroit. "Handsome David," as he was called, was a gay, dashing Kentuckian who had fallen in love with "la belle Soulange" when she had visited her friends in Detroit. He was a great favorite, and spoke French like a native, and his easy, débonnaire manner carried captive the hearts of the old and young. The amazement of the party was intense when they found that David's canoe was a wheelbarrow.* He laughed at their perplexed looks and briefly explained that

---

*Fact: A feat performed by Pierre Godfroy in fulfillment of a bet.

he had found no one to row him over and no boat to be had, so he had devised this new method— a feat as difficult as Leonidas swimming the Hellespont, and no less romantic. A summons from the house announced that all the things were in readiness to be carried to the church. As they wended their way, each laden with something, the gay peals of laughter that rang on their retreating steps told those who listened that David was in high humor, and amusing as usual with his sparkling jests and jeu d'esprit. In the sanctuary they arranged the *pain bénit* generally four in number and round in shape. The largest was placed first on a table, then layers of *cousins* and so on until the top loaf and its "couronne" covered the structure. Little silk flags were stuck here and there, forming a charming and unique pyramid.

Pentecost morning dawned bright and beautiful and the church was crowded. At the Credo the Sacristan, with his slow, measured step, approached Soulange and presented her with a silver plate he held in his hand. With nervous trepidation she had awaited this moment, for she was the "queteuse" of the day. She arose with a dignified composure, of which only the fleeting color, as it came and went in her cheek, betrayed the effort. She walked to the altar railing and knelt, then rising, presented her plate at each pew for the collection, acknowledging the offering by a sweeping courtesy, whose perfection was attained by many an anxious hour of practice. The bread was blessed. The Sacristan gradually stripped the pyramid, cut the bread and distributed it to each person, who making the sign of the cross, ate it in silence as a symbol of the unity that should reign among Christians, who are all members of the same family.

After mass there were hand-shakings and greetings. The scene was a most picturesque one. In front the broad river swept majestically; beneath the cool shade of the trees were spread snowy white tablecloths, forming a contrast to the green verdure, around which were seated those habitants who lived too far to return for vespers, awaiting their meal. A number had gathered about the *bedeau* (Sacristan), who, arrayed in his long blue redingote and *carrick* cape edged with red, was crying out in a stentorian voice: "Avertisement! Avertisement!" Newspapers being then unknown in those regions, this was the only medium of advertising an auction, a lost cow, or stray child. Soulange was joined by her lover, David, and they together visited the various groups seated on the grass, with whom they exchanged the compliments of the day. Several children, catching a glimpse of David, insisted on his taking them to one of the booths, which looked like wigwams covered with fresh branches of maple, and displayed a tempting array of maple sugar and "croquecignoles."

That evening David and Soulange agreed they would be married at midsummer, for then "the fairies would dance at the wedding" David laughingly said. Happy was Soulange these days; her voice rippled with the melody of joy which surged from a heart filled with love and tenderness.

> And "Merry! merry! merry!"
> Rang the bells of every hour,
> And "happy, happy, happy!"
> In her valley laughed the flower.

As the weeks passed which measured the time before Soulange's wedding a shadow was creeping over her horizon which would rob the smiling lips of laughter and smother forever her sunshine of happiness. Vague reports floated on the idle wings of rumor, of a disagreement between David and an officer, which, though contradicted, left an impression of uneasiness in those who knew the gallant, warm-hearted, yet reckless Fisher.

It was an open glade below Sandwich that the sun flooded brightly on an August morning. The sparkling waters were sporting with the first golden beams; the branches of the trees in the woods skirting the field swayed lazily to the woo-

ing breeze. The flowers were still bathed in dew
and in their moist mass were flung instruments
of death. In the midst of an awe-stricken group
lay a handsome, manly form, whose life was
slowly ebbing away. The glory of the sunrise
and the birds gushing forth their melodies,
seemed a mockery to that sad scene, whilst an
immortal soul was winging its flight to the unknown world. The surgeon who had knelt beside
the prostrate form arose ; the pulse was stilled
forever.

The news of the duel and its fatal consequences
was soon known, and the shore was lined with
people. Soulange attracted by the crowd, came
to inquire the cause. A hushed whispering and
sympathetic glances greeted her, whilst a pair of
loving hands imprisoned her and tried to lead her
home. With a great fear over her which lent
her strength, she wrenched herself away and flew
to the beach. Two canoes were being slowly
rowed up the stream towing a third, over which
a blanket was thrown, the ends trailing mournfully in the water. The heads of the rowers were
bowed and their attitude denoted grief and sorrow. The sun had veiled itself behind the clouds
as if in pity. A solemn silence reigned, born
only in death's awful presence ; men uncovered
their heads and furtively brushed away a stray

tear ; women clasped convulsively their babes to their breasts and murmured a prayer for that solitary figure which stood on the beach. A clear voice pierced the ominous silence. "Bring him here," it said, and those who heard it would long remember it, for a human heart lay broken in its accents. Unconsciously the imperious order was obeyed and the canoe allowed to drift to her feet. Quick as lightning, deaf to the expressions of sympathy which burst forth from the multitude, she raised the blanket and saw the dead face of her lover.

Years had passed since that sad occurrence, when one Sunday the good priest of the Church of the Assumption recommended to the prayers of the faithful the soul of Sœur Therese of the Grey Order of Montreal, who had recently died after a life of penance and mortification. In the world she had been known as Soulange Gaudet.

XXI

HAMTRAMCK'S LOVE.

A Legend of Wayne's Occupation.

A QUARTER of a century had passed since Pontiac and his savage hordes battled in vain against the cedar ramparts of old Fort Pontchartrain. The American Colonies had thrown off the yoke of the mother country and proclaimed their independence. Remote from the scene of conflict the French settlement along Le Détroit had begun to recover from the devastations of their Indian neighbors. Among the habitants it was whispered that for the third time their flag was to be changed. Without asking their consent their allegiance was to be claimed by the

"Bostonnais"* or Yankees, whose star at present was in the ascendant. This rumor gave rise to diverse sentiments. Some of the settlers felt the spark of liberty kindling in their breasts, and hailed the change as a merited overthrow of the haughty English, their hereditary foes. Others, now that the fleur de lis was withdrawn, saw their only safety and strength under the cross of St. George. The Elliots, Babys, Askins, and McKees were among the prominent Canadians of the latter class, while Robert Navarre, Jr., the Chevalier Chabert de la Joncaire, Louis Descomptes Labadie and their influential followers espoused the cause of the rising young republic. In 1786 Robert Navarre, eldest son of the old sub-intendant, accompanied by his beautiful daughter Marianne, visited Philadelphia. The French colonists sought through him to ascertain precisely what was to be their status under the new government. Among the many illustrious men of the day to whom Navarre was presented was Maj. Gen. Arthur St. Clair, a distinguished officer of the late revolutionary war. His spirited daughter, Louisa St. Clair, at once became interested in Marianne Navarre, the brilliant, piquante beauty of the fron-

---

* Bostonnais. A name given to the Americans by the French of Quebec, and from thence the term spread among all the Canadians. "The Bostonnais" is a charmingly written book by L'Esperance, a tale of the American invasion of Canada in 1775–76.

tier. On the organization of a government for
the North West Territory (which comprised all
the American possessions west of the Alleghanies)
Gen. St. Clair was appointed Governor, and a
number of the most popular officers of the revolution given important positions.* These pioneers,
who had crossed the mountains of Pennsylvania
on horse back, settled on one of the picturesque
bends of the Belle Riviere (Ohio). Here they
founded Marietta, so called after the lovely and
ill-fated Marie Antoinette of France, the fast
friend of the patriots in their struggle for independence.

Louisa St. Clair, who had not forgotten the
little Norman friend whom she had met in Philadelphia, wrote to her as soon as she was settled at
Marietta, challenging her to cross the intervening
"Black Swamp" and visit her in her new home.
Marianne came from too good a pioneer stock to
shrink from any hardships, especially where it
promised an adventure. So, accompanied by her

---

*A court was established and the judges authorized to prepare
a code of laws. Maj. Gen. Samuel Holden Parsons, the rival of
St. Clair for the appointment of Governor, was appointed Chief
Justice, with Judge Cleves Symmes and Gen. Jos. M. Varum as
Associate Judges. The former was great-grandfather of Theo.
Parsons Hall, of Detroit, and the descendants of Judge Symmes
reside in Louisville, Ky. In this first court of the North West,
Judge Solomon Sibley, Gen. Lewis Cass, Col. Ebenezer Sproat,
and others well known in Detroit, took their first lessons in law.

relative, Antoine Gamelin, with a band of friendly Indians and her faithful pani slave, she performed the perilous journey in safety. On her arrival she found Marietta a scene of life and excitement. The newly organized First Regiment of U. S. Infantry was then on its way to garrison Vincennes. Its corps of gay officers, among whom was Col. John Francis Hamtramck (then Major), made the days speed merrily and happily for the young maidens. Hamtramck had, much to the secret pleasure of the Governor, been attentive for some time to Louisa, yet she coyly and frequently said that her heart's desire was to be the bride of some "noble warrior of the forest." She cultivated all the Indian sports, became an expert with the rifle, and one of the most daring and fearless horsewomen in the country. Undaunted by the fate of Miss McRea, whose story every mother repeated to her child, she would make long excursions into the forests, returning with game, new specimens of flowers, or rare medicinal plants. Marianne was too accustomed to the pastimes of a frontier life to find novelty in them, and was happy in perusing the books which her friend had brought with her from Philadelphia. Maj. Hamtramck was frequently by her side. She touched hidden chords in his heart, awaking the slumbering melodies of bright dreams and fanciful ideals. Louisa seemed strangely anxious to promote the friendship between Hamtramck and Marianne, but not so the Governor, who frowned upon this new state of affairs.

Marianne had been with her friend about a month when it was announced that the dreaded Chief Thayendanegea (Joseph Brandt) had camped in the vicinity with a band of his most noted warriors. The Governor, anxious to conciliate so powerful a foe and to secure his friendship, contemplated sending an ambassador to him. The mission was a perilous and delicate one, and required more than ordinary skill and diplomacy. An envoy possessing these talents was not easily found, so the Governor was obliged to content himself by a written missive requesting an interview. Louisa, having heard the matter discussed, learned who the messenger was to be. She disguised herself as an Indian girl and slung on her shoulder her trusty rifle. Extracting by some womanly art the note from the soldier, by the aid of her fleet horse she was soon in the presence of the great chieftain. Brandt was startled by the fair apparition, admired her daring and courage, and was flattered by her remembrance. These two had met before in Philadelphia, when she was at school, and he a student at college. The young Indian had been much sought after; his birth, his influence with his tribe, his stately and graceful figure and rare talents, had made him even then a conspicuous object. It is not to be wondered that he became the hero of many a girlish heart. "Noble warrior," she said, "I have risked my life to obtain this interview; you must send some one to accompany me back to my father." The chieftain replied, "It is fitting that I alone should guard so courageous a maiden." With a few of his braves he accompanied her home, and thus the Governor obtained the interview he desired. Owing to some disagreement a satisfactory treaty was not made. The Governor censured Louisa for what he considered a foolish escapade, but his anger knew no bounds when shortly afterwards Brandt asked him for her hand, which was haughtily refused. He sought the presence of his daughter and told her that he would never consent to her union with an Indian. He had cherished other designs, and his ardent wish was to see her the wife of Major Hamtramck whom he esteemed highly. The sharp tones of the angry voice penetrated to the room where Marianne sat reading, and brought to her an explanation of the Governor's peculiar manner of late towards her, and made her in her indignation question the motive of Hamtramck's devotion to her. The pride of la belle France was aroused.

She doubted the young officer's loyalty to her, and finding a favorable pretext, returned to Detroit whilst Hamtramck was away upon temporary official business. Shortly afterwards the embers of war were rekindled, and Gov. St. Clair, attacked by the combined savage tribes of the West, met with a most disastrous defeat.* He was only rescued from total annihilation by Hamtramck and his regulars. In this battle Brandt took a prominent part. So anxious was he to capture St. Clair alive, that he gave orders to his savages to shoot the horse from under him, but not to kill him. He hoped that by sparing the General's life, and making him sensible of this generosity, he could gain his suit and win Louisa from "Le Crapeau a Cheval,"† as he called Hamtramck, whom he supposed his rival.

Several years had elapsed. Col. Hamtramck, who had so distinguished himself at the battle of the Maumee, where he commanded the left wing under Wayne, was ordered to Detroit. Here for the first time (1796) the Stars and Stripes were

---

*On hearing of St. Clair's defeat it is said that Washington, for once in his life, swore such a volley of oaths as to make his Secretary's hair stand on end.

†Le Crapeau a Cheval (The Frog on Horseback). Hamtramck was small and rather round shouldered, making a poor figure on horseback, hence Brandt's jealous epithets.

unfurled by Mad Anthony, and later the fort was named in his honor. Here Hamtramck again met his former sweetheart, and pleaded his cause a second time. He told her that he had been wounded and surprised by her sudden departure from Marietta, and had heard later of her rumored marriage to Col. Gratiot. He had endeavored to efface her image from his heart, had married and was now a widower; hearing she was not Gratiot's bride he had returned to his allegiance. Marianne again refused him; the love which once might have been his had been hopelessly blighted, and her heart was a tomb wherein lay the ashes of buried hopes and bright illusions. "Mademoiselle," said Hamtramck, "since we cannot be united in life, in death I shall be near you. I shall give orders to be buried by your side." "Oh, that is romantic, Colonel, but you are a soldier and cannot say where your last sleep shall overtake you," she laughingly replied. "No matter, mark me, I shall slumber within the shadow of your tomb." In 1803 Hamtramck died, and was buried near the Navarre lot in the old Ste. Anne's church yard. The following is the inscription on his tombstone:

"Sacred to the memory of John Francis Hamtramck, Colonel of the First United States Infantry, and Commandant of Detroit and its dependencies. He departed this life on the 11th day of April,

1803, aged 45 years, 7 months, 27 days. True
patriotism and zealous attachment to national
liberty, joined to a laudable ambition, led him
into military service at an early age. He was a
soldier before he was a man. He was an active
participator in all the danger, difficulties, and
honors of the Revolutionary War, and his heroism
and uniform good conduct procured him the
attention and personal thanks of the immortal
Washington. The United States in him have lost
a valuable officer and good citizen, and society a
useful and pleasant member. His friends will
ever mourn the loss of Hamtramck.

This monument is placed over him by the officers who had the honor to serve in his command, a small but grateful tribute to his worth."

Hamtramck's remains were placed in Mount
Elliott on the abandonment of the old Ste. Anne
cemetery.

Fifty years later Marianne died, and her body
has been recently removed to the Godfroy lot,
which is opposite the spot where Hamtramck is
buried. His prediction has been fulfilled and he
literally "slumbers within the shadow of her
tomb." Is there a fate in this? On the lower side
of Detroit on the river bank is Fort Wayne. At
the upper extremity of the city still stands the
old French house where Hamtramck died. The

majestic elm, like a sentinel by its side, is the land mark by which passing vessels take their course. The adjoining locality bears Hamtramck's name.

Thus the two old heroes, even in death, hold their favorite respective positions, guarding the left and right flank,* whilst the name of Hamtramck's rival is still perpetuated in one of our most prominent business avenues (Gratiot).

---

*At the battle of Maumee, August, 1794, Wayne commanded the right wing and Hamtramck the left wing. This great victory over the Indians gave the Americans their first actual control of Detroit and the surrounding country.

XXII

THE HAUNTED SPINNING WHEEL.

A Legend of St. Jean's Eve.

"MAD," impetuous Anthony Wayne first flung in triumph the Stars and Stripes over the fair City of the Straits. It was a gladsome beacon to many Americans to come and seek a home beneath its protecting folds. The Marietta colony in Ohio sent Cass, Sibley, Woodbridge and others to weave in history their distinguished talents with the city of their adoption. Many dashing Kentuckians, followers of Wayne, having conquered the English oppressors were themselves vanquished by the dark-eyed, piquante Canadian demoiselles.

Many intermarriages took place between the

French habitants* and the new comers. In the families of these descendants are still preserved the quaint traditions of the French, also some of the physical traits, particularly the shapely foot and hand, and to-day the sale of shoes from the so-called Créole last follows the line of French posts from Detroit, Monroe, Fort Wayne, Vincennes, and St. Louis down to New Orleans. It is from one of these old families that the incidents embodied in the following story are gathered.

In 1795 Didier Duchêne lived with his wife and little daughter Fanchette on the banks of the Rouge. His aged mother resided with him, a venerable dame who lingered seemingly forgotten, beyond her time. But not so, thought Fanchette, who would steal from her play to sit beside grandmère, nestle her curly head against her knee, and listen with flushed cheeks and eyes glowing with wonderment to the marvelous tales she told. There is something beautiful in the witchery which a pious, serene old age exercises over impressionable childhood. There seems to be a perfect union between them,

---

*Habitants. A word whose meaning has been singularly perverted. It meant formerly the permanent settlers who came to "habiter le pays" (inhabit the country), in contradistinction to the military and civil functionaries who were transient. The richest merchant might be an habitant, that is, a permanent settler.

a mystic tie which as we advance in youth and towards middle age appears gradually to weaken. Perhaps the spontaneous reverence which lisping childhood pays to the aged, arises from the shadow of the mystery of its own existence which still envelops it, and the subtle instincts of companionship which nature instills in those standing on the confines of unknown worlds. It is the unconscious tribute of the mystery of the cradle to that of the grave. Childhood and old age have no present; one lives in the past, the other in the future.

One day grandmère died, and Fanchette felt that the sunshine had all crept out of her heart and left a great void. It was Fanchette's first contact with death and she felt its awe-striking influence, and wandered about listlessly questioning everything why all was so changed? She would sob herself to sleep, and in dreamland would hear again the sweet, faltering accents of grandmère. One evening she awoke her parents by a ringing shriek; they hastened to her, and found her excitedly exclaiming: "Grandmère, grandmère; don't you hear her?" To soothe her they remained quiet a moment and distinctly heard the hum of the old dame's spinning wheel in the adjoining room. Terror seized them, and it was only at the earnest pleading of the child "to see grandmère" that they regained sufficient courage to open the door. But instantly the noise ceased; the room was quiet and nothing disturbed.

Night after night the same occurrence took place. To Fanchette the phantom hum of the spinning wheel was a sweet lullaby, and an assurance that the dear grandmère was near. But the parents who had always laughed at the old lady's superstitions, felt it a warning for their incredulity. The "Bon Père" was consulted, and after hearing the story, asked if they had left any promise unfulfilled to the dead. "Ah! Mon Dieu," cried Didier, conscience-striken, "I promised fifty masses for the repose of her soul and to distribute some things among the poor." The promise was soon after fulfilled, and the spinning wheel no longer sent forth its weird music on the midnight air.

Years rolled on until Fanchette counted 16, the marriageable age among the maidens of that day. Her mother favored the suit of a little Canadian, but the girl's heart inclined toward a brave Kentuckian. It was a severe struggle for that docile girl, between her obedience to her mother and her affection for her lover. The great Canadian festival of St. Jean Baptiste, or Midsummer Day, as the English called it, was nigh.

Towards nightfall the great bonfire (*feu de joie*)

was kindled. It was an octagonal pyramid about eight or ten feet high, erected opposite the church on the beach, and was covered with branches of fir stuck in the interstices of the logs of cedar of which it was built. The lighted taper was applied to each little heap of straw placed at each of the right corners of the verdant cone. The flames arose sparkling and scintillating amidst hurrahs, cheers and deafening volleys of guns. The custom was of Norman origin, and commemorated the time when the bonfire was the only medium of communication for those living on opposite shores, and especially in winter, when they were shut off from each other. Thus fire became a language and they who knew its alphabet could read in the swaying flames the message of death, sickness or joyful tidings. On the eve of the festival great bonfires were built along the beach of the Detroit and all kept the vigil, as it was thought if any one slept his soul would leave the body and wander to find the place where death was to overtake him. At sunrise if close watch was kept one might see the sun dance three times.

Fanchette had come to the fort to visit friends but her principal interest in the day was centered on a trial which she had decided to make as to whom she should choose for a husband. At the hour of twelve everything was quiet in the house.

She cautiously made her way to the garden surrounded by its high cedar pickets, and taking a handful of wild hemp seed, she scattered it on the ground saying,

"Hemp I sow, hemp I hoe,
Who is my love come after me now."

To her intense joy, a vague resemblance of the Kentuckian arose and stalked across the garden.

Then hastily plucking a few sprigs of vervain, a plant so useful in warding off goblins and possessing wonderful powers, she carefully picked a rose de France, which she felt would keep fresh until marriage time at Christmas, and returned to her room to watch with the others, and muse on her happiness in store.

The same belief and traditions repeat themselves in other lands as is seen in the oft quoted

POEM OF ST. JOHN'S WORT.

The young maid stole through the cottage door,
And blushed as she saw the plant of power;
" Thou silver moon glow, oh lend me thy light,
I must gather the mystic St. John's wort to-night,
The wonderful herb whose leaf will decide
If the coming year will make me a bride!"
    And the glow-worm came
    With its silvery flame,
    And sparkled and shone
    Through the night of St. John,
And soon has the maid her love-knot tied.

With noiseless tread
To her chamber she sped,
Where the spectral moon her white beams shed;
Bloom here, bloom there, thou plant of power,
To deck the young bride in her bridal hour;
But it drooped its head, that plant of power,
And died the mute death of the voiceless flower.

And a withered wreath on the ground it lay,
More meet for a burial than a bridal day;
And when a year was passed away
All pale on her bier the young maid lay.
    And the glow-worm came
    With its silvery flame,
    And sparkled and shone
    Through the night of St. John,
As they closed the cold grave on the maid's cold clay.

When Christmas came little Fanchette decked as a bride stood by the side of her gallant Kentuckian, and said the words which made her his "for weal or for woe." She told him afterwards the story of St. Jean's eve, and transformed him into a fervent believer in grandmère's superstitions. A few years later a group of merry children might have been seen in the Duchêne orchard burning bundles of straw under the trees, whilst they chanted:

    Taupes, chenilles, et mulots
      Sortez sortez de vos clos
    Ou, je vous brule la barbe et les os
      Arbres, arbrisseaux
    Donnez moi des pommes a minot.

Translated into English the rhyme means :
   Caterpillars, mice and moles
   On this instant leave your holes,
   Crawl forth from under bark and stones
   Or I will burn your beard and bones,
   And may the trees both great and small
   Be loaded down with apples all.

XXIII

THE CURSED VILLAGE.

A Legend of L'Anse Creuse.

IT WAS on a glorious September morning that our carriage rolled along the picturesque shore of Grosse Pointe. The soft, misty waves of fog which trailed over the smooth cut lawn and over the broad lake were gradually curling themselves into graceful, spiral wreaths, to dissolve in the sunlight. If there is a touch of sadness in Autumn, an indescribable yearning after something indefinable, there is a strength to resist the depression in the fresh, bracing atmosphere which lends roses to the cheek and buoyancy to the step. Nature, as if conscious of this tinge of melancholy, dons her brightest colors, throws around her that mystic, mellow light which rounds the sharpest outlines and softens the roughest landscapes, and whilst we are enchanted by her gorgeous devices we forget the sad reflections of this season of decay.

We passed the fashionable drive, bordered by its handsome villas with their evidences of culture and refinement, crossed the tottering bridge over Milk River, into a strange country and a past age. Occasionally signs of a well-to-do farmer greeted us, but these were rare. Silence, monotony and dilapidation were written everywhere. The lake here swept majestically into the shore forming a graceful curve. This was the Bay of L'Anse Creuse from which the village on its banks derived its name, we were told. Dim, shadowy memories of a legend connected with this place drifted confusedly through my brain, and asking the driver about it, he told us that there lived not far an old habitant who was well versed in all such lore, and who would be but too happy to have a listener. Ten minutes later we entered a humble cottage, stated our errand, and were received with that genuine courtesy, the peculiar heritage of the French, which caused Sydney Smith to envy the manners of his cobbler in Paris. The old raconteur introduced us to his children and grandchildren, who eyed us politely, but with curious, speculative eyes, unused to a sudden inroad of strangers. The habitant evidently relished telling a story, and smacking his lips after the manner of an epicure, told us the legend of L'Anse Creuse.

It was the feast of Corpus Christi in June, and the whole neighborhood of L'Anse Creuse was in a whirl of excitement. For to-day the Bishop was coming from the fort (Detroit) accompanied by the new pastor, to consecrate the little chapel. The young men on horseback with their guns to fire a salute, had gone to meet them, whilst the children, dressed in white, bearing flowers and looking like so many butterflies, were flitting to and fro, and the habitants in their Sunday attire were gaily chatting. All of a sudden a discharge of guns announced the near approach of the clerical party, and in a few moments all were formed in a procession. Banners were unfurled, voices were raised chanting the Te Deum, clouds of incense rose to perfume the air and the pathway was strewn with flowers.

Thus were they escorted to the church, and amidst that grand silence so appealing in its solemnity, the imposing ceremonies took place. They were followed by a short but eloquent address from their new pastor, Father Gabriel. He thanked them for their welcome and hoped that God would bless his efforts; he would endeavor to prove a true shepherd, but his flock must aid him to keep in the narrow path. He alluded lightly to that greatest of all temptations, excessive drinking, which brought so many evils in its train, and which was so difficult to overcome.

Perhaps the eagle eye of the priest had noted the recess on the banks, where old Francois Fontenoy, the celebrated Indian trader (who had buried a brass kettle of gold at Presque Isle, and which has caused as many explanations and conjectures as Kidd's treasure), had tapped a barrel of genuine eau de vie to appease the thirsty.

After the blessing all dispersed to give themselves up to the enjoyment of the day. The young men amused themselves by shooting in the air, which caused a stranger, who seemed by his manner and dress to take no part in the day's rejoicing, to say, "They are shooting the devil out of the neighborhood." One near him jestingly replied, "Perhaps he was never here until you came; you must have brought him." An angry flush crept over the swarthy face of the stranger, who with a muttered something, turned on his heels and joined old Fontenoy and his flowing glass.

This man, Lizon by name, had recently settled at L'Anse Creuse. Being reserved in his manner, he merely stated that he came from Montreal.

He formed a contrast to the light-hearted villagers, who lived as one family, shared each others joys and sorrows, and who were closely bound by the ties of early association and relationship. Lizon rejected in a morose manner their friendly overtures, and was soon left to the solitude he seemed to covet. He possessed means, for he had purchased land, and built an auberge where liquor was the chief inducement.

One day it was announced that Lizon had asked Julienne, the daughter of a respected habitant, to marry him. The amazement of the good people was intense, as Julienne was a sweet, pious girl, and had rejected half of the youths of L'Anse Creuse, whilst this Lizon was ugly, cross-eyed and had a halt in his walk, besides had never been known to enter the church.

How he won the damsel was a sort of mystery to all, a constant theme of conjecture. Some boldly said it was sorcery. The parents of the girl were opposed to the marriage, but seeing how headstrong she was, left her to her own devices.

Lizon refused to be married in church, as he would then be obliged to attend to his religious duties. Julienne besought him, but to no avail. What argument he used, what witchcraft he employed, is not known, but Julienne deserted her home and came to live with Lizon. Father Gabriel who had been absent, returned a few days after and found his community excited over the scandal. He immediately sent for both culprits. Neither obeyed his command. The following Sunday he hurled against them the fearful ban of excommunication, and stated that Lizon had a wife and children whom he had deserted, living in Montreal. From that day no one crossed the threshold of Lizon's door,—the grass grew rank, and seldom was Julienne seen. Lizon's rage knew no bounds; he repaired a dilapidated barn and there kept liquor for all who desired to procure it. Those who had feared to go to the auberge flocked to this new place and soon the evil influence of this drinking was felt. The peace which reigned in this Arcadia of Lake Ste. Claire was broken; dissensions, quarrels and scandals arose. The voice of the priest seemed powerless and his efforts paralyzed by the demon of liquor.

Julienne, who was seldom seen, startled the congregation one Sunday morning by standing in front of the altar and asking public pardon, through the priest, for the great scandal she had caused. All in the church were melted into tears, and the voice of the pastor was tremulous with emotion as he welcomed back the erring sheep into the fold.

When Lizon discovered the flight of Julienne,

that she had returned to her God and to her parents, his anger was fearful. He swore that he would have her back, that he would spurn anything that stood in his way. The bay would sooner break its bonds than he forego his design.

It was New Year's eve, and every household was making preparations, for each expected a visit from the d'Ignolée. This is an old custom, traced to France, and by fragmentary history and tradition away back to the Druids* and is still kept up at Grosse Pointe and in Lower Canada. A number of young men gather, masked and armed with stout sticks, and visit each house successively in the village. They halt at the door and sing their song. They are bidden in, and after greeting the host and hostess, continue their song in which they state that they come in accordance with their promise to visit them annually. "We ask but little," they say, "a little

---

*Freya, the wife of Odin, the Saxon god, made all things swear not to harm Balder, the Sun, except the mistletoe, a plant so diminutive that she did not think it worth noticing. Lake, god of evil, found out his weak point however, and tearing up the mistletoe gave it to Odin, the blind god, who with it fatally pierced Balder. That was the fable, and it was to prevent Lake from slaying Balder that the Druids solemnly sought the oak trees and gathered the mistletoe from their boughs with the joyous cry, "Au gui l'an neuf," of which La d'Ignolée is a corruption, meaning the mistletoe—the new year.

piece of chignee, nothing more. Will you give it? If not, say so, and we will take your eldest daughter." The chignee to which allusion is here made is a piece cut from a newly slaughtered hog, with the tail depending therefrom. It is invariably put aside, with clothing and provisions, for the singers who place the offerings of all in their cart, and afterward distribute them among the poor.

The d'Ignolée knocked for admittance at the door of Julienne's father; they were welcomed and received their offerings. Whilst the party was singing a sudden cry of distress caused all to rush to the door. Nothing was seen and the d'Ignolée immediately departed. The father called Julienne for the evening rosary and receiving no answer, went to her room; she was not there. Immediately they suspected that Lizon was among the d'Ignolée. The cry they had heard was hers and a warning to the rest of the d'Ignolée to leave. Messengers flew to stop the d'Ignolée and others ran to Lizon's, but they did not find Julienne. Father Gabriel was sent for and he went to demand Julienne of Lizon who laughed at him, saying he did not recognize his authority and did not understand why he, Father Gabriel, should interfere with what did not concern him. The priest answered that Julienne was one of his flock, she had willingly left Lizon and he had stolen her. A scream for help from the house was heard and Julienne's father and others rushing in, found her and brought her back. The night of horrors was too much for her; she became a maniac. Lizon, maddened by liquor and at the defeat of his plans, in his rage struck the priest in the face and blasphemed everything sacred. A few sprang forward to seize Lizon, but the majority looked on.

Father Gabriel raised his hands and said that Lizon has brought a curse on the place, and caused others, by his bad example, to follow in his footsteps; and he again pronounced the awful edict of excommunication against him. That unless he repented, even in the grave he should have no rest; and all who aided or abetted him in his evil deeds would suffer. *Their church would be swept away by the rising waters.*

Father Gabriel left for Fort Pontchartrain, and Lizon took every occasion to distribute his vile liquor and to malign the good character of the priest. But somehow nothing seemed to prosper. The season set in wet and stormy, the fruit failed to ripen and was blasted on the trees. The crops were all destroyed and clouds of locusts devoured the young grass. The people murmured among themselves and looked for the return of the good priest, whose interest in their behalf they had rewarded with ingratitude, and on whose departure disaster had come. One day the old auberge was closed, and it was said that Lizon had died unexpectedly. He was hurriedly placed in a coffin and a grave dug in unconsecrated ground. As the bearers were about to place the coffin in its final resting place, they suddenly felt it grow lighter, whilst out of the grave issued loathsome serpents without number. For many days these occurrences were common gossip. Phantasmagorial forms in white could be seen moving about, and those who looked towards Lizon's grave saw it roll and heave, whilst the feu follet skipped about in all directions.

A fearful storm set in, lashing the waves into foamy billows mountain high and dashing them against the shore with such force as to sweep over the road. Higher and higher the waters crept, climbing up towards the orchards of fine Colville apples and the stately pears, survivors of the days of "le grand monarch." Closer and closer the angry surf came to the little church; the water had undermined the quicksand beneath it, and with a groan and deafening crash it sank into the mighty element. The people frightened by the fearful disaster fled in terror to the woods, where they remained through the night. Day dawned peaceably; the habitants returned to their deserted homes, rebuilt their church, and by their prayers and the faithful observance of their duties, removed the curse which rested on L'Anse Creuse.

XXIV

SANS SOUCI AND OKEMOS.

The Legend of a Centenarian.

ONE of the best known houses in Detroit during the early part of this century stood on the north-east corner of the present Woodward avenue and Woodbridge street, fronting on the latter, then "par excellence" the fashionable street. A hospitable old French domicile was this, with its big fire place occupying nearly the entire side of a room in the centre of which was a stout oaken table with carved legs and rush-bottomed chairs around it. About the floor were deer and buffalo skins on which unexpected guests (frequently chiefs of the neighboring Indian tribes) might stretch their weary limbs and with their feet on the hearth beguile the night away.

This was the home of Gabriel Godefroy, agent of the Pottawatomies and Chippewas. Style then was not a ruling element as at the present time. General Cass relates that when he arrived he found benches instead of chairs in ordinary use, and that an old bottle was frequently the nearest approach to a candlestick; and servants being scarce he who served himself was best served. So his friends often saw him returning from market with a great yellow pumpkin under his arm, and on occasions of necessity he did not disdain to place across his broad shoulders the neck-yoke, a certain machine with two buckets pendent from its extremities, which constituted the primitive water works, the river then as now furnishing a never-failing supply of the beverage. Long intercourse with the Indian tribes had simplified the tastes of the habitants and brought with it freedom from care and the calls of the tax-collector.

The proprietor of this house previously mentioned, was one of the few born within the walls of old Fort Pontchartrain under French rule, who survived all the eventful changes and who lived to serve the American government forty years. His boon companions were Chabert de Joncaire, Descomptes Labadie, Francois de Lasclle, Jacques Campeau, Antoine Beaubien,

Pierre Navarre, Antoine De Quindre, Jacques Dupéron Baby, Whittmore Knaggs and other hardy pioneers of this outpost of civilization. Some of them were sure to happen in at Godefroy's during the long winter evenings and would meet there such chiefs as Tecumseh, Black Hoof, Walk in the Water, Okemos (a nephew of Pontiac) and others whose names are familiar. The law required an Indian agent to keep open house for all representative savages who chanced to visit the post. How often have I sat by the crackling fire of blazing logs, listening to the wild tales of Indian fights, wonderful hunts, hairbreadth escapes, etc., etc.! How they laughed as they told the story of old Sans Souci, a superannuated mare the date of whose birth was beyond the ken of the oldest habitant! This remarkable animal was the property of Godefroy's clerk, Jean Beaugrand, a mysterious old bachelor who was himself looked askance at by all the children of the fort on account of a strange habit he had of mumbling to himself. How old Sans Souci survived for so many years was inexplicable, for she was sure to visit each neighbor's cornfield or watermelon patch once a week, and before escaping therefrom had to run a wild gauntlet of stones and sticks. The more stolen provender she disposed of the leaner she grew, until at last she became a veritable scarecrow. No fence was high enough to keep her out, and there was a tradition that she had once jumped the pickets of the fort, twelve feet in height. In case some over-exasperated habitant shot at her she would merely kick up her heels and switch her tail by way of return salute. A whip or club had no effect on her except to cause a sort of scowl and a malicious laying back of the ears. On bright, sunny days she would saunter forth on the narrow streets or stand with downcast head on the corner for hours, evidently communing with herself on by-gone scenes, only aroused by a dog fight or a knot of idlers discussing politics in which she seemed to take a lively interest. Occasionally she would open wide her mouth in apparent laughter at the recollection of some old joke. At other times she would shake her head wisely and blink with the dignity of a sage judge delivering a profound opinion. What Sans Souci was thinking about no one could tell; that was the mystery. She would only brighten up when her master, Beaugrand, who seemed to have some private understanding with her, appeared around the corner and beckoned her to the barn just behind the house. For an instant a reminiscence of departed youth would animate her, causing her to prick up her ears and forget her usual snail-like pace, in expectation of fodder to come. Jean used to avow that years before his old mare had broken a leg in a race on the ice but that she kept right on and won the race in spite of it. Tradition has it that a line of steeds which sprang from this same mare have a peculiar habit of cutting up the same capers, even to this day.

It was in 1805, the year of the famous fire, that a number of French and Indians were seated around Godefroy's festal board. Numerous potations had exhausted the jug of cider, and Okemos, who was present, became clamorous for something stronger. "You will have to find Jean, then," said Godefroy, "he has the key to the cellar." The Indian immediately disappeared but soon after returned in evident terror. He announced that seeing a light in Beaugrand's window over the barn, he had looked through the chinks and saw Jean seated with the old mare, Sans Souci, before a table and that both were laughing and chatting together. It was not strange that an Indian should believe this, for they all looked on bears, wolves and beavers as reasoning beings, and only prevented from speaking by an evil spirit. Godefroy, to the great horror of Okemos, exclaimed, "We will see about this," and followed by several of his

French guests ascended the ladder leading to
Jean's room, determined to put an end to this
spiritual séance. A Frenchman who cautiously
peeked through a crack avowed that he could
see Jean playing "seven-up" with the old mare,
and that they were pouring into a pewter cup
and drinking what looked by lamplight like
melted brass. Godefroy, indignant at such nonsense, dashed his foot against the door which
yielded. Both the Frenchmen with him declared
they saw the old mare leap out of the window
when the door flew open, but Jean on being accused of diabolical work insisted that he was
only concocting a little "cidre au charbon" by
the light of his lantern, and that the mare would
be found in the stable below. Okemos, however,
who had followed, would not believe this story
but considered Godefroy a "big medicine" to
dare to disturb the evil spirit at his meals. Ever
after this Godefroy's influence with the Indians
was all-powerful. As to the old mare, her days
were numbered. A few weeks later the cry of
fire resounded though the post, and in a few
hours not a single habitation was left to indicate
where old Detroit had stood. The old barn, of
course, was burned, and the superstitious ones
who thought that Sans Souci was carried off
by the devil in a cloud of smoke, were shown her

charred remains the next day. There were many, however, who asserted that they saw the dreaded Nain Rouge (or little red man), the traditional fiend of the fort, on the roof of the barn just before it fell in, and that he grinned and chuckled as he did on the day the old French flag was hauled down. When war broke out with England, the United States Government by a mistaken policy at first allowed the British to secure control of the Indian tribes. But after Winchester's defeat and the cold-blooded massacre of Kentucky troops, Okemos and his Chippewas with many others, were secured to the American cause by Godefroy's influence.* It was one of his

---

*Narrative of Elizabeth Ann Godefroy, daughter of Judge James May: "About two weeks after the battle of the River Raisin, during the absence of my husband from home, I purchased a prisoner from a Pottawatomie Indian named Ta-tas-sa. This was in the month of February, 1813. The Indians were about to burn him at the stake in the yard before our house. I called on my husband's clerk and interpreter, Raumaine La Chambre, and said to him that he must devise some way to save the American. Being ill and near the period of confinement, the interpreter said that if I were to ask of the Indians, the prisoner as an adopted son they might give him up. So I followed his advice, and on hearing the request they shrugged their shoulders, saying, 'Oh! oh! it is bad medicine to refuse a woman in your condition anything, but this is a Yankee dog and we must burn him.' I then asked them what they would take for his ransom. They replied, one hundred dollars. Having but ten dollars at hand I offered them a fine black horse well saddled and bridled,

friendly Indians that brought Godefroy the first
news of Perry's victory, and the enthusiastic
Frenchman hastened to promulgate it from house
to house, lightening the hearts of a people almost

---

belonging to my husband, with two bundles of dry goods and a
lot of silver work (for Indian use) together with the ten dollars in
money, in all worth some two hundred dollars. But the Indians
replied, 'This is not money to us and we will not sell him.' I
then told them through the interpreter that we had in the cellar
a five-gallon keg of whiskey. At this they held a council among
themselves, and finally sold me the prisoner and went their way.
His name was John Henry, from Louisville, Kentucky. He said
his wife's name was Nancy Burnet, and that he had a child six
months old named Valentine. Immediately after the purchase I
gave him something to eat, and had the interpreter shave off his
beard and dress him in the garb of an old French voyageur, so as
to disguise him as much as possible, fearing that when the whiskey was all gone the Indians would return and demand the pris
oner, or more whiskey, which was not to be had at any price.
After a short rest I sent the prisoner under charge of a Frenchman to my father, Judge May, of Detroit, whom I desired to attend to his exchange, which he did by sending my brother, James
May, Jr., with him to Major Muir, British Commandant. As I
had anticipated the Indians returned by daylight and brought
back all that I had given them except the whiskey and demanded
the prisoner, or more whiskey. I told them through the interpreter I had given them all I had and they then began a search
about the house for the prisoner. La Chambre said to them:
'Now you see the poor woman after paying you well for the prisoner has lost all she gave and her adopted son also, for your British father sent his soldiers here last night and took him away from
her.' So half believing the story they left for the border of the
woods thinking he might possibly be concealed there. The prisoner on leaving promised to write to me but if he did, his letters
never reached us."

driven to despair by Proctor's tyrannies and the insatiable exactions of his savage allies.

While the site of the old house is still in possession of Godefroy's descendants, the ground on which the old barn stood is occupied by a police station, and from the shrieks and groans that often emanate from some of its frenzied occupants while under the influence of potations of strychnine (modern whiskey), we may well infer that the ghosts of both Sans Souci and the Nain Rouge still haunt the spot.

XXV

THE SIBYL'S PROPHECY.

A Legend of the Huron Village.

IT WAS in August, 1806. The Hurons, following their usual yearly custom had come to camp near the church in Sandwich, to celebrate what was then called "Le Festin des Sauvages," (The Indian Feast). After assisting devoutly at mass, they filed out one by one according to grade, for these monarchs of the forest were as tenacious of their rank as the Ancienne Noblesse of France, who even respected the rights of precedence in mounting the steps of the guillotine.

A grand feast was prepared in the grove to which were invited the clergy and those of the habitants whom the Hurons knew well and desired to honor. The menu was not in strict conformity to the rules of the superb epicure, Brillat Savarin. But those who partook of the repast were reared in that healthy atmosphere which demands no sauce piquante to suggest appetite to blasé palates. It consisted of a soup made of game to which were added corn and summer squash; fresh fish from the clear waters; abundance of game, well dressed; praline made of parched corn pounded between two stones and mixed with maple. sugar (supplying the place of the modern baker's loaf to the wayfarers of early times); sagamite, a porridge made of corn, and fruit completed the bill of fare.

Among those present was Angelique Conture who had been the "queteuse" for the collection in the church that day, a task she performed in that easy, graceful manner peculiar to the French girl. Another guest was Francois Navarre, whose father was prominently connected with the Indian traffic, and whose fluent tongue had won for him the sobriquet of Robiche (the speaker). Francois inherited his sire's facile and happy speech which, added to charming and persuasive manners, gained him many strong allies among the fair sex both of Sandwich and Detroit. He was distantly related to Angelique and made that slender tie a favorable pretext to seek frequently the society of the bright-eyed coquette who even carried the witchery of her charms so far as to captivate the hearts of the savage braves.

As soon as the meal was over the young men gave themselves up to their favorite game of ball, the chiefs smoked in dignified repose their beloved calumet. The children clustered around "le bon père" to hear some holy legend, whilst others more volatile pursued the many hued butterflies. The young squaws swept away the débris of the feast, pausing now and then to caress the little dusky papoose who, suspended in the birchen cradle on the bough of a tree, was swayed lazily by the breeze.

Angelique finding no amusement to divert her, proposed to two of her companions that they should seek the prophetess of the tribe, of whom they had heard most marvelous tales. The proposition rather frightened the timid girls, but Angelique excited their curiosity to such a degree that they eagerly followed her, and as they leisurely strolled along she kept up their courage by her inimitable mimicry until the forest rang with their joyous laughter.

Suddenly a turn in their path brought them

face to face with the object of their search. Leaning over and stirring a kettle on the smouldering fire, was the figure of a woman who was chanting in a low monotone a song of incantation to which she kept time by the swaying motion of her body. This was the dreaded Sibyl whose solitary habits, strange wanderings and wonderful gift of prophecy had thrown a veil of mystery over her which few had ever attempted to raise. No one knew her history save that she had been made a captive years before. She always followed the tribe to its various encampments, yet lived a apart, never crossing a threshold save in cases of severe sickness. Her knowledge of the different healing herbs was considered equal to, if not greater than that of the renowned medicine men. The old habitants involuntarily crossed themselves when the strange, stern woman passed them.

The girls on the impulse of the moment thought of flight, but were arrested by an unaccountable fascination. The woman evidently had heard their approach, for she turned slowly and raising herself up to her full height displayed a tall, commanding figure, a face bronzed by exposure, and eyes accustomed to lonely vigils. She asked in a deep, sonorous voice, "What do you seek?" Summoning up courage Angelique tremblingly replied, "Knowledge of the future." "Heedless ones," she replied, "read it for yourselves; it is written everywhere, on the broad face of the sky, on the leaves of the trees. Ere many moons this very soil will become the scene of carnage; the air will be filled with lamentations. These woods which have re-echoed to your careless merriment will resound to the savage warwhoop and the tomahawk will gleam in the upraised hands. Lovers will be separated, wives will be made widows and children orphans. Go, you have heard enough."

Passively obeying her imperious gesture the girls silently retraced their steps, with the gay smiles frozen on their lips and the sunlight faded from their eyes. But their other companions joining them, enticed them into the mysteries of the moccasin game, and with the careless insouciance of youth they forgot for the moment the Sibyl and her gloomy predictions.

The great comet of 1812 shortly afterwards appeared as a premonition of war, and to the superstitious there were other signs of illomen and disaster. War was soon declared and spread its devastating influence over the land, converting this fair region into a scene of bloodshed and rendering its peaceful homes desolate. Angelique's brothers fought under the banner of St. George, her lover, Francois, under the Stars and Stripes. These were days of anguish and suspense to the sad watchers at home, and Angelique's heart was divided in its allegiance. She heard of the battles, of the terrible massacres, of the sad fate of the prisoners, but received no tidings of her lover.

One day Proctor passed through Sandwich on his way to his encampment near the church, and elated by his recent success at the battle of the river Raisin, was displaying in proud triumph his captives, whose dejected mien, travel-worn and weary forms covered with dust, appealed to the tender sympathies of the spectators.

Among them Angelique recognized the stately figure of her lover. Stunned by the blow she did not realize its full meaning, until the sorrowful procession had passed. Shortly afterwards to her great surprise, Francois knocked for admission; being so well known he had been paroled until sunset, and one hour he had to spend with his beloved. Sad was the interview, bitter the parting; for them there was no morrow. The well-known character of Proctor whose cruelty equalled that of his savage allies, left no hope for intercession. The girl clung to her lover and frantically besought him to fly, to avail himself of his liberty, to escape the frightful death at the stake which awaited him on the morrow. Her tender pleadings might well unnerve a strong man, but honor triumphed and pointing mutely to the setting sun, Francois wrenched himself from her detaining arms and with her despairing cries ringing in his ears, reached the camp as the sun was sinking below the horizon.

This act of extreme honor commanded even Indian appreciation, and they left him unbound. Sad and melancholy were his thoughts. How much that parting with Angelique cost him, and his struggle with love and honor his altered face betrayed. Memories of the past greeted him everywhere, with no ray of hope to gild the gloom of sorrow.

Savage cries of exultation awoke the doomed man from his meditations. He saw the Indians had all rushed to the beach to welcome new prisoners who were landing, and in the hurry of the moment had left him ungaurded. His practiced eye took in the situation and commending his soul to his Maker, he had vanished into the forest before the barbarous warwhoops told him that his departure had been discovered, and that the red fiends were in pursuit.

A squad of Dickson's noted savages hideous in war paint and feathers, surrounded Angelique's home. The interpreter explained that Francois Navarre had reported himself as promised, but taking advantage of an unguarded moment had escaped. The Indians were impatient to enter, and the interpreter no longer able to restrain them, said that the house must be searched. Angelique thanked God that her lover had escaped but trembled at the idea of his capture, for it seemed impossible for him to elude his pursuers. The house swarmed with the savages who left no spot unvisited. Even the chimneys were examined and the beds pierced by bayonets, until satisfied that the fugitive was not there, the Indians leaving a guard in case he should seek refuge there, withdrew.

An Indian chief came to Angelique a few days later and triumphantly pointed to a fresh scalp which hung at his belt, which the wretched girl thought her lover's. The suspense, followed by what she imagined was his tragic fate, was too much for her to bear, and she gradually began to fade. Soon afterwards a well-known token from her lover found its way to her which brought life to her heart and health to her cheeks. She learned later that he had kept to the forest until he reached where now is Walkerville, where he found a canoe and crossed to the American side. After the war there was great rejoicing, for the happy lovers were united.

XXVI

CAPTAIN JEAN.

A Legend of the First Militia.

ALEXIS Trotier des Ruisseaux belonged to a distinguished family of Quebec ; he came to Detroit to join his brother-in-law, the brave and chivalrous Picoté DeBellestre, the last French Commandant of Fort Pontchartrain. Des Ruisseaux here met and wedded the beautiful and ascetic Catherine Godefroy de Marboeuf, whose pious deeds have come down in fragmentary traditions to her brother's descendants, who to-day reside in Detroit, and who revere and honor the memory of their saintly ancestress. Alexis was the first trustee of Ste. Anne's Church, and the first captain of militia.

In 1760, when the lily of France, which had

bloomed for sixty years on the fair soil of its adoption, drooped before the fiery standard of England, many of the old customs and traditions of the French régime lay cradled in its folded petals.

It was not until 1805 that the militia system was resuscitated from the dust and cobwebs of the past, though an attempt was made in 1796 by Acting Gov. Sargeant. But Gen. Hull after organizing the Territorial Government, formed the first regiment of militia. It consisted of eight companies, drawn from every part of the territory, except the District of Erie. Jean Cecire was among the first of the French habitants who joined the new militia. To the diplomatic policy of the Americans, anxious to conciliate the French element, was he indebted for his rank of Captain in the First Regiment of Michigan. He never fully recovered from the shock of the honor, and became so thoroughly imbued with the importance of his position, that every detail of his dress and every action, bore the impress of this great event in his career.

His conceit, pretentious manners, and exaggerated self-importance, were endless sources of merriment to the old habitants, who possessed exquisite finesse in quickly detecting the foibles of others, and were happy in their piquante remarks, to which the indescribable and expressive shrug of the shoulder, lent its humorous charm.

Jean would frequently go to see the regular troops drill. Their severe discipline and military exactness sorely puzzled him, and he thought it must be owing to the words of command being given in English, in which there was a hidden magic. His knowledge of the language was almost as limited as his use of the pen, though his ingenuity conquered the latter difficulty. The names of the men of his company were printed in order, so he used a pin to punch a hole after the name of the absentee. But that tongue of his, so facile, so easy to control in French, was positively frozen in English. By wonderful struggles he succeeded in thawing it into the semblance of broken English.

The American officers stationed at the fort, to the great delight of Capt. Jean, would frequently request to be present at the drills, and the recital afterwards by a graceful and graphic tongue of these rare and quaint manœuvres, awoke the echoes of the mess room. It is to be regretted that one officer at least, who had talent for sketching, left no record of these strange scenes. He would have won a debt of gratitude from even this unleisurely age.

The time of the general training had arrived, and Capt. Jean was ordered to drill his company on the commons. No haughty Scottish chieftain ever surveyed his tartan clan with prouder mien, or more happy feelings surging in his heart, than Jean his motley recruits. Some were in uniform, others in the gay dress of the habitants, and their pieces and accoutrements represented every variety known to the history of arms.

Gen. Hull was too exacting in his requirements in time of peace, and demanded the same nicety of order, dress, etc., as in the regulars, which caused anger and insurbordination. He forgot that these stepsons of France, though they inherited the bravery and love of glory inseparable from the French character, had been placed in a strange position by the various changes of government. They had been forced to adopt a passive policy, which had buried their enthusiastic natures beneath a crust of indifference and indolence. Their easy going life had little prepared them to assume at once the rigid discipline of the camp which Hull tried to enforce, though gradually they would have recognized its utility and quietly submitted.

Capt. Jean ordered the Sergeant to call the roll. He immediately proceeded to obey, the Captain standing by in the full glory of regimentals.

Sergeant—"Attention, Companie Francais Canadians! Answer your name when I call it, if you please. Tock Tock Livernois?"

No answer; at last a voice says, "Not here, gone catch his lambreuer (fast pacer) in the bush."

Captain—"Sergeant, put peen hole in dat man! Go head!"

Sergeant—"Laurant Bondy?"

"Here, sah."

"Claude Campau?"

"Here, Monsieur."

"Antoine Saliotte?"

Some one answers—"Little baby came last night at his house, must stay home."

Captain—"Sergeant, put one preek on dat man's name."

Sergeant—"T'enfant Riopelle?"

"Here, sah."

Sergeant—"Pitou Laforest?"

"Here, sah."

Sergeant—"Simon Meloche?"

"Not here. Gone to spear mushrat for argent blanc."

Captain—"Sergeant, take your pin and scratch dat man."

After the roll was called and the absentees pricked the Captain proceeded to drill his company.

Captain—"Marchée! Mes camarades, deux par deux (two and two) like oxen, and when you come to dat stump stop."

They all made for the place and got there in a heap, looking, with their various colored dresses, like a rainbow on a spree. Disgusted at their awkwardness, the Captain gave them a few minutes relaxation. Instead of resting "au militaire," they rushed off, one to smoke his beloved pipe, another to polish his carbine, whilst others amused themselves sitting on the grass and telling about the races.

The Captain called them to try again. This time he said: "Marchée as far as dat soulier de bœuf (old shoe) in de road, den turn! Right, gauche, left about! Shoulder mus-*keete!* Avance donc, back! Drill fineesh!"

An English Sergeant drilled the company during the war of 1812, and was a source of great admiration to Capt. Jean.

At the battle of Mongaugon Capt. Jean led his company. They fought well and bravely, but he lost his Sergeant and his men began to waiver. Jean was brave but powerless to rally them, or make them fall in ranks. He forgot the few words of command he was master of, and great beads of perspiration stood on his brow. At last he broke forth:

"Fix yourself, as pauvre Jim did, den, by Gar, follow me."

Many years afterwards a son of Capt. Jean, who had inherited his father's military taste and some of his peculiarities, once met old Oshkosh, Black Hawk's celebrated lieutenant.

The dusky warrior was quietly seated in one of the inns of the day, enjoying his calumet, enveloped in a soft mist of smoke which wove his thoughts with the past. Suddenly a loud voice resounded, and a gay figure entered with a swaggering bearing, rudely snapping the thread of Oshkosh's reverie. Many were present who knew the old brave's aversion to the militia, and thought of amusing themselves at his expense; so they introduced Lt. Cecire. From under his bushy eyebrows the Indian gazed at him and grunted forth:

"Infantry?"

"No," was the reply.

"Dragoon?"

"No."

"Artillery?"

"No."

Pausing a moment to think if there were another branch of the service in which to locate the Lieutenant, suddenly a light dawned on the Indian's mind. Hastily jumping up, he with a most disgusted expression hissed :

"Melish?"

"Yes," was the triumphant reply.

"Oh, h—l," said Oshkosh, and rushed from the house.

XXVII

KENNETTE'S VISION.

A Legend of Springwells.

A FEW years ago the figure of an old woman was frequently seen on our principal streets, whose quaint dress, erect bearing and keen piercing eyes, challenged the attention of every passer-by. She seemed to be a relic of a past age, who had strayed by accident into the present and was at variance with her surroundings. To-day, after slumbering for fifteen years, her restless spirit seems to revive and cause agitation in civil as well as political circles.

Marie Louise Thebault, generally called "Kennette," well known to the older portion of our French community and by tradition to its younger members, dwelt in a little old wooden house on the River road, opposite the Lafferty homestead. A stately elm threw its majestic shadow over the humble dwelling, seeming to shield it from rude winter blasts and to protect it from the summer's intense sun. Alone she lived here like a hermit. Her sister had married against her wishes, for Kennette was no advocate of matrimony. She believed in woman's rights; was a sort of pioneer in that doctrine among the people of those times, and to-day would have been a powerful ally to the leading spirits of the question.

A distinguished writer says: "Show me a man's room and I will tell you his character." Kennette's dress forcibly illustrated the application of the remark. It was stamped by her strong individuality. At all seasons she wore a calico dress, rather scant, short enough not only to clear the ground, but to bring out in bass-relief an ankle whose outline freed it from all suggestiveness of symmetry. Hooks and eyes, and even buttons, were superfluous luxuries when pins could be substituted, and failing these a thorn would answer. A red handkerchief around her neck was crossed on her breast; a coarse cotton cap with a deep frill, innocent of starch and fluting, emphasized each movement of that decided head; a check sunbonnet for outside wear, a blue umbrella and a pair of stout shoes of her own manufacture, completed a costume as characteristic as it was unique.

She seemed to scorn the usual gentler accomplishments of her sex, yet with a strange inconsistency frequently found in positive natures, she hated man, but adopted his pursuits. Never did her voice keep time to the music of the spinning wheel, nor did the steel needles flash through those fingers knitting stockings in which so many weave the history of their past, or build castles for the future. Seated on a wooden bench, with all the cobbler's implements, she would volunteer to make shoes for the children and warrant their durability, and even the most pronounced hoyden found Miss Kennette's sabots *pièce de résistance*, which defied everything save beauty.

No cat ever basked in the warmth of her hearth, no cow stood in her stall, no dog barked a joyous welcome as she crossed the threshold of her dreary and lonesome home. These were luxuries only for the wealthy, she said. Her means were more than sufficient to gratify her simple tastes and to allow her some indulgences, but she was penurious to a miserly extent. The neighbors along the River road all knew her well, and always gave her vegetables and fruits. Her evenings were invariably spent out to save light and fuel, and it was a rare treat and a token of particular good will if Miss Kennette brought her violin. She had a good ear for music, and with cultivation might have been an excellent performer, but her untutored efforts were rather crude. The children would cluster around her at a respectful distance, for Miss Kennette was a warm advocate of the doctrine that "children should be seen, not heard." Woe to the little urchin whose perceptive powers were too keen and who dared to ask why Miss Kennette used so much rosin, and was always shifting corners, complaining one was too warm, another too cool for her violin, and why she did not make it speak like George Maisonville's (a noted fiddler in those days). A tingling sensation and a peculiar redness of the ear warned the luckless boy not to repeat his questions.

She read much, and mostly works that tended to render her skeptical in religious matters. She had no patience with those who told her wonderful stories of apparitions. She was always ready for an argument, and would emphasize her declarations with expressions which, though original were more forcible than elegant. Toward the close of her life an incident happened which invested her with more than usual interest, caused a decided change in her religious belief and left its impress upon her character. There are many still living who have heard her relate it and who, knowing the strong, self-reliant nature of the woman, could not help being deeply impressed.

It was a bright moonlight night, and Kennette was spending the evening with a neighbor who lived near, and amusing all, as usual, by her quaint and piquante conversation. She was relating how she had allowed an elderly friend of hers to rent a room in her house, so that by the arrangement she would not only get a little rent, but could use the fire and light of her boarder; that this person was always preaching to her and destroyed all her pleasure, and that if her instincts of economy were not so well developed, she would not go near her. "It is not pleasant," she said, "to be told that the books I read are wicked, that they instill poison into my heart, and that when I am old I will be stranded on the shore of remorse and despair. Well, to hush her up I made an agreement. 'I don't believe in hell or purgatory,' I said, 'so if you die first come back; if I should, I will return. Just appear and I will know that there is such a place.'"

The bargain was made, and Kennette for a while sunned herself in the borrowed warmth of another's fire and had contentment. But the restless Kennette soon quarreled with the boarder, a good, pious soul, and told her she would never forgive her for some imaginary wrong she fancied the old woman had done her. Shortly afterwards the boarder died, and Kennette stood inflexibly and sternly beside the dying bedside and said she would not forgive, but their compact would hold.

Whilst she was talking to her neighbors one evening and sipping cider, of which she was very fond, one of the boys of the house returning from town, asked Miss Kennette why she left a light burning in her house, for knowing the old woman's miserly habits, he had thought it strange. Jumping up and seizing a poker, she said she would go over and find out who dared enter her habitation. Others accompanied her. Nothing but darkness reigned there, although the boy said positively he had seen a light; they thought probably it was the light of a fisherman's boat passing on the river, and dismissed the subject. But night after night the same occurrence took place and people spoke about it and avoided passing near the old house. It always happened on an evening when Miss Kennette was away.

Worried by the reports, and having witnessed this shifting light and searched everywhere for it, Miss Kennette determined to discover the cause, for she was not at all superstitious nor afraid of anything.

One evening she returned earlier than usual, softly let herself in by the back door and immediately retired. Hardly had she composed herself to sleep, when she saw the reflection of a dim light on the wall at the head of the stairs. The upper room was not divided and the staircase was in the center. The light grew larger and larger, as if a person were carrying it up the stairs. Seated bolt upright in her bed, which was in a corner of the room near the west window, Kennette watched for the solution of a mystery which had so long baffled her. A stranger, to fear she was cool and collected, and patiently waited the developments. At last the light seemed to have arrived on the top step. It was no candle, no lantern, but a peculiar vivid white light. It glided along the wall and as it came nearer to her bed, it suddenly assumed the outlines of a figure draped in clouds. Then a tremor ran through her. Her blood became chilled; new sensations crept over her. Rousing herself she rubbed her eyes, saw she was not dreaming and realized that it was no idle fancy but a fearful reality. Slowly was the apparition gliding along towards her. Seeing she must do something to arrest its progress, she said: "Come no nearer; I know you. I believe and I forgive," and as the mysterious light came, so it disappeared.

From that day forward all noticed a change. The dark hair was bleached, wrinkles were written on that stern face and a softer expression played over it. She returned to the faithful performance of her spiritual duties, and the Nemesis which had haunted her steps appeared satisfied, for the weird light was seen no more in her desolate home.

XXVIII

THE FISHERMAN OF GROSSE POINTE.

A Legend of the Grand Marais.

GROSSE POINTE was peculiarly congenial to the early settlers by its position, its beauty and other advantages. Perhaps a shadow of sentiment rested upon it in its suggestion of picturesque Normandy, souvenirs of which were tenderly cherished by the pioneers. Wherever we go we carry the image of our early surroundings, and unconsciously a new place or scene appeals to us, by the resemblance it bears to this revered picture. The imagination, like a skillful diplomate, catches its clue from the heart, and weaves its alluring net-work of enchantment. Even inanimate objects contribute to this deception, for we remain attached to the down on which our prosperity has slumbered, and still more to the straw on which we counted the days of our adversity.

The waters of Lake Ste. Claire grow shallow as they near the shores of Grosse Pointe, as if unwilling to break the harmonious silence by harsher sounds than the low breathing of its waves on the pebbles, thus affording a safe haven from severe storms, and allowing the timorous to stray a great distance out without fear of a worse fate than a ducking. Here, as along "La Cote du Nord Est," fishing was extensively carried on, and with the same avidity as at present. An old tradition says that here two bachelor brothers resided, whose skill in the manufacture of nets and whose successful hauls of fish were widely known, Hypolite and Pierrish Tremblay by name. The elder was surnamed Le Gascon, from the wonderful things he reported having seen, and from his supersti tious nature. They exchanged their daily catch of fish with their neighbors for corn, l'huile d'ours (bear's oil), a dainty edible then, and other necessaries.

Their pursuits, like the commercial ventures of modern times, were subject to fluctuations. One autumn their nets were frozen into the ice by a sudden sharp cold. When the early spring thaw came, it broke up the nets and carried them away.

More provident than the average fun-loving Canadian, they had sufficient "livres tours" (the currency of the day) to begin anew. Somehow luck deserted them and appeared to have drifted away in the broken meshes of the old nets, for morning and evening when they drew in the seine it was empty, save for a few meagre herring and hungry catfish, instead of the succulent white fish and muskallongé.* The prospect seemed dark for the fishermen, and a plenary court of Lent would soon reign if matters continued thus much longer.

"Let us consult le bon père," said Pierrish, the younger, after the brothers had been discussing the precarious situation. "Bah!" answered Hypolite with a feeble expression. He was much given to profanity, had received several rebukes on that score from the priest, and hence was not friendly toward him. "He can do nothing; some enemy has 'donnée le sort' (bewitched) our fishery, it is no use trying to do anything; I am going elsewhere, you may remain if you wish." So the brothers separated, one to search for new fishing grounds, the other to consult the priest. Pierrish laid the situation before the curé, who listened attentively, then said, "Mon fils, choose St. Pat-

---

*Muskanogé, corrupted into Muskallongé, is the finest fish o the lakes.

rick as your partner and divide each day's catch with him, selling the Saint's portion for the poor."*

On his homeward way, Pierrish revolved in his mind the advice of the priest, and made a solemn vow to follow it strictly. Full of hope, he cast his nets that evening, promising it to be the Saint's portion; the morning haul he would modestly reserve for himself. So when the net came in it was filled with fish, and while his catch in the morning was empty, the Saint's was always full. He pondered over the matter and was strongly tempted to keep the Saint's portion. Hypolite taunted him with his ill-luck, yet Pierrish remembered his vow and conscientiously brought the fish for sale, giving the proceeds to the poor. Finding that this mode was ruining him, he again visited the priest and told him of his misfortune. The priest, after hearing his story, said:

"Your simple faith and honesty will meet with its reward. Divide the proceeds of each net with your partner. You have stood a test of honesty which few in your position could have done."

From that time Pierrish became so successful that

---

* It was a beautiful custom then to bring to the church door the first fruits, fish or game, of the season, selling them to the highest bidder, the proceeds going to the poor, and for masses to relieve the suffering souls of purgatory.

he was known as "the lucky fisherman of Grosse Pointe."

Hypolite met with indifferent success, was always warning his brother, and looked with distrust upon this saintly partnership. His superstitious nature always conjured up some evil omen. "You will be inveigled into the lake and turned into a fish. Do you not remember the Indian legend relative to the origin of the poisson blanc, formed of the brains of a woman whom the Manitou had loved for a while, then cracked her skull on the rocks of Sault Ste. Marie? Your partner, St. Patrick, will play you a trick. Did he not eat pork chops on Friday by dipping them in water and changing them into orthodox trout? Beware!"

Pierrish would only smile at his vagaries. One day he was startled by Hypolite rushing into the house in a state of nervous excitement, wringing his hands and saying:

"Some terrible disaster is to befall one of us."

"Explain yourself," said Pierrish.

"Well," said Hypolite, "as I was leaving Baptiste Cochois, five miles from here, the cock crew and Baptiste said, 'You will meet company on the road, that cock tells you.' I was trotting along in my charrette (cart) when I spied a lady's muff by the wayside. Thinking it was strange to see such an article at this mild season, I got out to secure it. As soon as I approached it the muff began rolling. Becoming angry, and thinking the motion was caused by the wind, I still pursued it, but in vain; it eluded my grasp. Thoroughly frightened, I jumped into the charrette and trotted away as fast as I could, but the terrible thing followed me and actually jumped into and out of the cart. It must be the Manchon Roulant."*

Pierrish said, "If you had had holy water instead of brandy in that bottle, you could have exorcised that spirit. Go back where you saw the Manchon Roulant; if it is still there, cross yourself and boldly walk up to it, and before attempting to pick it up ask, 'What day of the month is Christmas day?'"† Hypolite, in fear and trembling, returned to the place, and

---

*Manchon Roulant. A superstition devoutly believed in many years ago, and still traditional among the habitants of Grosse Pointe.

†There were said to be two means to exempt oneself from any evil consequences arising from the tricks of the most malicious of goblins. The first was, on meeting the goblin to ask it, "What day of the month is Christmas day?" The goblin, which is never very well up in the calendar, will reply by asking the same question. Woe betide the traveller if he hesitates in answering. The second means was by placing two sticks in the form of a cross on meeting a goblin.

Parents were very particular in teaching their children to remember the day Christmas came on, to protect them from the feu follet.

sure enough the dreaded object was there. Fervently crossing himself, he cautiously approached the mysterious thing, which, strange to say remained immoveable. Closer he approached the mysterious ball of fur, and with eager, outstretched hands was ready to seize it, when suddenly bethinking himself of the question to put to it, in his excitement he blurted forth his usual oaths. Instantly there streamed forth a counter blast as from a fiery furnace, and a terrible odor filled the air, which struck him full in the face. Hypolite, nearly suffocated, in two bounds reached the lake, and as soon as he had recovered consciousness exclaimed, "La bête puante." His brother impressed it upon him that it was a punishment for his profanity, and whenever afterwards the Manchon Roulant was mentioned as a marvelous thing, it was observed, that Hypolite suddenly disappeared.

XXIX

THE GHOST OF MONGAUGON.

A Legend of Hull's Surrender.

THE dark, blackened ruins of a city, its poor stricken habitants gazing with tear-stained eyes on the gray ashes of their homes and hopes. Such was the scene which greeted the newly appointed Territorial Governor Hull, Stanley Griswold, the Secretary, and Augustus Woodward, the Chief Justice, on their arrival at Detroit the morning of the 6th of June, 1805. The night before a destructive fire had swept away every vestige of the old French town. Its quaint houses constructed of square logs, the steep roofs pierced with dormer windows and crossed with ladders in case of fire, its narrow streets of sixteen feet and sidewalks a foot wide formed of hewn logs, its

Norman and Indian relics, the quaint old furniture valuable only for its association with the past, decrees, deeds, letters and documents priceless legacies to the historian, perished in that night. Fate seemed to say, "This is a holocaust to departed memories. The cross of St. George, the lily of France have been dismantled, but the bright stars gleam like gems of promise through the tattered shreds. Cheer up, the past claims only your tears, the future will bring to you prosperity and happiness which you have sought in vain for an hundred years." Judge Woodward recognized the moment as a propitious one to win the hearts of the French settlers, and thus eloquently championed their rights, when it became necessary to divide the land and partition it among the dispossessed habitants: "He will not argue with you on your laws, or your forms, or your systems of policy and government. He looks only for that pittance of soil on which, perhaps, he drew his breath. He cannot be intimidated by threats, nor be induced to part with his lands, the hopes of himself and family, by any allurements of money. Tell him that you will dispossess him; he folds his hands with a pious resignation and commits the event to God. Amidst the collisions of nations, the incessant din of arms, the tide of revolution, he has lost a country to love and by which to be loved in return. Cast among strangers to his language, his jurisprudence and religion, he asks only a small, obscure spot upon the earth on which to spend in peace the fleeting transit of his existence."

A new town had sprung from the ruins of the old one, and the poor country-tossed settlers had thought that at last they were anchored in peace. The tocsin of war was sounded again in 1812. Gov. Hull, enfeebled by age, and perhaps too friendly toward the enemy, was defending the beleaguered garrison against a powerful force of British with their countless savage allies. The brave troops, under Cass, McArthur and other gallant leaders, were ready to shed their blood for the defence of the settlement. The militia, long versed in Indian warfare, felt confident of repelling the foe. A series of preliminary skirmishes were constantly going on. It was a trying crisis for the habitants; many families were divided, members of each being arrayed on opposite sides. Angus McIntosh, a Scotch gentleman, dwelt with his charming family on the Canadian shore. His daughter Marie was beloved by a young Canadian officer named Muir, but who was too timid to declare his love.

On the 9th of August an attack was to be made at Mongaugon on a body of Americans by a force

of British troops and Wyandot Indians under
their celebrated chieftain, Walk in the Water.
The command to which Lt. Muir belonged was
assigned the post of honor and peril, the forlorn
hope in the projected expedition. He felt that
now was the time to tell his love, that he could
fight better knowing that he bore Marie's color
and was cheered by her smile. Obtaining a short
leave, he presented himself at the McIntosh mansion and found his lady-love alone. He pleaded
his cause with all a soldier's ardor. Some unaccountable freak of coquetry made her turn an
indifferent ear to his passionate appeal. She had
been annoyed at his timid wooing, and reasoning
with a girlish logic, was determined to retaliate.
The young officer did not understand these tactics,
and overcome by the disappointment to his cherished hopes, he hastily left the house. Marie
thought he was only piqued. "He certainly
must know that I love him," she argued, "men
are so stupid and matter-of-fact; they take
months to make up their minds to woo a girl, and
if she do not immediately say 'yes' feel themselves aggrieved and wounded." Seeing that he
did not return she became anxious, and going to
the door, called him, but only the mocking echo of
his steed's retreating hoofs returned to her ear.
That evening when she retired to her room, the

shadow of a great impending woe seemed to hover about her. The long, weary hours of the night were measured by her tears and self-reproaches. Towards morning exhausted nature asserted her claim, and the anguish-rent heart lay in her embrace. But brief was the slumber. Marie was awakened by the sound of muffled footsteps near her bedside. Hastily drawing aside the curtain she saw her lover standing near her couch, the bright moonlight revealing every detail of his figure. His face was that of a corpse, whilst blood oozed from a ghastly wound in his forehead. A faintness seized her as she heard a far-away voice say, "Fear not, Marie, I fell to-night in honorable battle. I was shot through the head. My body lies in a thicket. I beg you, rescue it from the despoiling hand of the savage and from the wild beasts of the forest. The Americans will not long exult. Traitors sit around their camp fires and listen to their councils. Our blood has not been shed in vain. The standard of old England will float again over Detroit. Farewell, may you be happy." As he spoke he touched lightly her right hand. At that terrible sensation of coldness born only of the grave, she sank into unconsciousness.

The sun was flooding her room when she returned to her senses, and to a dim remembrance of a most frightful dream. Trying to recall each detail she suddenly glanced at her hand, and to her horror saw that it had been branded by the phantom touch; there was its impress left by deep, dark marks. It was not then a dream but a reality, and a sacred mission had been intrusted to her. Hurriedly throwing on her garments she called for her horse, bade a servant follow her, and rode at full speed to Brock's camp at Malden. Here all was in a state of commotion. She found Walk in the Water, whom she knew well, astonished him by telling him about the battle, and induced him to paddle her in a canoe over the river to the battle field. Here, in the thicket, with a bullet hole in his head, she found her dead lover, and ordered the savages to take his remains to Sandwich for burial. On that sad anniversary for many years afterwards, the ghostly form of a British officer could be seen gliding through the shady groves of Mongaugon towards the river. Marie won later the love of a noble man who had heard of her early romantic story. Ever afterwards she wore a black glove on her right hand, and every 9th of August, dressed as a mendicant, sandal footed, she went from house to house from Sandwich to Windsor asking alms for the poor. It was a penance self-imposed in atonement for her pride and coquetry.

The soldier's prediction proved true. On the

16th of August, whilst Judges Moran and Witherell (then mere boys, but who in their patriotism had enrolled themselves in Jacques Campeau's company) were on guard, they noticed a white flag suddenly hoisted. The excitement was intense when it was learned that it was the signal of surrender. So unexpected, so uncalled for an event caused the soldiers to doubt it. Gen. Cass, in his indignation, broke his sword in preference to giving it up to the enemy, an example followed by many others. As the British troops marched in triumph into the fort, the long line of French militia stood with bowed heads and tears of shame coursing down their bronzed faces, as for the fourth time they saw the flag they felt so able to defend changed for that of their hereditary foes.

WAYNE Co., from Gen. Anthony Wayne, who first raised the Stars and Stripes over Detroit.
WOODWARD AVE., from Augustus Brevoort Woodward, the first Chief Justice of Michigan.
GRISWOLD ST., after Gov. Hull's Secretary.
BATES ST., from Judge Bates.
SHELBY ST., from the gallant Kentucky Governor.
CROGHAN ST., from a young officer who distinguished himself in the war of 1812.
CASS AVE., also CASS ST., after Gen. Lewis Cass.
MACOMB ST., after Gen. Alex. Macomb.
Through the ignorance of street car conductors, and the lack of interest or veneration for the past evinced by some members of

the Common Council, the old system of nomenclature was changed and the numerical one adopted. The intelligence of those who advocated this system seems to have been limited to a knowledge of the letters of the alphabet and the numerals.

ARPENTS.—The French arpent is a square, the side of which is 19 feet 3 inches.

The American acre is a square, the side of which is 208 feet 8½ inches.

XXX

THE EVE OF EPIPHANY.

A Legend of Perry's Victory.

THE visitor to Detroit's "Hotel de Ville" (City Hall) will notice on either side of the main entrance, two "long nines" mounted on stone carriages. These grim sentinels are the trophies of the great "Battle of Lake Erie." The proud Mistress of the Seas for the first time in her history was forced to surrender an entire fleet, and to children whose grandsires she had cradled. Young America points to these cannons with pride and a glow of patriotism steals into his heart as he reads the thrilling account of the battle. The grey haired Octogenarian tenderly pats the guns and recalls memories of days that have gone, social pleasures, friends of his youth and beauty mouldering in the grave.

In 1801, some years before the outbreak of hostilities with England, the habitants of these "Cotes" had, with returning prosperity resumed much of their old time gaiety. In Winter the exciting races on the ice between the swift French ponies; in the Spring the annual crop of weddings with the long procession of "charrettes" (French carts) laden with a joyous, light-hearted freight of gay girls; and in Autumn the corn huskings, were again in vogue. Each feast day of the church had its peculiar and appropriate customs handed down from their Norman ancestry.

It was on the eve of one of these, the Epiphany, that in a hospitable old mansion on the present site of Windsor, was assembled a brilliant party of stately dames, fair demoiselles and courtly cavaliers, mingled with the élite of the young Scotch element. There seemed to be some latent chord of sympathy between these brave Highlanders and the French, for intermarriages were of frequent occurrence.

The table was laid for supper which was to be followed by games, fortune telling, etc. Seated near the head of the table, between two dashing gallants who had vied with each other for her bright glances, was a Kentucky widow on a visit to the settlement. Her husband had been killed a few years previous in one of the Indian raids, leaving her with a merry little boy to soothe her grief.

The large Epiphany cake was cut by the host, each lady present taking a piece. It was then customary to put in it a ring and a small white bean. The lady to whose lot the ring fell was crowned queen. The holder of the bean gave the entertainment the following year, and acted on the present occasion, as maid of honor. Madame Fairbairne found the ring and Julie Maisonville the bean. It was then necessary for the fortunate queen to select the king of Epiphany. Madame Fairbairne blushed as her eyes wandered from one to the other of her two gallants, and she said, "If we choose Monsieur Grant, we shall offend Monsieur Brevoort, if we choose Monsieur Brevoort we shall offend Monsieur Grant. We shall select the one who is to become the most distinguished, and to ascertain this we decree that our noble Dame D'Honneur, Mlle. Maisonville, shall take the grounds from the pot of tea and tell the fortune of all three of us. You know that she is a witch herself and in league with all the witches, so it is our royal pleasure that she shall explain to us what say the, fates, and to their decree we must bow."

A murmur of assent greeted the queen's proposition, and a large platter being brought Mlle. Julie, with many incantations in a wild jumble of words learned from the Indian magicians, turned the contents of the teapot out onto the platter, where the leaves assumed strange and wild forms that only the initiated could read. In those days clairvoyance and mind reading were but little known, and there was more of a disposition to impute effects to supernatural than to natural causes. Witchcraft was the name then given to modern spiritualism. Fortune telling was frequently and devoutly believed in, especially when the person was the seventh daughter of a seventh daughter. In those times of a plethora of children, this was no uncommon thing. Julie was the mystic seventh daughter, and she was noted throughout the colony for her wonderful powers of divination. Whilst her beauty was of a seductive, fascinating order, there seemed at times to be something beyond human ken in her lustrous eye. Though universally beloved there were many who looked with awe on her mysterious powers. After eagerly scanning the tea grounds she closed her eyes a moment as if communing with herself, and heaving a deep sigh said in a chanting tone to her profoundly interested audience: "My friends, I see here wonderful things. On this holy night of Epiphany when three wise men (the three kings) came from the East and learned the secrets of the future, it is fitting that I, the humble maid of our gracious queen, should reveal to you at her bidding what fate has ordained. This line," pointing toward the platter, "represents Monsieur Brevoort, and this Monsieur Grant, whilst this one describes the fate of our noble queen. These two young men are destined to wonderful careers. To-day they are intimate friends, later you will see them contending with one another but not alone. A great war is indicated accompanied by terrible bloodshed. The contest between these two seems to be on the water, the victory for a time is evenly balanced but later it seems to belong to you, Monsieur Brevoort. Your line of life is not ended, Monsieur Grant; you will both settle down by the lakes around happy firesides." Suddenly the prophetess turned deadly pale, as she scanned more critically the tea grounds. "I see here by your line, honored queen, the figure of a tomahawk; great trouble will come to you through the Indians. A little off-shoot of your line seems to cross that of Monsieur Grant, and ends with many branches. This, gracious queen, is all I see in the shadowy future." The queen then addressed her loyal subjects as follows: "My children, the words of the sibyl indeed perplex me, and in the absence of the wise kings of the East to whom I could appeal, I am compelled to decide for myself. Although Monsieur Brevoort seems to carry off the palm of victory, yet my line seems to cross that of Monsieur Grant. My ambition prompts me to select Monsieur Brevoort as my king, but fate seems to point in another direction. On two such charming cavaliers I would not bring the trouble that is in store for me. It is evident I need a strong arm to protect me, a king with an army at his back. I therefore choose as king of Epiphany (here her eyes glanced around until they fell upon Col. Brush standing near the door) the gallant Colonel of the Legionary Corps. His veterans will never suffer harm to come to their queen." At this Col. Brush came forward and was crowned king. The company, charmed with the graceful manner of the young widow, applauded her choice. The festivities were kept up to a late hour, but the union of the king and queen extended no further than Epiphany's eve. She soon returned with her little son to her home on the Kentucky border.

As the inspired Franklin had said years before, "The war of the Revolution has been fought, the war of Independence has still to be fought," the long smouldering element at last burst its bonds. Detroit disgracefully surrendered at the first onset. An English fleet built on the river, controlled the lakes, but the dying words of the heroic Lawrence were impressed on the American minds : "Don't give up the ship." Under the direction of the daring young Rhode Islander, Oliver Hazard Perry, a fleet was hastily constructed at Presque Isle (now Erie) on the south shore of Lake Erie. On the 10th of September, 1813, from his look-out on Gibraltar Island,* Put-in-Bay, Perry discovered the British fleet sailing out of the Detroit River to attack him. It was composed of six vessels carrying seventy guns. The Americans had nine vessels carrying fifty-four guns. In weight of metal and efficiency, the British fleet seemed superior and its commander, Barclay, was one of Nelson's veterans. Young Perry flung out his ensign with the legend, "Don't give up the ship," and was determined that day to conquer or die. When twilight had set in that night, American valor had enabled him to write this immortal despatch from his ship moored off one of the Three Sisters Islands :* "We have met the enemy,

---

* Now the summer residence of Jay Cooke.

* Three Sisters Island, said to have received the name from three Indian squaws whose tongues were so sharp that their father for peace sake had to exile them to three islands near the mouth of

and they are ours,—two ships, two brigs, one schooner, one sloop." This was the decisive blow of the war. Harrison soon afterwards drove the cowardly Proctor from Detroit and unfurled again the starry flag, where long may it wave.

In command of the marines on the American fleet was Lt. Henry Brevoort, of the 3rd regiment of U. S. Infantry detailed for duty on the fleet. Later he was known as "Commodore" Brevoort.* Congress voted him a medal for his gallantry and his grateful country will ever cherish his memory. Commodore Alexander Grant commanded one of the British vessels in the action. He married Miss Barthe at Detroit, and after the war built his residence, called "Grant's Castle," at Grosse Pointe, where it was the scene of much hospitality.

Shortly after one of the Indian raids into Ohio and Kentucky, Mrs. Grant heard that a band of savages had encamped at Belle Isle. They were going to hold a "pow wow" to celebrate their exploits, and to torture and burn a young white captive whose mother they had killed.

The Commodore was away, but his wife's moth-

---

the Detroit. They are called East Sister, Middle Sister and West Sister.

* Commodore Brevoort married Miss Catherine Navarre, named from her aunt, the mother of Gen. Alexander Macomb.

erly instincts were roused, and knowing the love and esteem of the Indians for her family, she determined to make an effort to save the poor boy from so terrible a fate. She was rowed to Belle Isle, made her way to the camp and asked the amount of the ransom for the child.* The Indians, who were making preparations for their horrible feast, would not at first listen to her. The courageous woman was not to be baffled, and at last partly by lavish presents and partly by threats that the black gown (priest) would bring some calamity on them, she succeeded in her mission. The little boy was brought home and adopted by his humane deliverer, who already had a large family (ten daughters) of her own. On the Commodore's return his good wife described to him her visit to the Indian encampment and its gratifying results. "What did the Indians call him?" suddenly exclaimed the Commodore. "I think they called him fair bairn or 'pretty boy'" she replied. The old veteran bowed his head, whilst memory was busy weaving the broken links of the prophecy on Epiphany eve, many years before.

---

*See chap. on Grants. The grandchild of the little boy still lives and remembers his mother's account of Mrs. Grant's trip to Grosse Isle.

XXXI

KISHKAUKOU.

A Legend of the Chippewas.

IT WAS an evening in the early spring of 1815; the moon had just risen and was flooding with soft radiance the restless waters of Saginaw Bay. On the banks was an open clearing fringed by the dark, primeval forest. Here and there were scattered tents covered with variegated mats, or formed of the fragrant boughs of the spruce.

In the center of the encampment was a bright fire, the flickering light from which mingling with that of the moon caused weird expressions to play over the dusky faces of the Indian warriors, who sat round in a semicircle. They were smoking in calm and deliberative silence and listening with solemn attention to a speaker who was explaining the object of the council.

In such assemblies decorum was never broken; the etiquette which forbade one speaker to interrupt the other was strictly enforced; calls to order were unknown.

At a little distance, closely guarded and with pinioned arms, stood an Indian prisoner, whose murder of a young brave of the tribe had caused this council. The squaw and children of the victim were the accusers, and demanded the fulfillment of the code, which was blood for blood, for according to Indian tradition, the soul of the deceased would be excluded from the happy hunting grounds of his ancestors, until the act of atonement had been made. There was something impressive in the passive grandeur of the Indian's stolid stoicism, in his supreme indifference to the deliberations of the council, as if it were another's fate it was deciding.

There seemed to be a division of opinion; dissenting grunts were heard, when suddenly a warrior of powerful form arose, who gliding towards the prisoner, ended all hesitancy by burying his tomahawk in his brain. Then, brandishing his reeking weapon towards the petrified group, robbed of the force of the fearful reality by the swiftness of the blow, he left the council. It was

Kishkaukou, the celebrated Chippewa chief, whose savage barbarity had made his name a terror all along the lakes, and the bare mention of which blanched the cheeks of the bravest. Not a murmur of disapproval was heard; his will ruled supreme. "Le roi le veut," was sufficient, and the warriors drew their blankets over their heads and filed one after another from the council.

Kishkaukou was reproved afterwards by an intrepid white for having broken the law by his peculiar mode of legislation, and replied with a ready wit which equalled that of Moliere's fagot boy: "I have altered the law."

The brave, notwithstanding his savage cruelties, was not impervious to Cupid's darts. Whilst in the vicinity of the River Huron (now the Clinton) he met a charming half-breed, Monique, who had the misfortune to make him the captive of her pretty eyes. Kishkaukou's manner of wooing, added to the terrible stories told of him, was not calculated to find favor in a timid maiden's heart, and it was not strange that she preferred another and more gentle lover, Louizon, the clerk of Judge Rielly.

Kishkaukou soon discovered his rival, and with his startling idea of facilitating legislation, disposed of Louizon as he had of the Indian captive and carried the maiden away. But he soon discovered that the law was not to be altered by the capricious will of a lawless despot, and the Chippewa chief was obliged to hide. For some time he eluded the vigilance of that power which he had so outraged. Trusting to his cunning and strategy, and to the terror of his name, he was rash enough to come near Detroit and encamp in Col. Louis Beaufait's orchard, now known as the "Bagg Farm." He was followed by his suite, consisting of several of his squaws and Indians, for he always travelled en grand seigneur, and, like Sapor of Persia, mounted his horse from the kneeling backs of his slaves. Among them was Monique, who, though compelled to follow the murderer of her lover, still cherished revenge, and only waited a favorable opportunity to punish him for his crime. Her very repugnance only served to inflame Kishkaukou's love, and he zealously guarded her. She eluded his vigilance one day, came to the fort, and revealed the whereabouts of the celebrated outlaw. Kishkaukou was captured and lodged in jail. The event created a great sensation. The captive became the lion of the day and was constantly visited by the curious, who had heard the marvelous tales told of this notorious chief. There are several who still live, who remember the haughty warrior with his stately tread and his ferocious expression, his

hand always resting on his tomahawk. All were
struck by the bold daring and almost insolent
recklessness which pervaded his every movement.
He was sentenced to be hung, the most degrading
punishment possible to an Indian.

It was the eve of his execution, November 21,
1822. Kishkaukou sat alone in his prison with the
thought of the morrow as his companion. Death
in itself had no terror for him, but the manner
revolted against the traditions of his race; how
was his spirit to be freed from its mortal tenement
if he were choked? Thus brooding over his fallen
fortunes, the images of faded despotism passed
before him, humiliation enveloped him like a
pall, and his proud spirit was broken. He would
become a by-word in his tribe, a scorn to his
people. The door opened, disturbing his reflections; two of his squaws came in, followed by the
jailer. Kishkaukou, as if by magic, suddenly
dropped his mournful and dejected manner and
conversed rapidly with them. As they left the
jailer noticed one handing him a small tin cup,
but thinking nothing of the occurrence let it pass.
The next morning the squaws again returned to
accompany their chief to his execution. The
gallows was erected opposite the jail, where the
First Presbyterian Church now stands. The jailor
knocked at the door of the chief, but received no

answer; he entered and found the warrior dead. Immediately the building resounded with the mournful wailing of the squaws who chanted the death song. How he killed himself was never definitely known, but it was strongly surmised that the cup given him by the squaw contained poison.* Thus the Chippewa chief's honor was saved and he left no legacy of disgrace to his tribe.

---

* The poison given Kishkaukou by the squaw was probably the distilled juice from the roots of the wild citron plant. Its effects are peculiar. Almost immediately after swallowing it the victim has two or three convulsive shivers and then dies. The fruit of this plant is not poisonous ; it is used for preserving.

A LEGEND OF L'ANSE CREUSE.*

A woodpecker sat on an oaken stump,
Pecking away with a ceaseless thump,
And now and then, as he cocked his eye,
Darted a glance so keen and sly,
You'd have thought, had you seen him that summer day,
Old Greenback has something queer to say.
When that stump was a stately tree,
Sturdy in trunk and sound in knee,
Forward a little from the wood,
Close by the edge of the bank it stood,
And acorns dropped where the ripples break
Over the brim of the smiling lake.
When that tree was at its best,
An emerald bird, with crimson crest.
All through the summer, from dawn till dark,
Hopped and tapped on its ridgy bark;
The limbs have dropped, the trunk is dead,
But the plumes are shining on back and head,
And the restless eye is clear and keen
As when the old oak's leaves were green;
But under his throat, perhaps you'd say,
Rubytop shows a spot of gray.
Orchard and field for many a rood
Cover the dust of the buried wood,

---

* I am indebted to the courtesy of Hon. James V. Campbell for the use of his charming poem, also for much historical information and flattering interest and encouragement.

And low-roofed houses, old and quaint,
Browned by the weather and bare of paint,
Shelter a people—so they say,
Brown and quaint and old as they.
The urchin tumbling in the grass,
The merry youth and the blooming lass,
The farmer who tills the teeming soil
When hunting and fishing leave time for toil,
And the jolly old man who sits and drones
Of the winter signs in the wild-goose bones,
Seem living over as in a trance,
The old, old life of sunny France.
This restless age,—this age so fast—
There fights at odds with the hoary past;
Vainly it matches its eager will
With those who win by sitting still,
And hears an adage old and worn,—
Who goes for wool may come back shorn.
There kindly nature spreads her stores
In rich profusion out of doors;
Bright gleam the apples, pears, and cherries,
The brambles bend with luscious berries;
The bullfrog, with his croaking harsh,
And the fat muskrat, haunt the marsh;
The wild duck floats among the reeds,
The red deer in the woodland feeds,
The grouse, the partridge, and the quail
Their bounteous larders never fail;
And, yielding more ethereal fare,
The daintiest creatures swarm in air.
But, if your feet are ever found,
O muses, on such level ground,
Come hither from Parnassus' hill,
Of melting whitefish eat your fill;
And from your lubricated throats
Will glide such smooth and pleasing notes
As never yet the pipes did follow

Of your precentor—bright Apollo.
In the fall weather, cool and hazy,
When the slow sun is getting lazy,
And from his cold bath in the river
Comes out all red with many a shiver,
With feet too chilly as they pass
To melt the hoar frost on the grass,
Northward his yearly journey takes
The shining "white deer of the lakes."
Swift through the lymph, in countless herds,
Thicker than thickest flight of birds,
The living shapes of silver dash,
Till all the rustling waters flash,
As when beneath the breeze of June
Their myriad waves reflect the moon.
Then all the dwellers in the land
Come trooping gaily to the sand;
Through day and night the populous shore
Echoes the clanking of the oar.
The meshes of the spreading seine
Are tried by many a grievous strain,
And the gay crowd, with jovial din,
Hail the rich harvest gathered in.
Then comes the kindly winter's reign;
Then mirth and pleasure scour the plain,
The rapid pacers come and go
Like phantoms o'er the beaten snow,
And where the summer shallops ride,
Swiftly the painted carioles glide.
Not Hector o'er the Trojan field
By his illustrious coursers wheeled,
In his mad circuit whirling round,
Thus saw his steeds devour the ground;
Nor Pindar, yielding loud acclaims
To the great victor of the games,
E'er saw upon the Olympic plain
Such ponies of heroic strain.

And should they meet at break of day,
Fresh baited with ambrosial hay,
The sun's team prancing up the cope,
They'd beat him half way down the slope.
But oh, my colts, too swift ye pace,
You've borne me past my stopping place;
Backward return in slower mood,
And while you whinny o'er your food,
Again upon the bank I'll stray,
And if he has not flown away,
Hear what the old bird has to say.

High on the stump the old woodpecker sat,
Twisting his neck this way and that,
And soon as he found an ear to listen,
He bristled his crest, and his keen eyes glisten,
On his breast feathers he wiped his beak,
Opened his mouth and began to speak.
Hearken, stranger, while I tell
Wondrous things that once befell
The people of this drowsy land.
Here on this pulpit where I stand
Preaching my sermon to only one,
Long ago I sat in the sun,
And saw a sight that shook with fear
The hunter fierce, and the trembling deer.
The bright warm rays of an August noon
Hushed each sound but the locust's tune;
But a gentle wind blew from the west,
Dimpling with ripples the water's breast,
And catching the swans' wings where they float,
Drove each one on like a well-trimmed boat,—
A stately boat, with canvas white
As a sheet of snow in a starry night.
Now here, now there, the great fish rise
To snap at the gaudy dragon-flies;
The loon like a porpoise rolls and dives,

Screaming as if for a hundred lives,
And solemn bitterns stand and think,
Each on a leg, by the rushy brink.
Just as the sun in his path on high
Stayed his course in the middle sky,
Speeding along with a foaming wake
A great ship sailed upon the lake;
And the loon dove down, and the white swans flew,
Scared at the sight of the wonder new;
For never had vessel along this shore
Cleft these quiet waves before.
No better craft was ever seen
Than brave La Salle's stout brigantine:
Out from the prow a Griffin springs,
With scales of bronze and fiery wings,
And the ship that earned so wide a fame
Bore on its scroll the Griffin's name.
For when the cunning Robes of Black
Troubled the zealous Frontenac,
And strove his venturous hands to keep
From reaching out to the western deep,
The wrath of the sturdy Norman rose
At the jealous arts of his patron's foes,
And the ship he built for his dangerous quest,
He named from the valiant noble's crest,
And vowed he would make the Griffin fly
Over the crows in the western sky.
A gilded eagle carved in wood
On the crown of the quarter-deck castle stood,
And from the staff astern unrolled,
Floating aloft with its lilies of gold,
The great white flag of France is spread,
And the pennon decking the mainmast head
Bears the chieftain's arms on a field of red.
Three black-nebbed falcons gaping wide
Scowl through the ports on either side.
And the old sergeant says they speak

Each for a common day in the week.
While the great bow gun with its heavy knell
Rings as loud as a Sunday bell.
But another standard is seen to-day
As the gallant cruiser wins the bay,
For the cross is waved, and the censer swings,
And the seamen kneel as the mass bell rings,
For to-day is the feast of the Abbess Claire;
And the corded priests, with chants and prayer,
Sprinkling the lake with holy water
Name it after the Church's daughter.
Then in a trice the gunners catch
Each in his place the blazing match,
And the flame leaps out, and the trembling shore
Quakes at the terrible cannon's roar.
And stout La Fleur with chuckling grin
Said as he patted his culverin—
In my church there's never a friar
Sings like the Abbot who leads the choir!
* * * * * * *
Out in the lake the Griffin lay
Wind-bound at anchor many a day,
While the ship's company explore
The novel wonders of the shore;
And as they reach upon the way
The bend at Pointe à Guignolet,
Before them spreads a lovely bay;
Its limpid waters softly glide
Like the slow creeping of the tide,
Upward and backward on the beach,
But ne'er beyond one margin reach.
And in its lonely beauty there,
So still, so smiling, and so fair,
To their charmed eyes it seemed to be
A sunny strip of Normandy,
Where mermaids in the moonlight play,
And happy children all the day.

Here,—said La Salle,—when history's page
Inscribes us of an ancient age,—
When populous cities rich and great
See ships in fleets ascend the strait,—
When this new world shall lead the van,
In the great onward march of man,—
Though men of other blood may press
More boldly through the wilderness,
And though the flag of France may be
Unknown upon this mimic sea,
Yet, something whispers in my breast,
Here shall be quietness and rest.
Though commerce through the forest break,
Or churn the waters of the lake,
The inland road shall not be nigh,
The busy craft shall pass it by.
And if our phantoms should be found
Exploring then this pleasant ground,
It still shall seem familiar earth,
As the old region of our birth.
Beside the shore a cross they plant,
The reverend priests an anthem chant,
And the stern soldier, as he went,
To seek the shelter of his tent,
Cast backward many a yearning look,
Made homesick by that fairy nook.
The ship sailed on, but the friendly shore
Saw it returning nevermore.
And many a day had come and fled
And many a fall the leaves had shed,
Before the early morning dews
On the white clover by L'Anse Creuse
Were dashed by footstep from their cup,
Ere the dry sun had drunk them up.
But when I grew to my chagrin
A little baggy about the chin,
And could not find sufficient cause

For a wrinkle or two around my claws,
The pleasing scene I daily viewed
No longer was a solitude.
Neat farms and gardens lined the strait
From Erie up to Huron's gate,
While on the narrow strips of land
The cottage homes so closely stand,
Their numbers stretching up and down,
Appear like one continuous town.
In front of each upon the bank,
A narrow wharf of single plank
Stretched out to where a steady hand
Might fill a bucket to the brim,
Sinking it down below the rim,
Yet never touch the bottom sand;
While to this simple jetty tied
Canoes float safely by its side.

Whenever Monday's morning ray
Brings to the world its washing day,
The busy housewives and their daughters
There with their labors vex the waters.
The garments in their fingers gathered,
With vigorous rubbing drenched and lathered,
And paddled with a cunning knack,
Resound with many a rousing whack;
While the fair laundresses at work
In no Carthusian silence lurk,
But skilled alike to wash and speak,
Gossip enough for all the week.
In the small hamlet of L'Anse Creuse,
One Monday, buzzed the stirring news
That the old Seigneur of Beauvais
Was busy all the previous day,
Devising how his daughter fair—
The arch and graceful Lady Claire—
Might find ere long an honest mate,

Of gentle blood and good estate,
Who by some valiant feat at arms
Might prove him worthy of her charms.
He was a man whose antique blood,
Traced backward to the very flood,
Had with such notions filled his brain
As once disturbed the knight of Spain.
He passed the vigor of his years
Roving among his gallant peers.
Exploring widely to advance
The glory of his native France.
And oft a pleasant hour had spent
With gallant Tonty in his tent.
Long years ago they made their way,
And camped beside this smiling bay,
To wait the gathering of the force
Destined to guard the northern course.
Then met the boldest hearts arrayed
That ever pierced the forest shade.
There met the venturous Beauvais,
La Salle's stout warden La Forêt,
And the sagacious Durantaye,
Whose flag had waved o'er many a post
On the remotest northern coast;
With his old comrade true and tried,
Renowned Du Luth, who far and wide,
Honest in heart, and strong in hand
Swayed the fierce tribes through all the land.
There, as they feasted at their ease
Beneath the stately forest trees,
With many a tale of savage fray
They passed the pleasant hours away.
And when the hallowed spot he knew,
Once honored by the Griffin's crew,
Said bold Beauvais, this cross so tall
Shall stand one day beside my hall,
When age from labor shall release,

To let me dwell at home in peace.
So, when he settled to retire,
And light anew his household fire,
He was the first who found his way
To dwell beside the cross and bay.
He mingled reading and the care
Of watching o'er his darling Claire,
And soothed his fatherly alarms
With chronicles of deeds of arms.
As up she grew to womanhood,
Merry and bright, as well as good,
He dreamed of noble cavaliers
Bearing her colors on their spears,
And jousting on the meadows green
To win the smile of Beauty's queen;
And a great tournament he planned,
The prize to be his daughter's hand.
The damsel having mother wit,
And some small will for using it,
Had been enabled to discover
She need not languish for a lover.
And though she knew that young Beauclerc
Was prompt enough to do or dare,
She was not anxious for her sake,
That he another's head should break,
Nor would it suit her views at all
Should others profit by his fall.
So, with a smile upon her face,
And many a blushing maiden grace,
She met her honest father's question
With a more practical suggestion.
The Greeks, in that heroic time
Which all the poets call sublime,
Instead of carving up a friend,
In public games did oft contend,
And deemed a vegetable crown
And name by Pindar handed down,

More likely to adorn the State
Than if they earned a broken pate.
When the hard winter's frost shall make
A slippery ice-field of the lake,
No ancient circus could compete
With such a course for flying feet;
And if no youth my hand may claim
But him who pleads a victor's name,
Then let his honors be my price
Who wins a race upon the ice.
The sire approved, and gave command
To publish it through all the land,
That on the coming Christmas day
A horse race o'er the frozen bay
Should by its fair results decide
What lucky hand should claim the bride.
Then to the shore in state he went.
Where the good dames, on work intent,
Their weekly store of clothes did scrub
In the great common washing tub;
And sought their willing aid to bear
His festive message through the air.
Swiftly it traveled toward the south,
Leaping from ready mouth to mouth;
And while its echoes still did play
In broken murmurs round the bay,
Past Windmill Point, on pinions quick,
It reached the mouth of Tremblé's creek;
And like a bullet from a gun
Crossed the ravine at Bloody Run;
Thence like the west wind on the main,
Shook the great flag at Pontchartrain;
Then like a brightly falling star
Gleamed on the household of Navarre,
And shot along its flashing way
Around the bend of Godfroy's bay,
Startling the ghost that lingered still

Sighing in Gobeye's haunted mill.
The violet banks of Bellefontaine
And the cool shades of Lover's Lane
Heard a low murmur, as of bees
Humming among the linden trees.
As up the Rouge the story sped.
Old Va-de-bon-Cœur, as he shook his head,
Marveled that any other place
Was chosen for a Christmas race;
But cracking all his knuckles bony,
Forthwith began to train his pony.
Beyond this region of the horse
The message reached the broad Ecorce,
Rousing the herdsmen as they roam
O'er the wide acres of St. Cosme.
Across the channel to Grosse Isle,
Shouted with sympathetic zeal,
And thence beyond, the tidings go
To the rich island dark with shade
By the gigantic lindens made,
Within whose woods the Wyandot
Had built his town in a charming spot,
Guarding Lake Erie's open door:
In the rough sailor pilot's lore
'Tis known as the island of Bobálo.
In the short passage of an hour,
Sped by this tireless motive power,
The news had entered at the gate
Of every household on the strait,
And the gay bachelors all prepare
To struggle boldly for the fair;
While pouting maidens—half offended—
Wish that the day had come and ended,
That they who fail to win the prize
Might find a better use of eyes;
Yet none the less they toil and fluster
To look their prettiest at the muster.

And, sooth to say, the gallant wrong
Would find his journey very long,
Who traveled till he found the graces
More prodigal of charming faces.
The summer into autumn glides,
The mellow autumn long abides,
Till dark December claimed a part in
The unruffled season of St. Martin;
And many a lovely bosom fluttered,
And many a savage youngster muttered,
As the sun neared his last decline,
While winter yet had made no sign.
But when the dreary solstice came,
The morning sky was all aflame,
And from the polar deserts vast
The wind came howling fierce and fast.
All day the clouds their snowflakes shed,
The sighing waves were dark as lead,
Sounding upon the gloomy shore
Like the dull plash of melted ore.
But in the night no vapor mars
The luster of the burning stars,
High in the firmament the moon
Shines dazzling as the sun at noon,
And the cold beams the waves congeal
Like a great floor of glimmering steel.
All through the night from shore to shore
The imprisoned waters moan and roar,
But vain are all their throes to break
The dungeon walls that hold the lake.
On Christmas eve the drowsy heads
Went early to their downy beds,
That all from sweet repose might borrow
More blooming roses for the morrow;
While even the watchful chanticleer
Forgot to blow his clarion clear,
And sitting snugly on his perch,

Was silent as the village church.
But when the rays of morning creep
Down the gray spire of St. Philippe,
And cast its shadows o'er the way
Just at the foot of Grand Marais,
The wooden cock that at its peak
Stood opening wide his gilded beak,
Thought surely there was something wrong
To make his brothers mute so long.
Uprising on his sinewy toes,
Far out his gorgeous breast he throws,
While of the bracing air he quaffed
A deep exhilarating draught;
Then from the bottom of his throat
He crowed so fierce a trumpet note
That all the country stared aghast,
Astounded by that sudden blast;
And every rooster, roused to feel
A rival worthy of his steel,
Met the fierce chapel guardian's crow
With a defiant *coquerico!*
Up from their beds the slumbering people
Sprang at that summons from the steeple,
And every bachelor and maid
In rustic garments neat arrayed,
With sparkling eyes and glowing face,
Prepared to figure at the race.
Too far from Fashion's halls to get
The work of Ma'm'selle Tond-Minette,
The blooming damsels managed still
To show the power of taste and skill.
And when they all had met together,
Rose tinted by the bracing weather,
They made philosopher and dunce
Fall swift in love with all at once.

The mass was over, and the sleighs
Came sliding o'er the crystal ways,

As shining birds from flower to flower
Dart swiftly in the summer hour.
The swan-necked carioles make the scene
Lively with scarlet, gold, and green,
The bright-eyed pacers, roan and bay,
Caper like little boys at play,
And toss their heads, as if they knew
As much as human horses do.
The lady Claire, with courteous mien
Beams like a radiant fairy queen;
But while she swiftly moved her eyes
O'er the contestants for the prize,
She turned a moment pale as snow,
Then blushed with such a ruddy glow
That all the maidens then and there
Owned there was none so good and fair,
And wished success to lovely Claire.
For well, with ready wit, they guessed
She had a purpose in her breast
That none from her devoted swain
The triumph of the course should gain;
And each with sympathizing face
Hoped that her own true lover's place
Would be the second in the race.
Then forth advancing in his sleigh
The stately form of old Beauvais
Appeared among the shouting throng,
And with a voice like Stentor's strong,
Taught by his daughter's shrewd device,
Who knew the mysteries of the ice,
Announced the scrupulous rules to guide
The contest for the peerless bride.
In a straight run the course shall reach
From where the trending of the beach
Rounds into Pointe à Guignolet,
To Huron Point across the bay;
Thence turning at the blasted elm,

The limit of Maconce's realm,
Back to the starting point again
Across the white and slippery plain.
And he whose steed's returning feet
Shall first upon the margin beat,
Shall take my mansion and my land,
And, if she will, my daughter's hand.

The greybeards shrugged their shoulders wide
At such a long and freezing ride;
Eight miles across the raven's flight
Must reach before his feet can light;
And when upon the glassy floor
That space must twice be traveled o'er.
The horse that wins without a founder
Must be as hard as an eighteen pounder.
But the swift pacers cocked their ears
In scorn at such unworthy fears;
And, ranged in order on the shore,
The friendly rivals reached a score,
Waiting the signal to begin
The race that only one could win,
Each in such sliding carriage placed
As suits his money or his taste.
Jumper and cutter, train and pung
Behind the nimble pony swung,
While the trim cariole's graceful wedge,
With its shafts hung low at the runner's edge,
Was decked in the spoils of the shaggy bear,
Ready to cleave the frozen air.
But what has troubled the Sieur Beauvais,
And what the cause of the long delay?
The course is long and the day is brief,
The night comes on like a stealthy thief,
And woe to the wight who rides astray,
Far from the land on the wintry bay.
Alas, the old man's eyes are dim;
For under his features hard and grim

His soul is soft and his spirit mild,
And his heart is aching for his child;
He knew her love for young Beauclerc,
And marveled why he was not there.
He was a youth of manly heart,
Lithe as a panther, straight as a dart,
And loved to share the hunter's toil
More than he cared for his costly spoil.
Changing their names with one another,
The Swan creek chieftain called him brother,
And a sturdy man he saw who met
The tawny or white Eshtonaquet.
The chief just come from a prairie trail,
Brought home a horse like a spotted quail,
With long slim neck and Arab head,
But a back that sloped like the roof of a shed,
And legs that raised his ample chest
Up to the height of an Indian's breast.
And he gave a hint to young Beauclerc
That none with this strange beast might cope,
Though he should train an antelope,
To run the race for his lady fair.
He framed a jumper of ironwood tough,
Limber and stout, but rude and rough,
His harness strong and his reins to guide
He made from thongs of bison hide,
And there he sat with the jeering racers,
Proud of themselves and their well groomed pacers,
Wrapped in the shaggy robes of skin
That his red brother clad him in;
And many a scoff and scornful laugh
Greeted the sleigh with the brown giraffe.
A whisper from the Lady Claire,
And the old man with dubious air
Shouted the signal. Off they fly,
Skimming like swallows across the sky,
But far behind, with drooping tail,

And swinging his legs like a clumsy flail,
The prairie beast goes steadily on
As if there were never a race to be won,
While the neat ponies their sinews strain
To reach the verge of the frozen plain.
But when they turn at the blasted tree,
Panting and foaming, lo, they see,
Jogging along as fresh and stout
As when from the shore they first set out,
The clumsy brute whose movements seem
Like the measured sweep of a walking-beam.
And as the home-bound rivals ride
Just in the midst of the basin wide,
The shambling nag with his terrible stride
Passes them all, and in his eyes
Gleams of a conscious triumph rise.
Wider and wider he spreads apart
His hoofs, and shoots like a fiery dart,
Till his nimble limbs so swiftly fleet,
He seems like a body without any feet
Shot like a ball through the midst of the air,
And he reaches the goal when there's nobody there;
For they thought it was safe to sit long by the fire,
Not dreaming this monster, with sinews of wire,
And never within a decent stall,
Would thus so horribly beat them all.
But the boys when they saw the meek young men
Moodily driving back again,
Shouted a mocking *mange l'avoine!*
And the merry maids with smiling lip
Welcomed them back from their leisure trip.
But they looked more blithe when the jolly priest
Asked them in to the wedding feast;
And never since that Christmas-day
Have the good dwellers by the bay
Danced at the bridal of lady fair,
Sweeter and brighter than lovely Claire.

INTRODUCTION TO THE FRENCH FAMILIES.

It is not the intention of the writer to give a detailed history of the French families, who first came to settle at Detroit, but to furnish such chronological data, as will be of value and interest to the descendants of this hardy Norman stock.

In order to simplify the work, as a rule, the names have been selected of those, who are still perpetuated in the farms, streets or counties. In many cases, their ancestral estates have passed into strangers' hands, whilst others have sought new homes and ties on the Canadian soil. Of the latter class are the families of Baby, Pillet, Goyeau, Parent, Montreuil, Marentette, Janis, Drouillard, Maisonville, La Butte, Jeanette and Berthelet, a name well and favorably known in Detroit, and still most prominent in Canada.

At the time of the English Conquest in 1760, many English and Scotch came to cast their destinies with the fortunes of the struggling French colony. They were followed later by a number of Americans, who lent their talents, industry and enterprise towards rendering Detroit, the most beautiful and prosperous city of the west. A history of the French families would be incomplete without even a brief mention of these noble pioneers: Cass, Sibley, Woodbridge, Forsythe, Larned, Brush, Visgar, Abbott, Audrain, Connor, Eberts, Knaggs, Leib, Hunt, Macomb, Williams, McDougall, Sterling, McNiff, Meldrum, Parke, Schwartz, Jones, Witherell, Palmer, Whiting, Roberts, etc., etc.

STE. ANNE'S CHURCH.

A history of Ste. Anne's Church would be a history of the early Colony. To more graphic pens than mine I leave this task. Like a tender mother she gathered her children around her, she smiled in their joys and mourned in their sorrows, she placed the signet of heaven on the brow of the new born, she blessed the nuptial pair, and laid to sleep within her consecrated bosom the weary pilgrim. She kept a faithful record of the names and places of birth of all her children. Through fire, wars and Indian devastations she was true to her sacred charge, and to-day many a claim to disputed property has been justly settled by her undeniable evidence. To the student of genealogy these old records with their musty yellow paper, blurred writing and odor of antiquity are most eloquent epitomes of the brevity of human life. Each generation like a wave of the sea rises, swells, then bursts on the shores of Eternity. He realizes the deep, profound truth hidden in the homely child rhyme of Solomon Grundy. The lullaby of the nursery only hides the De Profundes of the church.

The first Ste. Anne's Church was built within the portals of old Fort Pontchartrain, and was called Ste. Anne's, from the fact that the first mass celebrated therein was on the feast of that Ste. (who was the mother of the Blessed Virgin), July 26, 1701. This church built by Cadillac was destroyed by the Indians, but rebuilt shortly afterwards in 1723. It occupied the ground on the north side of Ste. Anne's street (now Jefferson Avenue), and stood opposite Joseph Campeau's homestead between Griswold and Shelby Sts. It was then customary to bury within its walls the trustees. Robert Navarre, Sr., Royal Notary and Sub-Intendant, Pierre Chesne, Pierre Godfroy de Roquetiliade, Chevalier Trotier des Ruisseaux and Dr. Chapoton were buried therein. The trustees also occupied a special pew, generally the first one on the right side of the aisle, near the altar. In 1805 the fire swept away the church. On the 4th of October, 1806, the Governor and Judges granted the petition presented by Father Richard for a deed to the ground to erect a new church. The following was the resolution passed:

"Resolved, That the Roman Catholic Church be built in the centre of the little military square on section No. 1 on the ground adjacent to the burying ground, the said lot fronting on East and West avenue (Michigan avenue) 200 feet wide and running back 200 feet deep, and bounded on the three sides by three other streets." For a few years subsequent to the fire, the people attended service in the Meldrum storehouse near the river, between Randolph and Bates streets, from thence Father Richard removed to Springwells, where mass was said in a house on the Laselle farm. The records of Ste. Anne's have been faithfully kept from 1701, when the first baptism administered in the colony was to Thérèse, daughter of La Mothe Cadillac. To show the care manifested in preparing these early records, below an instance is given (translation).

"The undersigned Recollêt Priest exercising vicarial functions at Fort Pontchartrain of Detroit, declares that the present book contains 13 sheets of paper, being the veritable first book or registry of baptisms and interments at Fort Ponchartrain, and that it has been prepared and arranged by the venerable Père Dominique de la Marche, formerly Professor of Theology and Recollêt Priest, my predecessor at this same mission of Fort Ponchartrain, and for the purpose of giving to this registry all necessary force and value, I have requested Monsieur Antoine de la Mothe Cadillac, commandant for the king at said fort, to honor it with his signature.

Done at said place the 15th of January, 1709.

FRERE CHERUBIN DENIAU.
Recollêt Miss Priest."

"We, Antoine De la Mothe Cadillac, Lord of the places of Douaguet and Mont Desert, Commander for the king at Fort Ponchartrain, certify that the present book contains 13 sheets, being the faithful registry of baptisms and interments. In faith of which we have signed.

Done at said fort, January 16th, 1709.

(Signed)   LA MOTHE CADILLAC."

The signatures attached to the different entries show that the officers and many of the colonists were familiar with the pen. The spirit of caste is apparent in the designation of titles and various employments. A glance at the signatures at the end of a marriage entry, at once gives a clue to the social position of the contracting parties. The officers, both civil and military, belonged to the old régime and many of them bore names which stood high among the noblesse of France. Louis XIV, anxious to promote the interests of his colonies, offered every inducement in the shape of grants of land and bounties to emigrants from France. By younger sons of the nobility, by those whose fortunes had been ruined, and by the adventurous, these opportunities were readily seized; whilst the feudal system was dying out in France, the king revived it in the colony of Canada, by granting to his officers, distinguished soldiers and prominent colonists, so called seigneuries, (a domain of half a league front and two or three leagues deep) mostly situated on the St. Lawrence and its tributaries, outside the grants to Cadillac. There were no seigneuries granted on the Detroit or along the lakes, save the one to the Chevalier Le Gardeur de Repentigny, at Saulte Ste. Marié.

but in place, were the grants of land, at present called farms, and which were only originally given to prominent colonists. The younger scions of French noblesse could enter into trade in these colonies without derogating from their rank, and at once opened an immense trade in bear, mink and other furs with the Indians. A merchant then, was a man requiring considerable wealth, for every article of use was brought from Quebec or Montreal by canoe, which was dangerous and perilous with tedious portages. The officers who came here were generally accompanied by their wives and some of their connections. Sometimes the love of admiration was greater than that of conjugal affection, as in the case of the beautiful Angelique des Meloises, the wife of Hugues Pean, who found Quebec and the society of Intendant Bigot, too interesting to accompany her husband to the uncivilized wilds of his new post. The Campeaus, Cuillerier de Beaubien, Trotier des Ruisseaux, Chesne St. Onge, Godefroy de Roquetilliade, and Godefroy de Marboeuf, Barthe, Cicotte and Godé de Marentette accompanied some of the officers to whom they were related. De Mersac, Chapoton, Reaume, Chabert de Joncaire and Mouet de Moras came as officers. The Morand Grimard, Des Comptes Labadie, De Quindre came between 1745 and the English conquest. The Macombs, Anthons, McDougalls, Riopelles and many others came in with the English conquest of Canada, in 1760.

The titles were dropped from the record entries, also the general designation of employment, place of residence and profession, in 1760. It was then customary to confer soubriquets or nicknames. These were either derived from the province, city or village from whence the individual came, viz.: Casse dit St. Aubin Cauchois (de Caux), Provensal (de Provence); or from some agricultural source, such as: L'oignon (onion), La Tulippe (Tulip), La prune (plum); from some marked peculiarity: Grosse Jambe (big leg), Momirelle (mummy); others from the estates, viz.: De Beaubien, de Bondy; De Quindre, de Marentette. A child born on a festival was pretty sure of perpetuating the event in his name, viz.: Noël, Pasques, Toussaint, Assumption. This custom prevails to some extent to the present day, among their descendants. ¶ ¶Some of these families have thus, in the course of two hundred

---

P. S.—CARIGNAN REGIMENT. In 1664, Louis XIV sent to Canada, the famous Regiment de Carignan commanded by Col. de Sallières. It was a famous body of troops, and had distinguished itself fighting against the Turks. It was consolidated with that of Sallièr named in honor of the Colonel of the Carignan. They were officered by fifty or sixty French gentlemen belonging to the noblesse. Many of them obtained concessions of land, settled upon them and became the ancestors of many of the French families of to-day.

years lost their original names and are either known by their title
or soubriquet or their names have become completely Anglicized.

The older officers who came with La Mothe or were stationed at
the post at different times, are usually designated in the records as
having belonged to the Carignan Sallières regiment or to a "Detachment of Marines." They were not marines in the present acceptance of the term, but troops sent out from France under the
auspices of the naval department, and responsible to that authority
alone.

Many think that the French Canadian spoke only a *patois* forgetting that at the period when these pioneers came, French literature was in its zenith. Being a conservative people, they preserved
not only the manners and customs of the mother country, but the
purity of its language, a fact illustrated by a request made recently
by certain French writers for the simple old Norman songs, which
the French Canadian alone retained in all their original purity.
Many words which are considered *patois*, may be found in the
works of Racine, Corneille, or Boileau. The language of France
like the human body is constantly undergoing a change. A
Parisian four years absent from Paris is liable to be detected when
he writes. One is reminded of the fish woman of Athens who
knew by a new customer's accent that he belonged to the suburbs
of the city.

Almost all the old families possessed slaves as servants; they
were called "Panis." Very few were of African origin, mostly
Indians, belonging to remote tribes who had been made prisoners
by the Ottawas or Iroquois. They were sold to the whites, in
some instances given as presents by a chief who wished to secure
the good offices of the pale face. They made exceptionally good
servants, and were much attached to their masters. The records
of Ste. Anne's, have faithfully chronicled their births, marriages and deaths.

PRIESTS STATIONED AT FORT PONTCHARTRAIN FROM 1701 TO
1832.

Father Valliant, S. J.; Frère Constantin Del Halle, a Recollêt,
—both accompanied La Mothe Cadillac in 1701; Del Halle was
killed by the Indians in 1706; 2. Dominique de la Marche, 1706–
1707,—he was sent to another mission; 3. Cherubin Deniau, 1707
–1714; 4. Hyacinthe Pelfresne, 1714–1718; 5. Calvarin, V. G. of
the mission of Tamaruas, 1718–1719; 6, Jean Mercier. 1719–1720,
of the foreign missions of Paris; 7. D. Thaumur, 1720–1722; 8.
P. Delino, 1719; 9. Bonaventure, 1722–1735,—Charlevoix mentions meeting him when visiting Fort Pontchartrain in 1722; 10.
P. Daniel, 1735–1738; 11. Bonaventure, again, from 1738–1754;
12. De la Richardie, S. J., residing at the Island of Bois Blanc,

1738–1754; 13. Simple Bouquet, 1754–1784; 14. P. Hubert, priest of the Assumption, Sandwich, afterwards Bishop of Quebec; 15. P. Payet, 1782–1786; 16. Pierre Freshet, 1786–1796; 17. Michel Levadoux, 1796–1802; 18. Gabriel Richard, V. G. of the Sulpicians,—allied on the maternal side to Bossuet, the great pulpit orator of France,—from 1789–1832.

This remarkable man was born at Sáintes, France, Oct. 15, 1764. He was educated at the College of Angers, and studied for the ministry at the Theological Seminary of Paris. During the Revolution, he left France, came to America and was appointed Professor of Mathematics in St. Mary's College, Md. He was a missionary to the Indians for six years. In 1798 he came to Detroit and built the present Ste. Anne's Church. He was a man of wonderful erudition; he spoke and wrote in seven different languages. So anxious was he to establish schools for the education of his flock that he sent to France for teachers. The first printing-press in the Northwest was brought to Detroit by him. All the laws of the Territory and the printed matter then required was done under his immediate supervision. He published the *Michigan Essay,* a French newspaper, which was later discontinued. Many an old French family to-day possess prayer-books and other religious works published by this pioneer press. He took an active interest in everything appertaining to the growth and advancement of the Territory.

In 1823 he was elected delegate to Congress, where his successful efforts for the good of the Territory earned him the grateful appreciation of every enterprising citizen. His acquaintance was eagerly sought by Catholic and Protestant. There were no fire engines, nor well-regulated fire departments in those days. At the first alarm all able-bodied citizens ranged themselves in two lines from the river to the burning pile, the leather buckets (which always hung in the front hall) were passed up one line, the empty ones down the opposite one. Father Richard always took his place with the rest. During the cholera he was indefatigable in attendance on the sick and dying. Two long months of incessant labor among the most harrowing scenes, told heavily on a constitution already impaired by great austerities and over-work. Yet the weary, worn, faithful guardsman of Calvary only left his post when disease placed its fatal impress upon him. Even then, mindful of his flock, he consoled them by promising that his death "would close the door on the cholera." The prediction was verified; his was the last case. Two thousand mourners followed his remains to their last resting place, the sublime character of the man conquering nature's selfish fear of contagion. For forty-three years he was intimately identified with the City of the Straits. In the history of Detroit Gabriel Richard will always be the central figure as an accomplished scholar, a spirited citizen, an able statesman and a saintly and heroic priest.

Vincent Stephen Badin, 1832,—the first Catholic priest ordained in the United States. In 1821 Rev. Father Fenwick became Bishop of Cincinnati and Administrator of Michigan. Bishop Rézé was the first Bishop appointed for the See of Michigan. Ste. Anne's then became the Cathedral and remained so until Sts. Peter and Paul (the present Jesuit Church) was completed by Bishop Lefebre. The corner stone of the third Ste. Anne's was laid in 1806 by Bishop Flaget, of Kentucky, though not finished until many years later.

To the kindness and courtesy of the present pastor of Ste. Anne's, Rev. Theophile Anciaux, I am under many obligations for access to the old and valuable records of this venerable church.

FRENCH COMMANDERS AT FORT PONTCHARTRAIN.

Cadillac, 1701-1714; De Bourgmont during Cadillac's absence, 1706; De La Forêt, 1711-1717; Du Buisson, temporary commander, 1712; Alphonse de Tonty, Baron de Paludy, 1717-1724; Deschamps de Boiéhébert, 1725-1730; Huges Pean, Lord de Livandière, Knight of St. Louis, hereditary Town Major of Quebec, 1734; Pajot; Augustin Le Gardeur de Courtemanche; De Noyelle de Fleurimont, 1739; Deschaillons de St. Ours; Dagneaux Douville; Pierre Payen de Noyan; Jacques Chas. de Sabrevois; Jean Bapte de Celeron; Paul Jos. Le Moyne de Longueil, 1743; Nicolas D'Ameau de Muy; Marie Francois Picoté de Bellestre.

Surgeons: 1. Antoine Forestier; 2. Jean Bapte Chapoton, 1718-1755; Gabriel Christophe Le Grand, 1755-1760; Dr. Chas. Christian Anthon, 1760-1764. He came to Detroit, November 29, 1760, with Major Rogers. He married in 1770 Marianne Navarre, widow of Jacques St. Martin. He was the father of the celebrated classical scholar, Chas. Anthon.

ADHEMAR DE ST. MARTIN.

To this family belong a branch of Navarre, Godé de Marentette, the Anthons of New York, the Scotch branch of McIntosh.

Antoine Adhèmar de St. Martin was appointed a Royal Notary at Quebec as early as 1660. He was the son of Michel and Cecile Gache, de St. Salvy, Haut Lanquedoc. He married twice. His descendants by his first wife are still in Canada. By his second, Michelle Cusson, whom he married in 1687, he had one son, Jean Bapte, born 1689, who in 1709, came to Detroit, and married there Marie Louise Dogon, by whom he had five children: 1. Joseph, married 1757, Madeleine Peuillet; he died in 1778; 2. Jacques, surnamed La Butte, married 1760, Marianne Navarre, daughter of Robert, the Sub-Intendant; 3. Francois; 4. Marguerite, married 1758, Col. Louis Jadot. She is the ancestress of the Anthons of New York; 5. Marie Louise, married 1760, Jacques Godé de Marentette.

Jacques de St. Martin, frequently called La Butte, was a noted interpreter. He was a brother-in-law of Lt. Geo. McDougall, whom he accompanied with Major Campbell to Pontiac's camp at that chief's suggestion that he wished to treat with them. The office of interpreter was a very important one, and the English suffered much owing to the rascality of some of these men. The French missionaries and French officers were mostly all familiar with the Indian languages and were seldom imposed upon. Bradstreet and Sir William Johnson complained of their interpreters, but always made honorable exceptions of Chabert de Joncaire Chesne La Butte, later of Henry Connor and Whittmore Knaggs. He married Marianne Navarre, who after his death in 1768, married Dr. George Christian Anthon. She died at the age of 36 leaving no heirs by Anthon, but three by St. Martin. They resided in the old Cass House which belonged to St. Martin. 1. St. Martin St. Martin, died in early manhood, unmarried. 2. Finon, married Philip Fry; 3. Archange, born 1766, married Angus McIntosh, who inherited the estates which belonged to the Earldom of Moy, the Earldom itself having been forfeited in the rebellion against the House of Hanover. He was noted for his lavish hospitality. The sons of this marriage returned to Scotland. Two of the daughters were well known in Detroit, Mrs. Henry J. Hunt, and Miss Kittie McIntosh who died a few years ago.

ANTHON BRANCH.

Marguerite de St. Martin married, 1758, Col. Louis Jadot, an officer in De Muy's regiment. He was the eldest son of Jacques Jadot, former Mayor and Alderman of Rocrois (France), and Marie Boland. Col. Jadot was killed in 1765 by the Indians, his wife had died in 1764 leaving an infant daughter, Geneviève, to the care of her brother Jacques and his wife Marianne Navarre. Little Geneviève was kindly taken care of by her aunt Marianne, who becoming a widow married Dr. Anthon. In 1773 Mrs. Anthon died, and Geneviève was left with her cousins, the St. Martin children, as the wards of Dr. Anthon and their uncle, Alexander Macomb. When Geneviève reached her fifteenth year Dr. Anthon married her; he was at the time forty-five.

A brief sketch of the Dr. whose life was an adventurous one and who gave to America its most celebrated classical scholar, Chas. Anthon, may be interesting to many. Dr. Geo. Christian Anthon, born at Salzugen in 1734, died in New York, 1815. He studied medicine in his native place, afterwards at Gerstungen. In 1750 he passed his examination before the medical authorities of Eisenbach. From thence in 1754 he went to Amsterdam, passed two examinations there before the College of Surgeons, and was appointed surgeon in the Dutch West India trade. He made several voyages but the vessel he was on was captured in 1757 by a British privateer from N. Y., and was carried into that port. At the age of twenty-three, he found himself in a new and strange country without friends and with no other resources than his profession. Confident of his ability he applied for a position in the military hospital at Albany. His talents were recognized and he was appointed Ass. Surgeon in the First Battallion, 60 Regiment, Royal Americans. In 1760, he was detached with the party which under Major Rogers took possession of Detroit. He married twice: 1st, Marianne Navarre, the widow of Jacques de St. Martin, by whom he had no heirs; in 1778 Geneviève Jadot, her orphan niece on the St. Martin side. In 1786 Dr. Anthon removed with his family to New York, journeying thither by way of Montreal. Three of the Dr.'s children were born in Detroit. George, born 1781, died, N. Y., 1865; John,* born 1784, died, N. Y., 1863; Dorothea Louisa, born 1786, died N. Y., 1786; Catherine, born 1787, died, N. Y., 1789; Jane, born 1791, died, N. Y., 1859; Louisa, born 1793; Henry, born 1795, died 1861, became the Rev. Henry Anthon of "St. Mark's" in the Bowery; Charles, born 1797, died 1867, the most accomplished Greek and Latin scholar of America; William, born 1799, died 1831; Marie, born 1801, died 1803; Edward, born 1805, died 1830.

BABY.

This family, strictly speaking, after the English Conquest became and remained English subjects. One of its illustrious branches was born in Detroit, and a few of its descendants still reside in the State. The founder was Jacques Baby de Rainville, son of Jean, Seigneur de Rainville and Isabeau Robin, of Guienne, France. Jacques was an officer in the famous Carignan Regiment, and thus came to America. He married, in 1670, Jehanne Dandonneau du Sablée. Their children were:

Marie Jeanne, born 1671, married 1689, Paul de Lusignan, and in 1700, Claude Pauperet.

Jacques, born 1673, married 1709, Madeline Veron de Grandmenil.

Marie Madeleine, born 1683, married 1708, Jean Bapte, Crevier de Duvernay, a noted family, allied to the Gamelins, Hertels de Rouville, Boucher and Gatineau Du Plessis.

Raymond, born 1638, married 1721, Thérèse Dupré, daughter of

---

*John was one of the most eminent lawyers of New York. Author of several valuable legal works.

Louis Lecomte Dupré and Cath. St. Georges. They were blessed with many children; of their daughters, one became the Mother Thérèse de Jesus, Ursuline nun at Three Rivers, one married Dr. Claude Benoist, of Montreal, another married Louis Perrault, the fourth married Jean Bapte, de Niverville Seigneur de Chamblay; of the sons, Antoine, died unmarried, Louis, married 1758, Louise de Couague, daughter of Jean Bapte, Capt. of Infantry, and Marguerite Le Neuf de Falaise.

Jacques Dupèron Baby settled at Detroit. His name is intimately woven in the history of the seige of Pontiac, in 1760. He was a man of great worth and integrity, gaining alike the respect and confidence of the French, English and Indians. He married in 1760 Susanne Reaume, daughter of Pierre and Susanne Hubert de la Croix. Jacques died in 1796, leaving eleven children to bless his name and to emulate his good example. Of the girls, one mar. Mr. Caldwell, one Mr. Allison, another Ross Lerin, and the fourth Mr. Bellingham, afterwards Lord Bellingham. Three of the sons became officers in the British army, and by their bravery won renown and high positions. They were Daniel, Antoine and Louis. Pierre studied medicine at Edinburg, Scotland. He returned to Canada and married a lady of Scotch extraction.

Jacques, the eldest of Jacques Dupèron and Susanne Reaume, after completing his studies at the Seminary of Quebec, went to Europe to perfect himself in certain branches. He married Eliza Abbot, by whom he had five boys and one girl:

Jacques became a lawyer, and died in Toronto; he had mar. the d. of an English officer.

Raymond was sheriff for Kent Co.

Charles settled in Sandwich and left several children.

William also settled in Sandwich.

Eliza married Hon. Chas. Casgrain, son of Pierre Casgrain, Seigneur de la Bouteillerie, whose sons and grandsons have reflected glory on their ancestry, Dr. Casgrain in surgery, Abbé Raymond by his gifted pen, Thomas Chase Casgrain, of Quebec, at the bar, whilst the daughters have devoted their lives to the service of God.

Francois Dufresne Baby, youngest son of Raymond and Thérèse Dupré, married at Quebec, in 1786, Marianne Tarieu de Lanaudière, granddaughter of Baron de Longueil. She died in 1844, leaving four boys and four girls. Francois, a son, married a sister of Bishop Pinsonnault.

BARTHE.

Theophile Barthe, armorer to the king, married in Montreal, in 1718, Charlotte Alavoine, daughter of a prominent merchant of that city. Two of their sons, Charles and Pierre, left home to seek their fortune in La Mothe Cadillac's colony. Charles became very prominent, settled for a while at Mackinaw. He met his fate in Thérèse Campeau, daughter of Louis and Marie Louise Robert, and married her in 1747. At their marriage at Fort Pontchartrain were present Joseph Lemoyne de Longueil, Knight of St. Louis, Commandant of the post, Jos. Douaire de Bondy, Chas. Chesne, Du Musseaux, Dr. Chapoton, Pierre Chesne, Father Bonaventure, priest. Charles and Thérèse were blessed with a numerous offspring, whose descendants all occupy prominent positions in Canada and in the United States.

1. Marie Archange, B. 1749. Dr. Chapoton of the French army, was her godfather. She married John Askin, Governor of Michillimackinac. The Askins are of Scotch origin and trace back to the Earl of Mar. A branch of this family settled in Ireland and from there emigrated to America. The proper name is *Erskine* but was converted into Askin by the Irish branch. The children of John and Thérèse were:

CHARLES JOHN, B. 1780; married Monique Jacobs. He dwelt in the old Askin homestead at Walkerville, Canada, called Strebane, after the ancestral estate in Ireland. Adelaide. B. May 30th, 1783; married 1802, Elijah Brush, Attorney General of the North-West Territory and Colonel of the Legionary Corps during the war of 1812. Four children were the fruit of this union:

    1. EDMUND, married Elizabeth Cass Hunt.
    2. Dr. Alfred, died unmarried.
    3. Charles, married Jane Forsyth.
    4. Cymethia, married Mr. Meredith.

3. Thérèse, married Col. Alexander McKee, the British Indian Agent. The only son of this marriage, Alexander, married Felice Jacobs, of Sandwich, Canada, where his descendants reside.

4. Ellen, B. 1788, married Mr. Pattinson, whose son Richard was a British officer, afterwards appointed Governor of Heligoland.

5. Archange, married Mr. Meredith.

6. Alexander, died unmarried.

7. James, afterwards Col. Askin, of the British Militia. He married Francoise Navarre Godé Marentette. He was Register of Deeds of Essex County, an office which has been held by his son and grandson. The children of this marriage are:

JOHN, married, 1st, Monique Navarre, daughter of Col. François Navarre, of Monroe; 2d, Melinda McCroskey, daughter of James and Susanne Godfroy.

ARCHANGE, married Henry Ronalds, of England, whose only child, Lucy, married George Harris, of London, Canada.

James, settled in Australia.
Thérèse.
ALICE.

CHARLES, was killed by a sentinel during the Patriot War.
Ellen.
JANE, married, 1st. Daniel Murray, of Toronto; 2d. Edward Skae.
2. Catherine Barthe, B. 1750, died young.
3. Jean Baptiste, B. 1753, married Genevieve Cuillerier de Beaubien, a niece of Piquoté de Bellestre. He left several children. One of his daughters, Thérèse, married Hubert Villier, dit St. Louis.
4. Bonaventure, B. 1756.
5. Charles André, died young.
6. Louis Theophile. B. 1760, married, 2nd time, 1802, Madeleine Des Ruisseaux de Belcour, daughter of François and Madeleine Adhémar de Lusignan.
7. Thérèse, B. 1758, married Commodore Alexander Grant.

PIERRE BARTHE, a younger brother of Charles, followed him later to Fort Pontchartrain, and was associated with him in his extensive trade at Mackinaw and with the Miamis. In 1760 Pierre married Charlotte Chapoton, daughter of Dr. Jean Chapoton, surgeon in the French army. Their daughter, CHARLOTTE, B. 1763, was the only survivor of four children. She married, in 1780, Lt. Louis Reaume, of the British army, who left her a young widow within the year. In 1784 she became the second wife of Antoine Louis Descomptes Labadie, surnamed "Badichon," and became the grandmother of Mrs. R. S. Willis, Mrs. Giesse, Mrs. Alexander Chapoton, Sr., the Lagrâves, of St. Louis, Mo.

Commodore Alexander Grant married, in 1774, Thérèse, daughter of Charles Barthe, and Marie Thérèse Campeau was of the clan of Grants of Glenmoriston, Scotland. He entered the navy at an early age, but resigned in 1757 to join a Highland regiment raised for the army of General Amherst in America. In 1759 he reached Lake Champlain. Gen. Amherst desiring able officers for his fleet on the lake, commissioned Lieut. Grant to the command of a sloop of sixteen guns. After the conquest of Canada, Grant was ordered to Lakes Erie and Ontario. Detroit was then an English garrison, and it was here he met his fate in Thérèse Barthe. He built his castle as it was called at Grosse Pointe. (Its site is at present occupied by Mr. T. P. Hall's summer residence, "Tonnancour.") It was a noted place for the courtesy of its host and his open, generous hospitality. Tecumseh and his warriors were frequent guests at the Grant castle. The Commodore belonged to the executive council in 1805 of Upper Canada. In a letter to his brother Alpine, dated from York (Toronto), July 5, 1811, he says: "My duty where my naval command requires me is such a distance from here that I cannot travel in the winter when the Legislature meets, but I come down at my ease in the summer and take some sittings in the council. A gentleman who has served his country upwards of fifty-five years requires some indulgence, and my superiors allow it to me." He was a man of commanding presence, a great favorite and a good officer. He had ten daughters, who are to-day represented by the English-Canadian families of Wrights, Robinsons, Dicksons, Woods, Duffs, Gilkersons, Millers, Jacobs and Richardsons. Mr. Jasper Gilkerson, of Brantford, whom the author had the pleasure of meeting, has been in charge of the Indians in Canada for many years. So faithful has he been to his charge, that any promise made to the Indians by him has always been kept by the government. A worthy representative of his grandfather, Commodore Grant, who when admistrator, with the power of giving free grants of land, never granted any to his family or their connections. Commodore Grant died at Grosse Pointe in 1813.

BEAUFAIT.

In 1796, Sargeant Acting Governor of the North West Territory, formed the new County of Wayne. Its boundaries extended from the Cayuga river on the west, to the dividing line now existing between Indiana and Illinois, on the north to the national boundary line, including all of the subsequent territory of Michigan, and a portion of Ohio and Indiana. The Courts of Common Pleas for Wayne county were organized, and the Judges chosen to preside over them were business men, upright, honest, and intelligent. Louis Beaufait was the first Senior Justice. He came directly from France, was the son of Luc and Gabrielle Sourceau, parish of St. Martin, diocese de la Rochelle. In 1766 he married Thérèse de Mersac, d. of Francois, and Thérèse Campeau. Their children were: THOMAS, B. 1768; MARIE IRENE, B. 1770, married Jean Bapte Rivard, son of J. Bapte and Catherine Iliax; LOUIS, B. 1773, afterwards Col. Beaufait. He lived on the old Beaufait farm, (to-day known as the Bagg). There the celebrated Chippewa warrior Kishkaukou came to encamp after the murder of Judge Rielly's clerk. He was made a prisoner and would have paid the penalty of his crime on the gallows, had he not poisoned himself on the eve of the execution. He married, 1804, Louise Saussier. A son of Col. Beaufait, LOUIS, married, 1835, Catherine Peltier, daughter of Charles and Martha Cecile Chapoton; ELIZABETH, B. 1778.

CAMPEAU.

This family still retains in the "City of the Straits" the same prestige it held in the early days of the colony. So numerous

were its branches that there is scarcely now a family of French descent in Detroit, which does not claim a Campeau among its ancestors. The first of the name who came to Canada was: Etienne, who married in 1663, at Montreal, Catherine Paulo. Their children were:
1. Etienne, b. 1664, mar. 1690 Jeanne Fouché; 2. Michel, b. 1667, mar. 1696 Jeanne Massé; 3. Francois, b. 1671, mar. 1698 Madeleine Brossard; 4. Jacques, b. 1677, mar. 1699 Cecile Catin, d. 1751; 5. Jean Baptiste, b. 1681; 6. Agathe, b. 1685, mar. 1701 Paul Chevalier; 7. Catherine, b. 1669, mar., 1685, Francois Blot.

Michel and Jacques came and settled in Detroit about 1710, and are the ancestors of all the numerous branches of the name in Detroit, Monroe, Grand Rapids, Mich., and Chicago, Ill.

ELDEST BRANCH.

Michel and Jean De Merles, were the pioneer merchants of Detroit. He mar. 1698, Jeanne Massé. Their children were:
1. Marianne, mar. 1734, Pierre Belleperche, son of Pierre and Gertrude Du-Buisson Guyon, a near relative of Cadillac's wife.
2. Antoine, mar, 1736, M. Angelique Peltier. He died in 1759 leaving the following children: 1. Alexis, b. 1737, mar. 1763, Madeleine Du Muy. His children were Antoine, Marie Madeleine, Thérèse, b. 1770, Alexis, b. 1778; 2. Josette, b. 1738, mar. 1753, Guillaume St. Bernard; 3. Catherine, b. 1742; 4. Charles, b. 1746, mar. 1772, M. Louise Borde St. Saurin. His son. Chas., b. 1773; 5. Antoine, b. 1754; 6. Therese, b. 1749, mar. 1766, Ambroise Riopelle.
3. Marguerité.
4. Paul Alexis, mar. 1742, M. Charlotte Pineau, whose children were: 1. Charlotte, b. 1744, mar., 1762, Jos. Drouin; 2. Paul, b. 1746; 3. Francois, b. 1749; 4. Catherine, b. 1751.
5. Michel, mar. 1740, Marie Josette Buteau, whose children were: 1. Marie Josette, b. 1745; 2. Charles, b. 1749; 3. Michel.
6. Charles, mar., 1751, Cath. Casse St. Aubin. He mar., 1754, Charlotte Montrais; his children were: 1. Charlotte, b. 1757, mar., 1772, Toussaint Grenon; 2. Charles, b. 1760; 3. Rosalie, b. 1761; 4. Bridgitte, mar. 1772, René Tivierge.

CADET BRANCH.

Jacques, brother of Michel, (held the position of armorer) mar., 1699, Cecile Catin. They had the following children:
1. J. Louis, b. 1702, mar., 1725, Marie Louise Robert.
2. Henri, b. 1704.
3. Marianne, mar., 1732, Joseph Douaire de Bondy, son of Jacques and Madeleine Gatineau Duplessis.
4. Nicolas (Niagara), b. 1707, mar., 1733, Agathe Casse St. Aubin. He died in 1756, leaving the following children: Agathe,

mar.,1758, Alexis Séguin Ladcroute; Marianne, mar., 1763, Alexis Bienvenu Delisle; Angelique, mar., 1759, Antoine Louis Descomptes Labadie (Badichon); Cecile, mar., 1784, Pierre Chesne St. Onge.
  5. Jean Bapte., b. 1710, mar., 1737, Cath. Perthius, d. of Pierre and Cath. Mallet, of Montreal, whose children were: Jean Bapte (Piniche), mar., 1764, Cath. Boyer; Hypolite, mar., 1768, Angelique Cardouet; Julien, b. 1755; Joseph, b.   ; Louis; Francois, mar., 1805, Susanne Morand.
  6. Claude, mar., 1742, Catherine Casse St. Aubin.
  1. J. Louis, the eldest son of Jacques and Cecile Catin, mar., in 1725, Marie Louise Robert. The following children blessed the union: 1. Marie Thérèse, b. 1727, mar., 1747, Chas. André Barthe, and is the ancestress of the families of Askin, Grant, etc.; 2. Francois; 3. Jacques, b. 1735, mar., 1760 Cath. Menard, in 1784, Francoise Navarre, widow of Lt. Geo. McDougall, of the British Army; 4. Simon, b. 1739, mar., 1764, Cath. Boyer. His children were: Henri, b. 1773; Simon Chas., b. 1769, mar. Josette Gamelin; Archange, b. 1766. 5. Jean Bapte., b. 1743, mar., 1767, Geneveive Godé de Marentette, whose children were: 1. Thérèse, b. 1769; 2. Alexis, b. 1771, mar., 1795, Agathe Chesne. A daughter Thérèse (of Alexis) mar., 1826, Philippe Chabert de Joncaire, son of the Chevalier Francois Chabert and Josette Chesne; 3. Geneviève, b. 1767, mar., 1793, Gabriel Chesne.

JACQUES, 3d child of Jacques and Cecile Catin, mar., 1760, Catherine Menard. He was one of the 1st Captains of Militia, and his services are frequently mentioned, with high praise in the early annals of Detroit. There is a tradition that Jacques' grandfather was La Mothe Cadillac's Secretary for a while. If handwriting were any recommendation, Cadillac's choice was a fortunate one, for, as a family, their chirography is peculiarly noticeable for its beauty and distinctness. Jacques possessed much property, which is still in the family, and with the rapid growth of the city, has become immensely valuable. In 1784 he mar. Francoise Navarre, d. of the Sub-Intendant, and the widow of the gallant officer, George McDougall. By his second wife he had no heirs, but by his first, several; among others the following ones:
  1. JACQUES, b. 1762, mar., 1789, Susanne Cuillerier de Beaubien, d. of Jean Bapte. and Marianne Lothmande Barrois. They had two children: Sophie, mar. James Dubois; Jacques (Binette), mar., 1819, Josette Chesne; 2. Angelique, b. 1764.
  3. CECILE, b. 1765, mar., 1781, Judge Thomas Williams, whose children were: Elizabeth, who so nobly consecrated her life to the education of youth as early as 1808; Catherine. b. 1784, mar. 1809, Jean Bapte Pelletier; John R. (Genl.) b. 1766, mar. Miss Mott, and his descendants are all well known in Detroit.

4. JOSEPH, b. 1769, mar., 1808, Adelaide De Quindre; 5. Barnabé, b. 1770, mar. 1st, Thérèse Cicotte, 2nd, 18 , Archange McDougall; Louis (Louizon), b. 1767, mar., 1789, Thérèse Morand. His children settled in Grand Rapids, Mich. Mrs. Cotrell; Mrs. Villers dit St. Louis; George mar. Mlle. Rivard; Antoine mar. Mlle. Cotrell; Toussaint mar. Mlle. Mersac; Louisonette mar. Sophie de Mersac.

JOSEPH, b. Feb. 25, 1769, died in 1860, was for many years one of the central figures in the history of Detroit. He inherited some of his property, but by untiring industry, careful management, aided by the rapid increase and prosperity of the city encircling him on all sides, he was able to leave to his heirs one of the most valuable estates in the North West. He mar. in 1808, Adelaide, d. of Antoine Daigneaux Douville De Quindre and Catherine des Rivières de la Morandière. He had a large family, viz.: 1. Joseph, died unmarried.

2. DANIEL, mar. Marie Palms, d. of Ange Palms, of Antwerp, and Jeanette Catherine Peëters. Ange had been Quartermaster of one of the divisions of Napoleon's Army, at Waterloo. By his successful efforts to save the ammunition at that disastrous battle, he was made by Napoleon, on the field, a Chevalier de la Legion d'Honor. During the stormy period of the dethronement of Charles X., and the elevation of Louis Phillippe, the Citizen King, Mr. Palms was obliged to leave Belgium. He remained two years at Mayence, in Germany. He was an ardent admirer of Chateaulriand, and his description of America, with its grand primeval forests, its wonderful Niagara, roused his desire to travel through the country which had won such enthusiastic praise from France's most gifted son. Mr. Palms brought letters of introduction from his intimate and personal friend, the Prince de Liège, Archbishop of Malines, to Bishop Dubois, of New Orleans, La., also a letter to President Van Buren, who introduced the Belgian exile to New York's most cultured society, to the Van Ransselars, Minturns, Roosevelts, etc., where he was a welcome guest. On his travels he had proceeded as far as Detroit, where, Aug. 26, 1833, his wife died of cholera. Thus a new land became her tomb, and the cradle of the race on American soil. He abandoned all thought of returning to Belgium, for he had given to America his most sacred deposit. Ange Palms' parents were: Francois and Marie Rosenboeck, Jeanette Peëters his wife's parents were: Pierre and Jeanne Catherine Tumen, of Malines, Belgium. Ange had several brothers and sisters: 1. Francois, a distinguished priest, noted for his scholarly attainments; 2. Françoise; 3. Jerôme, a wealthy banker of Antwerp; 4. Baptiste; 5. Marie Anne, mar. William Van Dick; 6. Elise, mar. Mr. Calhouy. Ange's children settled in Detroit

and in New Orleans, La.; they were: 1. Jean Pierre; 2. Francois, mar. at Detroit, Catherine Des Rivières, d. of Joseph Campau and Adelaide de Quindre, who died in 1880, leaving one daughter, Clotilde. By a former marriage Francois had one son, FRANCOIS, who resides at present at Detroit, and who had married, in New Orleans, Mlle. Péllerin, a descendant of the Acadian family of that name; 3. Thérèse, married Wm. Wilder, of Rochester, N. Y.; 4. Marie Francoise, married Danl. J. Campeau, son of Joseph, whose children are well known in Detroit. Danl. J. is a lawyer. Louis Palms; and Adèle, wife of Wm. G. Thompson. Ange and Louis Palms married in New Orleans, La., and both reside there.

3. LEILA CAMPEAU married Mr. Johnston, of Grand Rapids, Michigan.

4. CATHERINE Des Rivières married François Palms. She died in 1880, leaving one daughter.

5. DENIS died unmarried in 1878.

6. JACQUES married Alice Edwards, daughter of Major Edwards, U. S. A., and Miss Hunt, and left three sons.

7. EMILIE married Lewis.

8. MATILDE married Eustache Chapoton, son of Eustache and Adelaide Julie Sérat dit Coquillard; one heir survives.

9. Theodore married and left no heirs.

10. Timothy Alexander married, and resides at Detroit.

BARNABE married 1808, Thérèse Cicotte, daughter of Jean Bapte and Angelique Poupart Laboise. He was called L'Abbié from the termination of his name. Two girls were the result of this union.

EMILIE, died unmarried at Washington, in 1880.

ANGELIQUE married 1836, Jean B. Piquette, son of Jean Bapte and Eleonore Descomptes Labadie. The Piquette family was originally from Picardie, and the name is frequently seen in the "Amorial General of France." The first in this country, was EUSTACHE, who married 1680, Jeanne Boucher. His son JOSEPH married 1706, Marie Thérèse Merienne, daughter of Jean Merienne de Lasolavye, who was godfather in 1685 for Marienne, daughter of M. de Brissay, Marquis de Denonville, Governor of Canada. FRANCOIS EUSTACHE, born 1734, married Charlotte Gaudry. JOSEPH, born 1753, married 1776, Marguerite Renaud. JEAN Bapte married 1808, Eleonore Descomptes Labadie. To this family belongs the celebrated Sulpician Francois Picquet, who, in order to attach the Iroquois confederacy to the French, founded a mission at the mouth of the Oswegatchie in 1748. He erected a substantial stone building and placed this inscription on the corner stone. "Francois Picquet laid the foundation of this building in the name of the Almighty God, in 1749." This inscribed corner stone occupies a conspicious position in the State Armory, erected at Ogdensburg in 1858.

The children of Jean and Angelique Campeau were: JOHN, died unmarried; ELISE, married first in 1870, Ombsy Mitchell, U. S. A., son of the distinguished astronomer and soldier, Gen. Mitchell; second, 1880, James Hoban of Washington; CHARLES married 1876, Fanny Ellston Perley, by whom he had two children. He died in Paris, France, in 1876; EMILIE married 1876, Francis Preston Blair Sands, a prominent lawyer of Washington, D. C., son of Rear Admiral Sands, U. S. N.

In 1821, BARNABE married a second time, Archange McDougall, daughter of Jean and Archange Campeau. The McDougalls were a prominent family of Scottish origin. The first who came to Detroit was Lieutenant George McDougall, a British officer who accompanied Major Campbell to Pontiac's camp at Bloody Run, in 1763 to attempt to negotiate with the wily chief. He treacherously kept them as hostages. Fortunately Lieutenant McDougall escaped. He married 1765, Francoise Navarre, daughter of Robert, the Sub-Intendant and Royal Notary, and Marie Louise Lothman de Barrois. After his death she married, in 1784 Jacques Campeau, father of Joseph and Barnabé, by whom she had no children, but left the following by Lieutenant George McDougall: JEAN R., born 1766; GEORGE; JOHN Robert, the eldest, married, 1786, Archange Campeau, daughter of Simon and Veromique Blondeau, whose children were: GEORGE, born 1706; ROBERT, born 1789; CATHERINE, born 1797.

ARCHANGE, who married, 1820, Barnabé Campeau. The McDougalls acquired considerable property, and among their land grants was Belle Isle to Lieutenant George McDougall, at the same time that Grosse Isle was granted to his brother-in-law, Alexander Macomb.

Barnabé had two sons by his second wife: BARNABE Jr.; ALEXANDER Macomb. Barnabé, Jr., married Alexandrine Sheldon, daughter of Thomas Sheldon and Eleonore Descomptes Labadie. Two sons were the fruit of this union: THOMAS Sheldon; Dr. ALBERT Campeau.

ALEXANDER Macomb, married, 1843, Eliza Throop of New York, a member of that family so well and favorably known in the political world. He had a large family who fully justified the traditional beauty of the Navarres; GEORGE Bliss married Minnie, daughter of Commodore Woolsey, U. S. N. He died in the flower of youth, leaving four children, ALEXANDER is unmarried.

BARNABE married Alice, daughter of Admiral Stevens, U. S. N.; EMILIE married Lieutenant Fitch, U. S. N.; MONTGOMERY died unmarried; FRANCES married Frederic Sibley, a rising lawyer and worthy scion of the distinguished name he bears; McDOUGALL married Miss Batcheler of Pittsburg and is actively interested in some of the new manufacturing interests which has placed Detroit in the foremost ranks among manufacturing cities.

CHABERT DE JONCAIRE.

This name figures conspicuously in the annals of Detroit, especially from the time of the English conquest. In France it is still found among the nobility, in the navy, and on the tablets of the French Academy. THOMAS was a nobleman, came to Canada as an officer, having an aptitude for languages, he soon mastered the Indian dialects and became royal interpreter for the five nations. He married at Montreal, Marguerite LeGuay of Rouen. Their son DANIEL, born 1714, was a Lieutenant in the French army, and later succeeded to his father's position of interpreter. He married in 1751, Ursule Marguerite Elizabeth de la Morandiere, of the distiguished Rocbert family of Canada. He died at Detroit, in 1770, three years later he was followed to the grave by his wife, leaving several children, among whom were: 1. LOUIS; 2. PHILIPPE, married 1783, Judith Gouin, daughter of Claude Thomas and Josette Cuillerier de Beaubien; 3. ANGELIQUE Marguerite, named from her godmother Angelique Cicotte, wife of Medor Gamelin. Philippe at the baptism of his daughter JUDITH, signs himself Chevalier. Francois Chabert de Joncaire, was a nephew of Daniel, son of Gabriel, Captain of Infantry, and Marguerite Fleury de la Gorgendière, one of the most aristocratic and powerful families of Canada. The Chevalier was a man of great ability and took an active interest in promoting the growth of the city of Detroit. He, with Solomon Sibley and Jacob Visgar, represented Wayne county in the Legislative Assembly of the North West Territory, held at Cincinnati, Ohio, in 1799, at which General William Harrison was chosen delegate to Congress. In 1780, the Chevalier married Josette Chesne, by whom he had several children, to-day represented by a branch of the Loranger family of Detroit and Monroe: M. CATHERINE, born 1783, married 1808, Francois La Fontaine; Francois, born 1784; ROSALIE, born 1782, married 1808, Joseph Loranger, son of Claude and Marguerite Monouson, parish of St. Antoine, Quebec; HENRIETTE, married 1825, John Norton Hubble, son of Isaac and Eunice Hilton of New York; PHILIPPE, married 1826, Thérèse Campeau, daughter of Alexis and Agathe Chesne.

CHAPOTON.

The numerous branches of this family so well and favorably known in Detroit all descended from JEAN, son of Tendrez and

Dearne Cassaigne, Cazolle, Diocese of Duges, Lanquedoc. He was a surgeon in the French army with the rank of major, and was ordered to Fort Pontchartrain to relieve Forestier, the first physician who came to the post. For forty years Dr. Chapoton's elegant and stereotype-like signature is affixed to every death notice in the colony. He retired from the army several years previous to the English conquest, and settled on the land which he had received as a grant. He died in 1762. In 1721, he had married M·rguerite Esténe or Stebre, by whom he had twenty children, only seven of whom arrived at maturity:
1. JEANNE, born 1734, married 1749, Paul de Meuchel.
2. MARIE'CLEMENCE, born 1736, married 1747, Pierre Chesne de St. Onge, son of Charles and Catherine Sauvage.
3. MADELEINE, born 1739, married 1758, Gabriël Christophe Le Grand, surgeon in the French army, eldest son of Gabriël Louis Le Grand, Sieur de Sintré, knight of the royal and military order of St. Louis, and of Anne Henriette de Crenay, parish of Roch, France.
4. LOUISE CLOTILDE, born 1741, married 1758, Jacques Godefroy de Marbœuf. She died in 1762, leaving one child, Gabriël.
5. CHARLOTTE,—Lieut. Duburon was godfather and Madame De Noyelle de Fleurimont godmother—born 1742, married 1760, Pierre Barthe, a brother of Charles, the ancestor of the family of Askins, Brushs, etc. Her daughter Charlotte, born 1763, married twice: 1st, in 1780, Lieut. Louis Reaume, an English officer; 2d, in 1784, Antoine Louis Descomptes Labadie (Badichon), whose descendants are Mrs. Willis, Mrs. Giesse, Mrs. Alexander Chapoton, Sr., the Lagrâves of St. Louis, etc.
6. JOSETTE, born 1746, married 1764, August Chaboyé, of Mackinaw.
7. JEAN BAPTIST, born 1721. He was the one who held a parley with Pontiac in 1763. In 1755 he married Felice Cecyre by whom he had a large family: 1. Jean Baptiste, Jr., born 1758, married in 1780 Thérèse Pelletier. He died in 1836; 2. Benoit, born 1761, married 1788, Thérèse Meloche; 3, Louis Alexis, born 1764, married 1783, Catherine Meloche, whose daughter Catherine married in 1809 Major Antoine De Quindre; 4. Catherine Angelique, born 1769; 5. Josette, born 1771; 6. Isabelle, born 1773; 7, Nicholas, born 1776. Eustache, born 1792, son of Jean Baptiste and Thérèse Pelletier, married 1819 by Bishop Flaget, of Bardstown, Ky., Adelaide Julie Sérat dit Coquillart, daughter of Alexis and Cecile Tremblay. Eustache died in 1872. Many remember him; he was an exceptionally handsome man, of a fine, stately presence and courtly manners. Through some unfortunate accident his father lost the large property which had been granted to Dr. Chapoton. Eustache by energy, industry and untiring perseverance acquired considerable wealth which he left to his children, but what they

prized more, a name synonymous with honor and integrity. His
children are all worthy representatives of their sire.
1. ALEXANDER, married Felice Sédilot de Montreuil, daughter
of St. Luc de Montreuil and Isabelle Descomptes Labadie.
Several children blessed this union, viz.: 1. ALEXANDER, JR.,
married Marianne Pelletier, daughter of Charles and Eliza Cicotte;
2. ELIZABETH, married Alex. Viger; 3. EMILIE, married Edward
Bush; 4. JOSEPHINE, married Raymond Baby, of that well
known Canadian family, and resides at Sarnia, Canada; 5. ED-
MUND, one of the rising surgeons of Detroit, married 1883, Martha Sherland, of South Bend, Ind.; 6. Felice is unmarried.
2. BENOIST, married Miss Bour. He died in 1880 and left no
heirs.
3. EUSTACHE, married Matilda Campau, daughter of Joseph
and Adelaide De Quindre.
4. THÉRESE, married Louis St. Aubin.
5. WILLIAM, married Sarah Connor.
6. Julie, married John Cicotte.
7. FELICE, married Capt. Paxton.
8. THEODORE is unmarried.

CHESNE.

As early as 1717 the name of Chesne appears on the records of
Ste. Anne's, and one is attracted by the beautiful and picturesque
signature. So clear, precise, full of character and individuality.
PIERRE, the founder of the race on the soil of the New World,
married, in 1676, at Montreal, Jeanne Bailly, of a family of considerable importance. Two of his sons, Charles and Pierre, came
to Detroit as early as 1717, and are the ancestors of that name in
Michigan. They were active and enterprising and at once took
leading positions in the colony. CHARLES married, in 1722,
Catherine Sauvage; PIERRE married, 1728, Madeleine Roy, in
1736, Louise Lothman de Barrois, a sister of Marie Lothman,
wife of Robert Navarre, the Sub-Intendant. Pierre was called
La Butte, though St. Onge was the proper title. Many of his
descendants are only known under the name of La Butte. He
was interpreter for a number of years, and fulfilled his office
most satisfactorily. He had many children. All died unmarried
save PIERRE TOUSSAINT, who continued this branch. Pierre,
Sr., died in 1774. Agathe married Wm. Sterling. CHARLES
and Catherine Sauvage had ten children: 1. Catherine, B. 1722,
married Pierre Testard de Fortville, cousin of the Chevalier
Testard de Montigny; 2. PIERRE, B. 1724, married 1747, Clemence Chapoton, daughter of the surgeon; 3. Agathe, B. 1727; 4.
Bonaventure, B. 1731; 5. Charles, B. 1732, was also an able interpreter. He married, 1754, Josette Descomptes Labadie, daugh-

ter of Pierre and Angelique de Lacelle; 6. Leopold, B. 1734; 7. Isidore, B. 1737, married 1758, Thérèse Bequet; 8. Antoine, B. 1742. Isidore was noted for his great bravery, and figures conspicuously in the military annals. To him was deeded a tract of land by the Pottawatomie at the same time as the one to Robishe Navarre. The grant to Isidore was confirmed by Lieut. Gov. Hamilton in 1777. He married Thérèse Bequet. In 1780 his daughter Josette married the Chevalier Francois Chabert de Joncaire. Charles, son of Charles and Catherine Sauvage, married Josette Descomptes Labadie and was blessed with several children, viz.: 1. Pierre, married 1784, Cecile Campeau, daughter of Nicholas (Niagara); 2. CHARLES, B. 1758; 3. CATHERINE, B. 1763, married Fontenay de Quindre; 4. Agatha, married 1795, Alexis Campeau; 5. Gabriël, B. 1772, married 1793, Geneviève Campeau. Gabriël (dit Caousa), son of Charles and Josette Labadie, married Geneviève Campeau, daughter of Jean Baptiste and Geneviève Godé. Their children were: Gabriël, B. 1796, married Oct. 23, 1821, 1st. Cecile Séguin Laderoute, daughter of Joseph and Archange Campeau, whose children by this marriage were: Emilie, married Gagnion; Charles, married 1st. Eliza Parent, 2d, Catherine Baby; Mathew, married Agnes Parent; Joseph, died in infancy; Alexander, died in infancy; Elizabeth, married Edmund Baby; Isidore, married Mary Martin; Pierre, married Sarah LeMay; William, married Miss Bird, of New York; GABRIEL, married a second time, Mlle. Campau, widow of Antoine Parent. His children by this marriage were: MARIE, died young; Gabriël, married Antoinette Barien; Alexander, married Miss Barien; Felice; Rosalie, married Mr. Charest; JOSETTE, sister of Gabriel, married, 1819, Jacques Campeau, son of Jacques and Susanne Beaubien; Genevière, B. 1800.

CICOTTE.

Cicot or Chiquot as it was sometimes written, is found in the early pages of the registry of Fort Ponchartrain. The founder of this family in America was Jean, born 1631, son of Guillaume and Jeanne Farfart, de Bolu, Diocese of Rochelle. He married at Montreal 1662, Marguerite Maclin; the children were: CATHERINE, born 1663; JEAN born 1666. Catherine married 1679,Joseph Huet of Boucherville, whose mother a Jacquelien, belonged to the family of the celebrated de la Rochejacquelien the Vendean chief. The Amblers, Jacqueliens and other Virginia families claim descent from the Huguenot branch which passed into England, thence to Virginia.

Jean married 1679, Catherine Lamourieux; ZACHARIE their son born in 1708, married in 1736 Angelique Godefroy de Marboeuf.

He had come to Fort Ponchartrain in 1730 as a merchant. The quantity of handsome plate possessed by this family has frequently been mentioned; with the exception of Miss St. Martin (afterwards the wife of Angus McIntosh) there was no such complete collection of silver in the colony. The fate of war, pillage by the Indians, extravagant living and reckless trust in the honor of others, soon scattered this superb property. Some few remnants are still in the possession of the descendants. Zacharie's children were: 1. Angelique, born 1741; 2. Catherine, born 1744; 3. Zacharie, born 1746; 4. Jean Baptiste, born 1749, married 1770, Angelique Poupart Lavoise whose marriage contract is given below; it is dated 1770. By the Treaty of Paris the French inhabitants preserved some of their privileges, rights and ancient customs. It is selon les "Contumes de Paris."

JEAN BAPTE, had fifteen children, thirteen of whom lived to maturity. They resided upon the Cicotte farm, the present Peter Godefroy farm, which was confirmed to Angelique Cicotte (Jean Bapte's widow) by the U. S. Commissioners in 1819. The children were:

Angelique, born 1771, married 1767, Medor Gamelin son of Ignace and Louise Dufros de la Jemerais, nephew of Madame D'Youville, foundress of Les Soeurs Grises (Grey Nuns), of Montreal whose life has been so charmingly written by L'Abbé Faillon.

AGATHE, born 1773, married 1790 Jacob Visgar one of the representatives with Solomon Sibley, and the Chevalier Chabert de Joncaire in the Legislative assembly at Cincinnati in 1799, to elect Genl. (afterwards president) Harrison, a delegate to Congress. The children were: Joseph, married Mlle. Godefroy, daughter of Col. Gabriel Godefroy; Catherine, married 1819, WHITTMORE KNAGGS, son of Wm. and Josette Des Comptes Labadie, a name well known in the history of Michigan; CATHERINE married 1797 Antoine O'Neale, of St. Louis, Mo.; SUSANNE, married Jacques Peltier; FRANCOIS X. born 1787, married 1819, Felice Peltier widow of Capt. P. Tallman, U. S. A.; LOUIS married 1815, Veronique Cuillerier de Beaubien; GEORGE, born 1796; JEAN BAPTE. Jean Bapte. de Celeron was his godfather. he died unmarried; THERESE born 1790, married 1808, Barnabé Campeau; MARIANNE born 1791, married 1809, Chas. Descomptes Labadie, son of Alexis and Marie Francoise Robert; ZACHARIE born 1775; JOSEPH married 1825, Susanne Drouillard.

Francois X. born 1787, married 1819, Felice Peletier, the widow of Capt. Peter Tallman, an artillery officer in the U.S.A. Francois was commissioned as a Capt. by Genl. Hull in 1812. His small company mostly composed of men innured to the toils, dangers and privations of frontier life, were noted for their discipline and undaunted bravery. After the defeat of Winchester at Monroe, an Indian chief brought a Dr. Brown, a Kentuckian, to Mr. Francois

Cicotte to sell as his prize. The Indian wanted $100 for the ransom of his captive, which was paid to him. Dr. Brown afterwards visited his deliverer when he came again to Detroit with Genl. Harrison's army. Francois died in 1860. He was a fine specimen of the early Frenchman, possessing that rare charm of manner which seemed a peculiar legacy to these descendants of the first pioneers. His children are well known in Detroit.

1. EDWARD for many years occupying many positions of public trust, married 1st, Miss Bell of N. Y., by whom he had one son, GEORGE; married 2nd time Lucretia Abbott, daughter of Robert and Elizabeth Audrain.

2. Francois X. married 1st, Victoire Beaubien, daughter of Lambert and Geneviève Campau, by whom he had two daughters: Victoire married Mr. Bagg; PHILIS married Mr. Rankin; both reside in Detroit. He married a second time Elizabeth daughter of the Patriot, Theller, by whom he had three girls and a son. The son Francois resides in California, with one of his sisters, Mrs. Wm. B. Hunt; Emma and Annie married two brothers and reside at Detroit.

3. SUSANNE married 1831 Chas. Beaubien son of Lambert and Geneviève Campau. Four girls and one son were the fruit of this union. 4. Eliza Van Meter married Chas. Peltier, son of Chas.——; 5. CATHERINE married Dr. Allen of New York; 6. JOHN married Julie Chapoton daughter of Eustache. He left one son and one daughter: Madaleine; Askin married Mr. Lawson.

Marriage contract between J. B. Cicotte and Angelique Poupart:

JULY 27, 1770.

Before Philip De Jean, Royal Notary, by act of law residing at Detroit, were present Monsieur Jean Baptiste Cicotte, merchant, eldest son of Zacharie Cicotte, also merchant, and Madame Angelique Godefroy de Marboeuf, his father and mother, natives of Detroit of the one part; the Sieur Joseph Poupart La Fleur, also merchant, and the Dame Agathe Reaume residing at the same place, stipulating for the Demoiselle Angelique Poupart, their daughter accepting and of her own consent for herself and in her name of the other part. The said parties in his presence and by the advice and councils of the Sieurs and ladies, their parents having assembled their friends as follows: on the part of the Sieur Jean Baptiste Cicotte, the Sieur Zacharie Cicotte and the Dame Angelique Godefroy, his father and mother, Pierre Chesne de la Butte, Jean B. Chapton, Jacques Godefroy de Marboeuf, his uncles; Medor Gamelin, his brother-in-law, Ignace Boyer and Jacques Gabriël, his cousins; the dame widow Trotier des Ruisseaux, his aunt; Chas. Rivard, Antoine Gamelin, Alexis Maisonville and Joseph Lamoureaux; also on the part of the Demoiselle Angelique Poupart La Fleur, the Sieur Joseph Poupart and the Dame

Agathe Reaume, her father and mother, Lt. Gov. John Hay, her uncle, Jean Poèrpart, her grandfather, Nicholas de Lacelle, Hyacinthe Reaume, her great uncles; Chas. Reaume, Pierre Barron, Pierre Descomptes, Labadie Baptiste, Joseph Reaume, her uncles; Dupèron Baby, her cousin. Madames Hay and Barron, her aunts, and the Sieur Dr. George Anthon, Madame Baby, their relatives and friends, have made convention and agreement of marriage as follows: "That the Sieur Jos. Poupart and Madame Reaume have promised, and do promise to give the said Angelique Poupart, their daughter, to the said Jean Baptiste Cicotte, who promises to take her as his future and legitimate spouse by law of marriage and to have the same solemnized in the face of our holy Mother Church, and this as soon as can be done or whenever one of the two parties shall demand of the other. They shall be the future espoused couple, one and common in their goods, moveable and immoveable, and their acquisitions according to the usages and customs of Paris, (Coutume de Paris) in express derogation of all other laws and customs, contravening appropriating to themselves the said Sieur and Demoiselle, future husband and wife jointly and severally the goods and dues to them appertaining, whatever they may consist of without there being any necessity of making a designation. The future husband has given and does give to the said Demoiselle his future spouse the sum of three thousand "Livres Tours" to be paid in one stated payment, to have and to take so soon as the dower shall become a lien upon all the goods of the future husband, which are hereby hypothecated to furnish and make available the said dower which the said future spouse shall enjoy and become seized of without being held to make a demand in her own right in a court of justice. The aforesaid dower shall belong to the children who shall be born of the said marriage, and in default of children, in her own right to the future wife. Arriving at the dissolution of the said marriage by the decease of the aforesaid future husband, the said Demoiselle future wife shall have and shall take for the marriage 2000 "Livers Tours." To her it shall be lawful and to her children if there are any, and in default of children to the next heir to accept or refuse a community of goods and in the latter case the said Demoiselle, future wife, will take all that she brought to said marriage; her wardrobe and jewels, her furnished apartments as well as any goods that have fallen to her by inheritance. And in consideration of the sincere affection which the future husband and wife bear each other, they have made and do make by these presents to the survivor two free gifts equal, mutual and reciprocal of all their goods, furniture, acquits, gains moveable and immoveable which shall be found to belong and appertain to the one first deceased to enjoy at such decease all such sums and quantities as said goods may amount to, or consist of and wheresoever they may be situated. And for making a registry of these presents at the clerk's office of the aforesaid City of Detroit, and wherever else there may be any need, the said parties have appointed their Attorney General and special, the bearer of these seals giving him full power, thereby relinquishing, promising and agreeing the things done at Detroit in the house of Sieur Jos. Poupart, situated in the Fort on the 7th day of June after mid-day, the said future husband and wife after reading the same have signed with us as follows, their relatives and friends:

(Signed)   JEAN BAPTE CICOTE.
ANGELIQUE POUPARD.
HAYCINTHE REAUME.
PIERRE DES COMPTES LABADIE.
PR. BARRON.
DUPERON BABY.
ANTOINE GAMELIN.
CHARLES REAUME.
JOHN HAY.
BAPTE CHAPOTON.
GEO. ANTHON.
MEDOR GAMELIN.
JOSEPH LAMOUREUX.
JACQUES GODEFROY.

(*Signed*)   DE JEAN,
NOTARY.

With regard to the division of property in general according to the civil law of Canada, it consisted of moveable and immoveable property.

MOVEABLE was anything that could be moved without fraction.

IMMOVEABLE was anything that could not be moved, and was divided into two kinds, propres (personal), and acquits (acquired). *Propres* (personal), is an estate inherited by succession in the direct or collateral line, and *Acquit* is an estate or property that is acquired by any other means.

COMMUNITY OF PROPERTY, was the partnership of husband and wife contract on marrying; but they could stipulate in their marriage contract that there should be no community of property between them.

The dot or dowry was all the property which the wife put into the community whether moveable or immoveable. But immoveable property falling to her in a direct or collateral line is a proper or personal estate to her; and does not fall into the community. The dower was a certain right given by law or by particular agreement to the wife; it was of two kinds, the *customary* Dower, and the *stipulated* Dower. The former consisted of half the property which the husband was possessed of at the time of their marriage and half of all the property which might come to him in a direct line. The stipulated dower was a certain sum of money or portion of property, instead of the customary dower during her lifetime; at her death it fell to her children who did not accept the succession of their father, but her heirs succeed to the stipulated dower. Hence by the community which existed in marriage, no man could dispose of any or part of his property without the consent of his wife.

CULLERIER DE BEAUBIEN.

This family still stands among the most distinguished in Canada. It is known under the names of Trotier de Beaubien, des Rivières Trotier des Ruisseaux, Hay de Montigny. The branch which settled in Detroit was formerly called Cuillerier. In large families it was then customary to add the mother's family name to distinguish the different branches, viz.: Des Rivières de la Morandière—Cuillerier de Beaubien.

René Cuillerier, son of Julien and Julienne Fairfeu de Clermont, near La Flèche, came to Montreal, married there Marie Lecault in 1665. Their eldest son, René, born in 1668, was sent to France to be educated but was lost at sea returning to Canada. Jean, born in 1670, married in 1696, Catherine Trotier de Beaubien, from whom the Beaubiens of Michigan descend. Jean died in 1708, and Catherine married in 1712, Picoté de Bellestre, and accompanied him to his post at Fort Pontchartrain. He was ensign in the French army, brother-in-law of de Tonty and de Celeron, former commandants of Fort Pontchartrain. He died there in 1729, leaving one son, Francois Marie Piquoté de Bellestre, the last French commander of that fort. By the first husband, Jean Cuillerier, Catherine had two sons: 1. Jean Baptiste dit Beaubien, born 1709, married in 1742 at Detroit, Marianne Lothman de Barrois.

2. Antoine, born 1697, married in 1722 Angelique Gerard. Jean Baptiste married in 1742 Marianne Lothman de Barrois, by whom he had the following children: 1. Catherine, born 1743; 2. Jean Marie, born 1745, married Claire Gouin his son Antoine married in 1829 Monique DesComptes Labadie, daughter of Pierre and Thérèse Gaillard. Antoine had no children and left a portion of his estate (known as the Antoine Beaubien farm) to charitable purposes. The present site of the Sacred Heart Convent in Detroit was their residence. Pierre, Jean Marie's son, married in 1824 Catherine Edesse Dequindre, daughter of Antoine and Catherine Des Rivières de la Morandiere, whose daughter Lydia married Joseph Lewis.

Antoine married Angelique de Lacelle in 1722, whose children were as follows: 1. Marianne married in 1750 Pierre Chesne La Butte; 2. Alexis, born 1732. He was implicated in 1769 in the murder of Fisher's child, but was honorably acquitted. He was called Cuillerier dit Beaubien (the descendants have dropped the former name and retain the latter); 3. Angelique, born 1735, married in 1760 James Sterling; 4. Antoine married in 1784 Catherine Barrois, widow of Pierre St. Cosme. Their son, Jean Baptiste, born 1789, settled in Chicago and was known as Col. Beaubien, married Josette Laframboise. Medard and Marc, two of Antoine's sons, went to Kansas, where their descendants reside; 5. Lambert married in 1788 Geneviève Campeau, whose son Lambert married in 1821 Felice Morand, daughter of Louis and Catherine Campeau. Charles married in 1831 Susanne Cicotté.

DEMERSAC.

Jacob L'Ommesprou de Mersac was one of the officers who accompanied Cadillac to Detroit in 1701. He died there in 1747 leaving several children by his wife Thérèse David. The family had several titles, Marcas de L'Obtrou, de Lommesprou, and Desrochers. Jacques, born 1704, died young; Jacques, born 1707; Francois, married 1734, Thérèse Campeau by whom he had, 1. Francois, born 1736, married 1767, Charlotte Bourassa; Thérèse, married Louis Beaufait; 3. Jean Bapte, born 1740, married 1773, Geneviève Séguin Laderoute; 4. Marie Louise, born 1744, married 1762 Robert Navarre, Jr.

Francois de Mersac, married 1767, Charlotte Bourassa, who was allied to the families Le Ber, Testard de Montigny, De Langlade, Gregnon, &c. Their children were: 1. Cecile, married 1776, Vatal Sarazin de Pelleteau; 2. Francois, born 1769; 3. Jacques, born 1772; 4. Robert, born 1774; 5. Antoine, born 1776; 6. René, born 1777, married 1806, Eulalie Gouin; his daughter Sophie, married Louis Campeau of Grand Rapids, Mich.

Jean Bapte (Benjamin), married 1773, Geneviève Séguin Laderoute; the children were: Archange, born 1774; Rose, born 1776; Genevieve, born 1777, married 1797, Henri Campau; Charlotte, born 1779.

It is a tradition in the DeMersac family, that its founder at Detroit, Jacob, after he had resigned his position of officer in the French army, cultivated the land granted him; it was no unusual sight to see him ploughing with his sword at his side.

DE QUINDRE.

This family is known under the titles of De Pécanier, Pon chartrain, Fontenoy, de La Saussaye. Daigneaux Douville, gallant officer, stationed at Fort Pontchartrain as early as 1736, received for his distinguished services a grant of land on Lake Champlain. Daigneaux Douville is the family name of the De Quindre, and is borne to-day by the Marquis Daigneaux Douville in France. Louis Cezar Daigneaux Douville De Quindre, Col. of Militia under French rule, settled about 1745, at Detroit. He had married Louise Catherine Piquoté de Bellestre, a sister of the Commandant of that name. He generally signs his name FONTENOY.

Francois, his eldest son, was Sieur de Pécanier, an officer in the British army, married 1779, Thérèse Boyé, daughter of Ignace and Angelique de Cardonet. The children were: FRANCOIS, born 1780, married 1822, Marie Renée Petit; ANTOINE, born 1782; Louis, born 1786; Thérèse, born 1787; Pierre.

Antoine was called De Pontchartrain, on account, it is said, of being the first child of European parents born within the walls of the French fort. He married Catherine Des Rivières de la Morandière, of a celebrated and illustrious family. The children were: 1. Catherine, b. 1782; 2. Antoine, b. 1784; 3. Catherine Edesse, born 1797, married 1824, Pierre Beaubien. A daughter by this marriage married Joseph Lewis; 4. Adelaide, born 1788, Philip Chabert de Joncaire and Claire Gouin were her godparents. She married 1808, Joseph Campau; 5. Louis, born 1790, married Marie Desnoyers. The children were: Henry, who died without leaving heirs, and Annie, who married Edward Lansing; 6. TIMOTHY married Jeanette Godé-Marentette, daughter of Dominique and Archange Louise Navarre. The children were: Sara, married Columbus Godfroy, of Monroe, Mich., son of Jacques and Victoire Navarre; Elizabeth, married Oliver Edwards, son of Major Edwards, U. S. A.; Emilie, married Chas. Hayes, of Kalamazoo, Mich.; 7. Julie, born 1799, married Judge Chas. Moran.

Antoine, born 1784, generally called Col., served with great distinction at the battle of Monguagon, in 1812, and received the thanks of the Legislature for his gallantry. He was offered the rank of Major in the U. S. army, but declined. He was a prominent merchant, and noted for the grace and courtliness of his manner. He married, in 1809, Cath. Chapoton, daughter of Louis Alexis, by whom he had several children.

DESCOMPTES LABADIE.

This name is among the most conspicuous in the early days of the colony; and the numerous descendants to-day are scattered throughout Canada and every part of the United States, many of them proudly preserving their rank and prominence.

FRANCOIS, son of Francois and Marie Renoult de St. Leger,

Diocese of Xaintes, France, born 1644, married in Canada in 1671, Jeanne Hébert, a name well known in Canada. There was a title of LeCompte in the Hébert branch from whence perhaps comes the Descomptes in the Labadie. Their children were: JEANNE, born 1674, married Nicolas Sylvester; CHARLOTTE, married Jean Borneau; FRANCOISE, married 1723, Marguerite Cotty; LEWIS Jos., married Gabrielle LaRoche; PIERRE, married, 1725, Louise Gervais; JACQUES was Major in the French army and died at Three Rivers in 1707.

In 1732 the name was borne in France by Alexandre Etienne Ravielt, Claude Labadie, Colonel of an Infantry regiment, Chevalier, Seigneur de la Chausseliere. He was the son of Francois. A son of Alexander was Francois Patrice Alexandre Vincent Ravielt de Labadie, Captain in the navy. He was born at Rochelle, 1732. PIERRE, born 1702, son of Jean Bapte of the Diocese of LaRochelle, came to Quebec and married there in 1727, Angelique de Lacelle, daughter of Jacques de Lacelle, Savigny Sur-Oise, Diocese of Paris and Angelique Gibaut of Poitiers about 1747. He came to Detroit and immediately took a foremost rank in the affairs of the colony. His children were: 1. ANTOINE LOUIS, born 1744, married, 1759, Angelique Campeau. In 1784, he married a second time, Charlotte Barthe, widow of Lieutenant Louis Reaume, of the British army; 2. ALEXIS, born 1746, married 1769, Francoise Robert; 3. JOSETTE, married 1755, Charles Chesne, the Interpreter; 4. MARGUERITE, married, 1760, Claude Solo; 5. PIERRE, born 1742 married Thérèse Gaillard Livernois.

ELIZABETH, born 1749, married 1766, Joseph Lupien Barron. On the twenty-sixth of February, 1759, ANTOINE LOUIS, (called Badichon by the Indians) married Angelique, daughter of Nicolas Campeau (Niagara), in the presence of Pierre Des Comptes Labadie, Hyacinthe Reaume, Claude Campeau, Charles Chesne, Jean Gaultier, Pierre Testard de Fortville, Robert Navarre, Sub-Intendant, Pierre de St. Cosme. Simple Boquet, Missionary Recollêt. By this marriage he had three children; ANTOINE, (Didine) married Chesne La Butte; ANGELIQUE, married Seguin Laderoute.

CATISHE, married J. Peltier. In 1784, LOUIS, (Badichon) married Charlotte Barthe, daughter of Pierre and Charlotte Chapoton, widow of Lieutenant Louis Reaume, of the British army. Their children were: 1. CECILE, married, 1803, Angustin Lagrâve, son of Antoine and Thérèse Duberger, dit Sans Chargrin. Her descendants reside at St. Louis, Mo., and intermarried into all the old French families of that city. 2. FELICE, married John Hale, one of her daughters, ANTOINETTE, married Jos. Langly, of New York; the other, LIZZIE, married William Driggs. Her son, William Driggs, is an officer in the

U. S. A.; 3. ISABELLE, married St. Luc Sedillot de Montreuil.
One of her daughters, Felice, resides in Detroit, is the wife of
Alex. Chapoton, Sr. A son, Luc, married Marie Roberge, who is
known as the "Sister of Mercy" of Walkerville, on account of
her unselfish devotion and charitable deeds ; 4. EUPHROSINE,
married Petrilnouc ; 5. MARGUERITE, married 1829, Elias John
Swan, of Albany, N. Y., son of Elias and Elizabeth Palmer
6. Eleonore, married, first J. Reid, second in 1806, Jean Bapte
Piquette, son of Jean Bapte and Francoise Archevêque de
Rouen, by whom she had two sons, Jean Bapte and Charles ;
third, in 1825, Thomas Sheldon ; by this marriage she had three
children : THOMAS, married Winnie Clark, niece of Governor
Fenton, of Michigan ; ROSE, married Henry Geisse, of a distinguished Philadelphia family. Her daughter NELLY, married
Orville Allen and resides at Detroit. One of the sons, THOMAS,
possesses a superb voice. Music seems to have been a peculiar
legacy which the DesComptes Labadies have left to their
descendants ; ALEXANDERINE MACOMB, married first, Barnabé
Campeau, son of Barnabé (L'Abbé) and Archange McDougall, by
whom she had three children : CHARLOTTE, died in infancy ;
THOMAS SHELDON ; ALBERT, who is a physician at Detroit. She
married the second time, Richard Storrs Willis.

SECOND BRANCH.

Alexis, (Badi) married Marie Francoise Robert, daughter of
Antoine and Marie Louise Beconon, of Amiens, France, in presence
of Le Chevalier Chabert de Joncaire, De Lacelle, Jacques
Duperon Baby, C. Le Blont, Nicolas de LaCelle, Charles Chesne,
Louis Nicolas DesComptes Labadie, SIMPLE BOQUET, Missionary
Recollêt. The children of this union were : MARIE FRANCOISE,
born 1774, married 1795, Isidore Navarre; MARGUERITE, born 1773,
married Etienne Dubois ; CHARLES, married 1809, Marianne
Cicotte ; MONIQUE married 1813, Francois Cadot ; ELIZABETH,
married 1808, Charles Gouin ; LOUISE ADELAIDE, married Hyacinthe Saliotte; ARCHANGE born 1787 ; PIERRE married 1809,
Marie Barron; ALEXIS married, 1811, Anne Bourgeois ; second,
1823, Isabelle Rousseau ; CECILE married, 1802, Pierre LeDuc.

THIRD BRANCH.

PIERRE, brother of Alexis, (Badi) and Louis, (Badichon)
married Thérèse Gaillard, of a most distinguished family of
Quebec. Their children were : 1. PIERRE married, 1812, Eliza-
beth Bienvenu Delisle ; 2. ELIZABETH married, 1820, Jean Bapte
Beseau ; 3. MONIQUE, married, 1829, Antoine Beaubien, son of
Antoine and Catherine Lothman de Barrois ; 4. Josette, mar-
ried William Knaggs ; 5. MARGUERITE married Judge James
May, one of the earliest Justices of the Territory of Mihigan. He

had previously married Adèle de St. Cosme. The only child by this marriage, ELIZABETH ANNE married Gabriël Godfrey, Jr., son of Col. Gabriël and Angelique de Couture.

By Marguerite. Judge May had many children: 1. MARIE married LouisMoran of Grand Rapids, Mich. Some of her descendants still reside there.

Marguerite Anne married Col. Edward Brooks, U. S. A. Her children were mostly girls and proverbial for their beauty, brightness of intellect and supurb musical talent. 1. MARGARET ; ANNE BROOKS married Charles W. Whipple, son of Captain Whipple, U. S. A., and Archange Pelletier. He was a very able lawyer and held the office of Chief Justice of Michigan. She died at the early age of thirty, leaving two daughters EUNICE, wife of Judge William Jennison, of Detroit, ADELINE widow of Mr. Johnson ; 3. ADELINE died unmarried.

4. REBECCA married Dr. J. B. Scovile, a most able and prominent physician of Detroit. Two children were the fruits of this union: 1. EDWARD Brooks, whose wonderful voice has won him a national reputation, married Marcia Roosevelt, daughter of Judge Roosevelt of New York ; 2. MAY married Richard Cornell of Buffalo, N. Y., and is known as May Fielding to the histronic and musical world.

4. OCTAVIA married J. C. W. Seymour. Three children of his marriage are still living : WILLIAM ; ELIZABETH, wife of Lieutenant Waterbury, U. S. A.; MARGUERITE, wife of Rush Drake, formerly of Detroit, but now of Denver, Col.; MARY married Mr. Whitney, of Philadelphia, and is noted in New York society as one of its most beautiful and brilliant women; 6. WILLIAM died unmarried; 7. EDWARD; 8. EMMA died unmarried; 9. EMILY married Francis Markman and resided in New York ; ELIZABETH married Henry Scovil ; CARRIE married Philip Guliger and resided in New York, where her wonderful voice was highly appreciated.

4. NANCY, fourth daughter of Judge May, married James Whipple, son of Mayor John Whipple and Archange Peltier. In 1823, she married Francois Audrain ; 5. CAROLINE married 1829, Alexander Frazer, the leader for many years of the Detroit bar. The only child of this marriage was ALEXANDER, who married Milly Miles, of New York : ALEXANDER, Jr. died, leaving one daughter; CARRIE, who died unmarried.

DESNOYERS.

There are many families of this name who settled at an early period in this country. The Detroit branch traces direct to France through Pierre Jean Desnoyers, who established himself at Detroit shortly after the American possession in 1796. He was the son of

Jean Charles and Marie Charlotte Mallet, St. Bartholomi Parish, Paris. Pierre immediately took an active interest in the affairs of the little town which he had chosen for the cradle of his race. He was universally respected as a thorough Christian, an upright, enterprising citizen, a courteous and charming companion.

July 30th, 1798, he married Marie Louise Gobeil, whose saintly life is mirrored in that of her daughters. Many children came to bless the union of this happy couple: 1. Pierre, married in 1821, Caroline Leib, daughter of John and Marguerite O'Connor of Philadelphia. She left two children, Dr. Edmund Desnoyers and Emilie who married the talented artist Emile St. Alary. Pierre married a second time, Anne Hunt Whipple, daughter of Capt. John Whipple, U. S. A., and Archange Peltier, by whom he had many children, but only two at present living. Kate, married J. Newton Powers; Fanny, married 1875, Wm. B. Moran. Pierre held many offices of public trust, and died in 1880, at an advanced age; 2. Marie Rose, married 1817, Louis de Quindre, whose daughter Annie married Edward Lansing of New York; 3. Emilie, married Louis Leib. She died young, and left no heirs; 4. Victoire, married 1825, Henry S. Cole, of Canandaigua, N. Y., a most able lawyer, who had settled at Detroit. Their family consisted of three sons and four daughters: Augustus Porter Cole; Charles Seymour, died unmarried; James Henry, died unmarried; Marie Louise, married E. M. Wilcox; Isabelle, died a nun of the Sacred Heart; Marie Antoinette; Harriet S., whose beautiful and pious life is a repetition of that of her mother and grandmother; 5. Elizabeth, married 1835, James J. Van Dyke, one of the most brilliant lawyers of his time, who died before he fulfilled the brightest expectations which his talents promised, leaving a large family as follows: Geo. W., married Fanny Perley, widow of Chas. Piquette; Marie Desnoyers, married Wm. Casgrain, a member of that distinguished family of Canada. She resides at Milwaukee, Wis.; Philip James D., married 1st Marion King, 2nd Sarah Beeson. He was one of the most promising lawyers Detroit has ever produced, inheriting in an eminent degree the brilliant talents of his distinguished father. He died in the flower of his age, leaving four boys by his second marriage: Ernest D. is the worthy and respected pastor of the Pro. Cathedral, (St. Aloysius) Detroit; Josephine Desnoyers, married Henry F. Brownson, an officer in the U. S. A. He resigned in 1871, became a lawyer and partner of Philip J. D. Van Dyke. He is a son of the celebrated writer, Dr. Orestes Brownson. Major Brownson is one of the most scholarly men of which Detroit is justly proud. He has a large and interesting family, the members of which though young already give promise of the talents doubly inherited; Victoire, is a nun of the Sacred Heart Order; Elise, married 1872, William B. Moran. She died in 1874, leaving one child Catherine; 6. Charles Desnoyers. married

Elizabeth Knaggs, by whom he had three sons; 7. Francois, married Louise Baird, of Erie, Pa., settled at Green Bay, Wis. His children still reside there; 8. Josephine, married Henry Barnard, son of Chauncy Barnard and Elizabeth Andrus, Hartford, Conn. Mr. Barnard, is a thorough scholar, and has held many important positions. He was President of St. John's College, Md., Chancellor of the University of Wisconsin, U. S. Commissioner of Education. One son and two daughters are the children of this marriage. The son, Henry D., resides in Detroit, is an accomplished, studious gentleman, ambitious and likely to obtain eminence in the political world, in which he has already attained position and reputation of which many an older man might well be proud. He married in 1878, Kittie, daughter of Judge Chas. Moran, and Justine McCormack.

DOUAIRE DE BONDY.

This family is still to be found among the *haute noblesse* of France. It was once very influential in Canada, allied to the Fleury de la Gorgondière, de Vaudreuil, Joliet, Godefroy, d'Amours, and others. Thomas Douaire de Bondy came to Canada in 1650, and married Marguerite de Chavigny, daughter of François, Seigneur de Champennois in France, and the great heiress, Éleonore de Grandmaison. This Eleonore though married three times always signed her maiden name to deeds and documents. Thomas was drowned whilst bathing near his residence, the Isle d'Orléans, leaving a rich young widow and four children. She married in 1671, Alexis de Fleury d'Eschambault and became the ancestress of the powerful Fleury de la Gorgondière family whose deeds and exploits fill the annals of Canada. By her first marriage with Douaire de Bondy she had the following children: 1. DOROTHÉE, married, in France, Count Fabian d'Albergati. Her son, Marie Luc, Marquis d'Albergati, married, in 1757, Charlotte d'Aubert, of the Juchereau family; 2. LOUISE MARGUERITE, married, 1st, Pierre Allemand, in 1693 Nicolas Pineau; 3. AUGUSTIN, married, 1693, Catherine Testard de la Forest. A grandson of his married, in 1780, in France, Charlotte Testard de Montigny, daughter of Chevalier Jean Baptiste and Charlotte Trotier des Rivières; 4. Jacques, married 1660, Madeliene Gatineau du Plessis, daughter of Nicolas, Sieur du Plessis and Marie Crevier. 1. JACQUES, married, 1728, Marie Damours whose family goes back to 1496, François Seigneur du Serin who belonged to the royal household of Louis XII. Marie's grandfather, Seigneur de la Morandière, came to Canada in 1652. His brother was a Maréchal de France.

2. JOSEPH, son of Jacques and Madeleine Gatineau du Plessis,

came to Detroit in 1730, married, in 1732, Marie Anne Campeau, daughter of Jacques and Cecile Catin. Their children were: 1. ANTOINE; 2. DOMINIQUE, married 1799, Charlotte Saliotte, whose descendants are still in Michigan and Indiana; 3. LAURENT, was a very brave soldier and was killed in 1812; 4. BENJAMIN; 5. CATHERINE, married Antoine Baron; 6. JOSETTE, married Joseph Beaubien; 7. THÉRESE, married Col. Gabriël Godfroy; 8. JOSEPH, married 1758, Josette Gamelin; 9. VERONIQUE, married Bernard Campeau.

DUBOIS.

Several branches of this family settled at Detroit: Dubois dit Filliau; Dubois dit Durebois, or Brisebois. It was the family name of the sixth French Governor of Canada, Pierre Dubois, Baron D'Avaugour. In 1754 Jean Baptiste Dubois (Durebois), son of Jean Francois and Marianne Prudhomme of Quebec, married, at Detroit, Charlotte Des Hestres, daughter of Antoine and Charlotte Chartier. Their children were: 1. Pierre Amable, born 1755; 2. Jean Louis, born 1758, died young; 3. Susanne, born 1759; 4. Marianne, born 1760. In 1760 Francois Dubois, a brother of Jean Baptiste, married Susanne Durivage. The one who left his name to the present Dubois Farm was Etienne, son of Etienne and Marie Charlotte de Lacelle of Montreal. He came to Detroit several years previous to the American possession; in 1792 he married Marguerite, daughter of Alexis (Badi) Descomptes Labadie and Francoise Robert—to whom he was distantly related through his mother. James, a son of this union, married, in 1829, Sophie Campau, daughter of Jacques and Josette Chesne. He died a few years ago, leaving to his children his large estate, and the reputation of an honorable man and upright citizen. His children are: Louis, married Julie St. Aubin, daughter of Louis and Thérèse Chapoton; Emilie, married M. de Girardin; Elizabeth, married Julian Williams.

GAMELIN.

This name ranks among the most celebrated in Canada, and is still found in France. Michel came to Canada as a surgeon, and married there, in 1662, Marguerite Crevier, a member of that historic and aristocratic family. Their children were: Ignace, born 1663, married 1673, Marguerite Le Moyne; Marguerite, born 1664, married 1657, Léger Hébert; Jean, born 1670; Pierre, born 1675, matried 1699, Jeanne Maugras; Genèvieve, married Baptiste Le Gras. Ignace married Marguerite Le Moyne, daughter of Jean and Madeleine de Chavigny. His son Ignace married 1698, Louise DuFros de la Jammerais, whose sister Marguerite, after the death of her husband, Francois You, Sieur de la Découverte, became the celebrated foundress of the Grey Nuns at Montreal. Louise was the daughter of Christopher DuFros, and Renés Gaultier. The sons of Ignace and Louise came to Detroit in 1760. They were Medor and Antoine—the former married, in 1767, Angelique Cicotte; he was very prominent in getting up the first militia under French rule and was appointed Major; he died in 1778. Antoine, his brother, married his cousin Catherine Gamelin, daughter of Laurent, who had come to Fort Pontchartrain before his cousins; he was the son of Pierre and Jeanne Maugras, allied to the Boncher de Boncherville. He had married Josette Dudevoir Lachine, by whom he had the following children: Marie Jeanne, born 1743, married Jean LeGras; Catherine, born 1744, married 1765, Antoine Gamelin, son of Ignace and Louise DuFros de la Jammerais; Josette, married 1758, Joseph Douaire de Bondy, who was related to her through the De Chavignys; Francois, married, 1772, Thérèse Cabassier; second mar., 1786, Marie Joachine Fouché, of Montreal; Laurent, born 1755; Francoise, born 1756; Paul, born 1757. Francois and Thrèse Cabassier's children were: Catishe, married Simon Campau; Josette, married, 1796, Jean Baptiste Campeau. Francois' second wife, M. Joachine, daughter of Antoine, a lawyer of Montreal, and Joachine Chesnay de la Garenne; her brother was an eminent judge, Solicitor and Inspector General, and Member of Parliament of Three Rivers, Canada. The children of this marriage were: Francois, died unmarried; Susanne, born 1796, married Audrain Abbott, son of Robert and Elizabeth Audrain. She still lives, having outlived every member of her family (save a grandson) and the friends of her youth. Few, in conversing with her, would imagine that her years numbered eighty-seven. The kindling eye, dark hair, and charming grace and courtesy of manner make her an attractive companion to the young and old. She is a thorough type of the Old Regime, which in her will lose one of its last representatives.

GODÉ DE MARANTAY.

This family counts among its descendants a branch of Le Moyne de St. Hélène, Le Gardeur de Repentigny, St. Ours, Guyon, Godefroy, Reaume, and others equally well known. Nicholas B., 1583, a native of Perche, was a man of considerable ability; he was killed with his son-in-law, Jean de St. Per, by the Iroquois, in 1657; he left several children by his wife Francoise Gadois: Francois, married 1649, Francois Bugon, de Clermont, Auvergne; Nicolas, married 1658, Marguerite Picard, de Paris; Mathurine, married 1651, Jean de St. Per, Royal Notary of Montreal; he was killed by the Indians in 1657. Their daughter Agathe, born 1657, married 1685, Pierre LeGardeur de Repentigny; one of Agathès daughters, married in 1705, Jean Bapte de St. Ours, Chevalier de St. Louis, whose family can be traced back to the 13th century; he was a distinguished officer, and commanded at Fort Pontchartrain; when he came to his post he was accompanied by his cousins, Jacques and Francois Godé; Mathurine, married a year after her husband's tragic death, Jacques Le Moyne de St. Hélène, brother of the Baron de Longueil, Governor of Canada, an uncle of Iberville, and De Bienville, the founder of New Orleans, La— Seigneur de la Varennes, and de la Trinité. Jacques, son of Nicolas, Jr., married Marguerite Du Guay, daughter of Dr. Jacques Du Guay and Jeanne de Baudry-Lamarche, of the renowned Boucher de Boucherville family. Two of their children established themselves at Detroit. Jacques, Jr., married 1747, Louise Adhèmar de St. Martin; his children were: Chas. Joseph, born 1749 ; Marie Angelique, born 1750, married 1775, Francois Gouin; M. Louise, born 1756; Geneviève, born 1751, married 1767, Jean Baptiste Campeau.

Francois, who received the title of de Marantay (corrupted into Marentette) which his descendants adopted later as their proper name. He married Jeanne Parent, daughter of Laurent and Jeanne Cardinal; their children were: 1. Francois, born 1756; 2. Angelique, born 1757; 3. Jacques Francheville, married 1795, Geneviève Reaume, daughter of Claude. A daughter Jeanette, by this marriage, married Wm. Macomb: 4. Dominique, married 1796, Marie Louise Archange Navarre, daughter of Robert, Jr., and Marie Louise de Mersac; 5. Laurent, married Marie Louise Chesne La Butte, daughter of Pierre and Marianne Cuillerier de Beaubien, whose numerous descendants still reside at Windsor and Sandwich, Canada, whose son Pierre married Mlle. Groue. His sons are all noted for their great musical gift, and reside at Sandwich, Canada.

GODEFROY.

This name, at present written Godfroy, is among the oldest in Normandy. In some of its branches there is a tradition of a descent from Godefroi de Bouillon, the crusader. In the chambers of the courts of Normandy at Rouen, we find many of the names enrolled among the "haute noblesse." Several were eminent as priests and historians. Denis, Councillor in the Parliament of Paris, 1580, was the author of several valuable legal works, his son Jacques was Secretary of State and Syndic of the Republic, his grandson was made historiographer of France, in 1640, and wrote the history of the Constables and Chancellors of France. A branch of this family resided in Normandy in 1580, whose head was Pierre. His son Jean Bapte came to Canada about 1635. His marriage contract, a copy of which is before the writer, is dated Dec. 15, 1636, and is supposed to be the oldest one recorded in Canada. His wife was Marie Le Neuf de Herison. His sons and kindred were ennobled in 1667, and received the Seigneuru de Linctot and the fiefs de Normandville, de Vieux Pont, de Roguetiliade, de Tonnancour, de Marboeuf, &c., &c. A sister of Jean Bapte, Anne, married Jacques Testard de Montigny, whose descendant Jean Bapte Montigny de Louvigny, commanded at Detroit, married there a d. of Lt.-Gov. Hay and Julie Reaume, another Pierre Testard de Fortville married Catherine Chesne, of Detroit. René de Tonnancour, of Three Rivers, was Procureur du Roi, Lt.-Gen., &c. His branch was at one time very prominent, and several of its members were decorated with the Cross of St. Louis, Maurice being among the last to receive it in 1784. The old church at Three Rivers, richly endowed by the Godefroys, still has the arms of this family superbly curved on the Banc d'Oeuvres.

In 1715 Pierre Godefroy de Roguetiliade, grandson of Jean Bapte de Linctot, came to Detroit. He was followed shortly afterwards by Jacques Godefroy de Marboeuf. In 1750, Jean Bapte Godefroy, called the Chevalier, came to Detroit with his wife, Jeanne Veron de Grandmenil, and died there in 1756. Pierre and Jacques both married into the same family. Jacques married 1716, Marie Cuesne St. Onge. Pierre married 1724, Catherine Sanduge, and his step-daughter married Charles Chesne St. Onge. Like others of the name they were interested in the fur trade, which was originally a monopoly carried on by a company called the Hundred Associates, and later by the Companie des Indes. As early as 1687, it was said that 25,000 beaver skins alone were exported from Quebec in a single ship. The immense destruction of fur bearing animals led to the extension of the trading posts to the far west. Pierre's line died out.

The children of Jacques were: Catherine, b. 1717, at Three Rivers, named from her godmother, Catherine Godefroy de Roguetiliade, married Nov. 21st, 1733, the Chevalier Alex. Trotier des Ruisseaux, of an illustrious family. He was the first trustee of Ste. Anne's and first Capt. of Militia. The witnesses of this marriage were : De Noyelle, Commander of the Post; Le Gardeur de Courtemanche, Lt. of Marines; Sieurs Chas. and Pierre Chesne; Louis Campeau; Barrois, Beaubien, Alexis Bienvenu Delisle. In 1777 she died, and she is recorded as the daughter of the deceased nobleman Godefroy de Marboeuf; this is the last time that the title is mentioned; Angeliqua, born 1719, married Jan. 8th, 1736, Zacharie Cicotte, a wealthy merchant ; the marriage contract is given under the Cicotte family; the witnesses of the marriage were : Hughes Pean, Chevalier of St. Louis, Pierre Chesne La Butte, Francois

Prejent, Dagneaux Douville, Jean Bapte Chapoton; Jacques, born 1722, was very young at the time of his parents' death, and was brought up by his eldest sister, Catherine des Ruisseaux. Like his father he was interested in the fur trade. He was thoroughly familiar with the Indian tongues; and exerting great influence with the chiefs, by reason of his bravery and family connections, he soon became widely known as interpreter and negotiator between the savages and whites. He was ensign in his brother-in-law's, Alexis des Ruisseaux, company. After the fall of Quebec, Detroit was ceded to the English. Pontiac was at first disposed to resist the new comers, and had he been aided by the French settlers it is doubtful whether the conquest of the country would have been effected. But they, relying upon the promises made in the treaty that all their rights would be respected, no resistance was made, and the garrison under Mons. de Bellestre surrendered, and were escorted to Philadelphia, leaving the French settlers at the mercy of the English troops. French accounts say that in the face of the treaty they were robbed of their property, deprived of their fire-arms, leaving them without defence against the Indians. It is not to be wondered that bitter feelings were engendered, and the English commanders, ignorant for the most part of the French and Indian languages, were suspicious of constant plottings against them. It is a matter of surprise that the settlement, aided by their old Indian allies did not exterminate the English garrison, and their conduct under the circumstances is a convincing proof that the characteristic honor and loyalty claimed for them existed in the highest degree. In 1763, the haughty Ottawa warrior, who could no longer brook the arrogance of the British, attacked the fort at Detroit and the other English posts. Jacques and Dr. Chapoton were sent by the English commander to parley with Pontiac and endeavor to dissuade him from his purpose, but the savage chieftain would not be influenced. Jacques and other prominent French inhabitants were suspected of encouraging Pontiac, and on the advent of General Bradstreet, they were arrested and charged with treason. In 1758, Jacques married Louise Clotilde Chapoton, daughter of Jean Chapoton, Surgeon in the French army. She died in 1764, leaving one son, Jacques Gabriel. Jacques devoted the remainder of his life to the care of his son, and the rebuilding of his fortune, which had suffered since the English conquest. He figures prominently in many of the Indian transfers of land. In the American State papers is a curious deed in French from Jacques Godefroy to his son conveying to him farming lands, implements, cattle, silver and slaves. The land conveyed comprised the tract between 20th and 22nd streets from the river to some three miles back, some of which is still owned by his descendants. He died in 1795. He evidently was very popular and generous, for he seems to have been for several years godfather to almost every child that was born, for pages of baptisms on the records have his name affixed, in his strong, bold handwriting.

Jacques Gabriel, born 1758, within Fort Ponchartrain. He was named Gabriel from his godfather and uncle, Gabriel Le Grand, Chevalier de Sintre. About the time he came of age the American revolution was in progress. Though the colony was far removed from the scene of war, Gabriel's sympathies were with the colonists. His early years were spent in extending the fur trade and establishing trading posts on a large scale from Monroe to Fort Vincennes; the firm of Godfroy & Beaugrand was one of the largest and best known in the West. After the American possession he received an appointment as sub-agent and deputy-superintendent of Indian affairs from Gen. Harrison (afterwards president of the U. S.). The records which have been preserved of his success in negotiations with the Indians are abundant, and he retained the position until his death in 1832. The ordinary duties were to repair to any post where difficulties might arise, and to reclaim from maurading Indians stolen property, to pay the Indian annuities and to receive at his house all Indians who might arrive. Gabriel was Major of the 1st Regiment of the Territory; on the resignation of Augustus B. Woodward was made Colonel. He married Angelique de Couture, by whom he had five children: Gabriel, Jr., married Elizabeth, daughter of Hon. Jas. May; his descendants reside at Grand Rapids; Jean Baptiste settled at Fort Wayne, Ind. In 1796 Gabriel married Thérèse Douaire de Bondy, by whom he had several children. He died in 1831. He was one of the few who lived under French, English and American rule in the same place, and saw a change of flags five times. He married a third time Monique Campau, by whom he had no issue.

Those by his second wife were: 1. Susanne, born 1794, married Jas. McCloskey. Her children were: Henry, married Thérèse Soulard, of St. Louis; Elizabeth, married Hon. Isaac P. Christiancy; Caroline, married Mr. Calwell; Susanne, married Mr. Morton, brother of the late Julius Morton, of Detroit; Melinde, married John Askin, of Sandwich, Canada.

2. Pierre, "Le Prince" as he was generally called, was born 1796. He removed the last remnant of the Indians about Detroit to their reservation in the far West. He was active and enterprising, and the firm of P. & J. Godfroy was well known. He married Marianne Navarre Marentette, daughter of Dominique Godé de Marentette and Archange Louise Navarre; she and her sister, Mrs. De Quindre (afterwards Mrs. Wm. B. Hunt), were considered the most beautiful women in the Territory. It is a family tradition that Prince Godfroy once won a wager by paddling himself in a wheelbarrow across the Detroit river to visit his fiancée, who lived on the Canadian shore, a feat quite as difficult

as Leander swimming the Hellespont, and no less romantic. The
children of this union were: 1. Jacques William; 2. Elizabeth, married John Watson; 3. Franklin Appolonaire, died young; 4, Melonnie Thérèse, died young; 5. Caroline Anne; 6. Alexandrine Louise,
married Theo. Parsons Hall; 7.Charles Cass; 8. Nancy, married
Joseph Visgar, a name well known in the early days of the territory;
4. Josette, married 1821, John Smythe, son of Col. Richard Smythe
and Prudence Brady, of Lexington, Ky. After his death she
became a nun, and died whilst Superior of the Order of the
Immaculate Heart of Mary. 5. Jacques B. was educated at Bardstown, Ky.; he studied law but abandoned the profession of it on
account of ill health. He was a partner for many years in the
firm of P. & J. Godfroy. He married, 1820 Victoire, daughter
of Col. Francois Navarre, of Monroe. He died in 1847, leaving a
large family: Jacques Louis Columbus, married Sarah De Quindre;
Celestine, married Mr. Waldruff; Frederick; Alexandrine; Hilaire;
Philippe; Victoire; Augustus; Marie; Zoe, married Benjamin
Abbott, son of Robert, Auditor-General and Treasurer of the Territory of Michigan; Sophie, married James Whipple, son of Major
John Whipple, U. S. A.; 6. Richard, married Anne Villier dit
St. Louis, by who he had a rage family.

NOTE.—*Fief.* Fief is an estate held and possessed on condition
of fealty homage and certain rights payable generally by the new
possessor to the Lord or Seigneur by whom the fief is held; these
rights are *Quint* and *Relief.* The *Quint* is the fifth part of the
purchase money, and must be paid by the purchaser. *Relief* is the
revenue of one year due to the Seigneur for certain mutations. If
a fief came to a vassal by succession in the direct line, there was
nothing due the Seigneur but fealty and homage; but if in the
collateral line, then a fine was paid to the Seigneur upon taking
the estate which had lapsed or fallen by the death of the last tenant. Fiefs were divided by the "Contume de Paris" into two
kinds: 1st, those held nobly; 2d, those held by villainage. The
estates held nobly are the fiefs, and Franc Alen noble. The
estates held by villainage, were held subject to *cens* or *censive*, and
Franc Alen villain. Franc Alen was a freehold estate held subject to no seigneurical rights or duties, acknowledging no lord,
but the king. Censive was an estate held in the feudal manner,
charged with a certain annual rent which was paid by the possessor of it; it consisted of money, grain, fowls, etc. It was thus
that most of the habitants in Canada held their farms. The "lods
et ventes," or fines of alienation, were one-half part of the purchase money, and were paid by the purchaser on all mutations of
property "en roture" to the Seigneur in the same manner as the
quint was paid upon mutations of fiefs. The succession to fiefs
was different from that of property held "en roture" or by vil-

lainage. The eldest son took, by right, the principal manorhouse or chateau, and the yard adjoining it; also an acre of the garden joining it. If there were any mills, ovens or presses within the seigneuree, they belonged to the eldest son; but the profits arising from the mills, ovens and presses, if common, were equally divided among the heirs. When there were only two heirs, the eldest took, besides the manor house, etc., two-thirds of the fief, and the youngest son the other third. But when there were more than two heirs, the eldest son took one-half, and the other heirs the remaining half. When only daughters were the heirs, the fief was equally divided among them. If the eldest son died, the next did not succeed to his birth rights; the estate was then equally divided among the heirs.

GOUIN.

This family was allied to the most distinguished of Canada. Mathurin, born 1638, son of Vincent and Charlotte Gaultier, diocese de Poitiers, married 1663, at Three Rivers, Canada, Marie Madeleime Vien, daughter of Etienne and Marie Denot de la Martinière; their children were: Thomas, born 1667; Pierre, born 1679; Louis, married 1720. Jeanne Marchand; Joseph, married 1701, Marquerite Roy, daughter of Michel Roy Chatellereau and Françoise Hobbé, Diocese of Poitiers (France); Marianne, married 1703, Francois Trotier, son of Antoine Trotier Sieur des Ruisseaux and Catharine Lefebvre. Claude Thomas, son of Joseph and Marguerite Gouin, established himself at Detroit, and married there in 1742, Josette Cuillerier de Beaubien, by whom he had the following children: Joseph Nicolas, born 1746, married 1771, Elizabeth Rivard; Francois, born 1748, married 1775, Angelique Godé, daughter of Jacques and Louise de St. Martin; Claude Pierre, born 1751; Judith, born 1763, married 1783, Philippe Chabert de Joncaire, son of the Chevalier Daniel Chabert and Marguerite Ursule Elizabeth Rocbert de la Morandière; Claire, married Jean Marie Beaubieu, son of Jean Bapte Cuillerier de Beaubien and Marianne Lothman de Barrois. Joseph Nicolas, married 1771, Eliza Rivard, whose children were: Charles, born 1778. married 1808, Elizabeth Descomptes Labadie, daughter of Alexis (Badi) and Françoise Robert; he was very prominent, was chief surveyor under the British rule; Pierre, born 1780, married Irene Rivard, daughter of Jean Bapte and Irene Beaufait. Joseph Nicolas, married again in 1790, Archange Boyer—the daughter by this marriage was Colette (Clotilde), who married in 1809, Antoine St. Bernard, and in 1818, Dominique Riopelle, thus uniting the large landed interests of the Gouin and Riopelle families. A son of Dominique Riopelle married again into the Gouin family, (the branch which settled at Sandwich, Canada.)

LOTHMAN DE BARROIS.

Many French families of to-day claim among their ancestors a Lothman de Barrois. Antoine Lothman de Barrois was sent to America in 1665, as Secretary, Councillor and Agent General of the East India Company. He was also interpreter of the Portuguese language. He was the son of Jean and Marie Fournel, Chantel le Chateau, Diocèse de Burges, Berry. He married, 1672, Marie Le Ber, whose family was a very distinguished one. She was a niece of Jeanne Le Ber de Senmenville, whose life has been written by the Historian Abbé Faillon. A branch of the Le Ber returned to France, and the descendants all acquired fame and wealth. One was a page to Madame la Dauphine, another a gallant officer, killed on the field of Magenta. The Chevalier Benvoist, through his mother, belonged to the Le Ber family. Francois Lothman and Marie Le Ber had several children, among them were: Marianne, born 1680, married 1697, Francois Houdoin; Philippe, born 1672; Francois, born 1676, married at Detroit 1717, Marianne Sauvage; Charles, born 1678; Antoine, born 1683. Francois, born 1676, married Marianne Sauvage, and established himself at Detroit—their children were: Marie, born 1719, married 1734, Robert Navarre, the Sub-Intendant and Royal Notary, and is the ancestress of the Navarres; Louise, born 1722, married 1736, Pierre Chesne La Butte, the interpreter; Catherine, born 1727, married 1747, Pierre de St. Cosme, who was one of the earliest Justices of Peace. One of the daughters, Theotiste St. Cosme, married in 1776, Philippe De Jean, son of Philippe, Councillor and Sénéchal of Toulouse and Jeanne De Roque. De Jean was a Judge under Enlish rule. A great grand-daughter of Pierre St. Cosme became the first wife of Judge Jas. May. Catherine married again, Antoine Cuillerier de Beaubieu, by whom she had many children. Antoine, born 1733; Agathe, born 1735, married Jean Bapte Reaume, son of Hyacinthe and Agathe de Lacelle; Laurent, married 1757, Catherine Cecyre.

MORAND.

The descendants of this family are very ably represented to-day in Detroit. Pierre, its founder in America, was born at Batiscan in 1651, married Madeleine Grimard 1678. His branch is frequently known as Morand dit Grimard, it being then customary to add the mother's family name, especially if she brought a large dower to her husband. Of this marriage many children were born whose descendants in Canada were noted as clergymen, lawyers, and landed proprietors. Jean Bapte, a son of Pierre's, married 1707, Elizabeth Dubois, at Quebec, whose son, Charles Morand Grimard came to establish himself at Detroit some time before the English Conquest in 1760. There was at that time another branch of the same family, who settled at Detroit; another Charles, who married in 1751, Catherine Belleperche, who belonged to the celebrated Couillard and Guyon De Buisson family, thus closely allied to La Mothe Cadillac's wife; their children were: Louis, born 1756; Charles, born 1755; Joseph, born 1762, married 1790, Catharine Boycé; Louise and Thérèse, born 1769; Maurice, born 1775, married 1800, Felise Meloche; Marthe, married 1800, Louis Campeau; Susanne, married 1805, Francois Campeau, son of Jean Bapte. Chas. Morand-Grimard, married in 1767, Marguerite Simard Tremblay, whose family possessed the Seigneurie du Tremblay as early as 1681. She died in 1771, leaving two children: Louis, born 1769; Charles, born 1770. Louis, married 1794, Catherine Campeau, daughter of Jean Bapte and Catherine Boycé. One of his sons, (George), married 1826, Therese Tremblay, whose decescendants reside at Grosse Pointe. Charles, married 1794, Catherine Vessier dit Laferté, whose only child was the late Judge Chas. Morand. Charles, Jr., married 1822, Julie De Quindre, daughter of Antoine Daigneaux Douville De Quindre and Catherine des Rivières de la Moranddière. The children were: 1. Matilda, married James Watson; 2. Charles; 3. Julie, married Isaac Toll; 4. Virginie, married Francis St. Aubin ; 5. Mary Josephine, married Robert Mix, of Cleveland, O., Aug. 3rd, 1836; Judge Chas. Moran married Justine McCormack, of N. Y., by whom he had the following children: 1. James, died unmarried; 2. William B., married 1872, Elise, daughter of James J. Vandyke, in 1875, Frances, daughter of Pierre Desnoyers. His administrative faculty, his successful land operations have placed him in the foremost rank of Detroit capitalists. 3. John Vallié, married 1880, Emma Etheridge, daughter of the distinguished orator and politician, Emerson Etheridge, of Tennessee. He is one of the most successful business men of Detroit, and his sterling personal worth has made him deservedly popular; 4. Catherine, married 1877, Henry D. Barnard, of Hartford, Conn.; 5. Alfred is a lawyer, and in partnership with his brother, Wm. B. Moran. He married, 1878, Satilda Butterfield. Judge Chas. Moran died in 1876, leaving the most valuable estate, with the exception of the Brush and Campau, in Detroit. Charles inherited this magnificent property from his grandfather, Charles Moran Grimard. The family dropped the d at the end of the name, and also the title Grimard about 1796. To the peculiar conservatism of the French settler to-day, so frequently and unjustly misunderstood, are their descendants indebted for the preservation of their ancestral estates; 5. A brief glance at the early history of Detroit will convince the candid and unbiased reader, that the position of the habitants during the various political changes which Detroit underwent was one requiring delicate tact and diplomatic ability.

Early French Families. 307

Five successive flags waved over the fair "City of the Straits." One form of Government had scarcely enforced its laws and explained its policy before it vanished and gave place to another power. A disastrous fire destroyed their records. It is not strange that these country-tossed settlers looked with suspicion and indifference upon new ideas and improvments, their experience not having taught them to place much confidence in the existing orders of things. The old traditional Conservatism has fulfilled its mission, and handed to the present generation valuable estates, which, under the propessive management and enlarged ideas, founded upon a permanent form of Government, will bring not only princely revenues to its owners, but be later a source of pride to the city.

NAVARRE.

This family so illustrious in the early days of the colony traces back in an unbroken line to Antoine de Bourbon, Duke de Vendôme, father of Henry 4th, whose natural son, (1) Jean Navarre, married 1572 Perette Barat; (2) his son Martin Navarre de Villeroy married 1593 Jeanne Lefebre, whose son (3) Jean Navarre, married 1623, Susanna Le Clef ; their son (4) Antoine Navarre, du Plessis en Bois, married 1665, Marie Lallemant, whose son (5) Antoine Marie Francois Navarre, married 1695, Jeanne Pluyette, whose (6) Robert Navarre, was sent to Fort Pontchartrain as Sub-Intendant and Royal Notary, where he married, 1734, Marie Lothman de Barrois, his son Robert (Robiste) married, 1762, Marie Louise Archange de Mersac, whose daughter Archange Louise married, 1796, Dominique Godé de Marantette, whose daughter, Marianne Navarre married 1822, Pierre Godfroy. Antoine Navarre du Plessis' other sons remained in France, and one of them married Catherine de la Rue; their only daughter married Jean Navarre de Livry (her first cousin) whose daughter in turn, Marie Jeanne Navarre, born 1709, married Jean Louis Navarre de Maisonneuse (her cousin) brother of Mons. de Navarre, Marquis de Longuejoue, whose wife, born at St. Luce, was lady of honor (Dame d'Honneur) to Madame Elizabeth, sister of Louis 16th of France and the Duchess of Bourbon. Catherine Antoinette, Jeanne Martine Petronille, remained the only daughter by the death of her two sisters. She married Louis Francois Marguelet de la Noue, from whom Geneviève Celeric Marguclet de la Noue, eldest sister of Madame de Penteville, espoused Count Leoud Perthins, whose daughter Marie Celine Leonetine de Perthius, espoused Alex. Jacques Marie Clement de Blavett, whose son Edward married Marie Clement le Boulanger de Montigny, whose son Count Léon Clement de Blavett married Isabell de Brossard, de Versaille, France.

Robert Navarre, son of Antoine Francois. Marie and Jeanne Pluyette came to Detroit to fill the most important position in the colony. He was responsible to no one save the Intendant at Quebec. He added to this office that of Royal Notary. Following an old manuscript copied from the *Cabinet*, a scarce periodical issued at New York, 1827-1831. Robert de Navarre came to America and landed at Quebec. He was of a noble French family, a man of extensive erudition, was appointed under the French government subdéléqué and Royal Notary at Detroit. He married there in 1734, Marie Lothmande Barrois. At the marriage were present Hughes Pean, Seigneur de Livaudière, Hereditary Mayor of Quebec, Chevalier of St. Louis, Commandant of Fort Pontchartrain, Pierre Godefroy de Roquettliade, Duburron, Ensign, Daigneaux Douville and Chas. Chesne, Bonaventure Ptre. Robert Navarre's children were: (1) Marie Francoise, born 1735, married Geo. McDougall, Lt. in the British Army, by whom she had two sons, Jean Robert and George. In 1774 she married Jacques Campeau, father of Joseph and Barnabé, by whom she had no heirs, but Barnabé in 1820 married her granddaughter, Archange McDougall, whose sons were Alexander and the late Barnabé.

(2) Marianne, born 1737, married, 1760, Jacques Adhèmar St. Martin, frequently called La Butte, a most celebrated interpreter. They lived in the old Cass House, which was the St. Martin homestead, the ground being deeded to him in 1750. St. Martin died in 1766, leaving a young widow with three children : (1) St. Martin, who died unmarried; (2) Finon who married Philip Fry; (3) Archange, born 1765, married August McIntosh, who later on inherited the estates which belonged to the Earldom of Moy, the Earldom itself having been forfeited in the rebellion against the House of Hanover. The McIntosh homestead was on the Canadian shore opposite Belle Isle, and was celebrated along Le Détroit for the princely and lavish hospitality of its genial owner. Ten children were born to Angus McIntosh, the boys returned to Scotland to take possession of their estates. Two of the daughters were much loved and esteemed in Detroit, Mrs. Henry J. Hunt and Miss Catherine McIntosh. In 1770, Marianne Navarre widow of St. Martin, bestowed her hand upon Dr. Geo. Christian Anthon who had come to Detroit, in 1760, with Mayor Rogers. She died Oct. 11th, 1776, leaving no heirs by Anthon.

Robert, eldest son of Robert, Sr., surnamed Robishe the Speaker, was born in 1739. He married, 1762, Louise Archange de Mersac, daughter of Francois and Charlotte Bourassa. Another Charlotte Bourassa, a cousin, married in 1760, Chas. de Langlade, the pioneer settler of Wisconsin, whose family belonged to that of the Count of Paris. To Robishe was deeded by the Pottawatomies, their village, which was on a beautiful eminence commanding a fine view and which even then was pronounced by them in "Ancient Village,"

"We the chiefs of the tribe of the Pottawatomies nation at Detroit have deliberated and given of our own free will a piece of land of four arpents in width by the whole depth, situated at our ancient village to Robishe, son of the Scrivener. We give him this land forever, that he might cultivate the same, light a fire thereon, and take care of our dead, and for surety of our words we have made our marks." This grant was ratified by Henry Bassett, commanding at Detroit, July 15, 1772, in presence of Geo. McDougall. On one of Navarre's quit rent receipts it is stated that this tract was confirmed by Gen. Gage. Robishe resided on his land and in the house known to-day as the Brevoort homestead. It was later enlarged by Commodore Brevoort (Robishe's son-in-law). Robishe was the great great grandfather of the writer, and there still lives an old lady who remembers him. She speaks of him as a preeminently handsome man, with courtly manners, most engaging and charming in conversation. He was blessed like all the French of that period, with an exceptionally large family: (1) Robert, born 1764; (2) Jacques, born 1766, he settled on the River Raisin; (3.) Francois, born 1767, early removed with his brother Jacques and Jean Marie to Monroe, where twenty-six arpents had been deeded to the Navarres by the Ottawas. Francois was Colonel during the war of 1812-13, and figures most conspicuously. His house was the headquarters of Generals Wayne, Winchester, St. Clair and others. Thirty-six Navarres served in his regiment. He was thoroughly conversant with the peculiar habits and warfare of the savages, and spoke with facility several of their languages. He was captured at Brownstown, whither he had gone ahead of Col. Johnston to negotiate with the Indians; he was taken as prisoner to Sandwich, but fortunately escaped. His son Robert served under Capt. Richard Symthe, and told the writer many amusing anecdotes of the war. The only French pear trees along the Raisin, are those that were brought there by Col. Navarre from his father's place in Detroit. Francois was the personal friend of Wayne, Winchester. St. Clair, Cass, Macomb and Woodward, and his correspondence with several of them has been preserved.

4. Isidore, born 1768, married 1795, Francoise Descomptes Labadie, daughter of Alexis and Francoise Robert. Their eldest son Isidore, born 1795, though a mere stripling served in the war of 1812.

He married, 1790, Marie Suzord, daughter of Louis and Marie Josette Lebeau; his children were: Robert, born 1792; Francois, born 1793; Victoire, married 1823, Jacques Godfroy, son of Col. Gabriel and Thérèse Douaire de Bondy. Agathe was exquisitely beautiful; Julie died at an advanced age unmarried; Monique married John Askin eldest son of Col. James Askin, of Sandwich.

5. Archange Louise, born 1770, married 1796, Dominique Godé de Marentette, whose daughters were : Francoise Marie, married Col. James Askin, son of John, Governor of Michilimackinac and Archange Barthe; Marianne Navarre, married Pierre Godfroy, son of Col. Gabriel and Thérèse Douaire de Bondy; Jeanne, married 1st, Timothy De Quindre, son of Antoine and Catherine des Rivières de la Morandière; 2nd William B. Hunt.

6. Charlotte Soulange, born, 1774, married Cajetau Tremblay; Antoine Freshet, born 1772, married 1806, Madeleine Cavallier. He served with distinction during the war of 1812. Jean Marie, born 1778, named from his uncle ; 7. Marianne, born 1780, was a great belle. She was very gifted, possessing fine musical ability and decided talent for painting. Cols. Hamtramck and Gratiot, were rival suitors for her favor, both pleaded in vain; she was faithful to the memory of a former lover who had died suddenly. Several of her letters have been preserved—the style is admirable, the handwriting characteristic and beautiful.

8. Catherine, named after her aunt Catherine Macomb, born 1782, married Commodore Henry Brevoort, of Lake Erie fame, and a member of the Brevoort family of New York. The children of this marriage were: John, married Marie Navarre; Robert, died young; Anne, married Charles Bristol; Elias, settled in New Mexico; Henry, married Jane, daughter of Wm. Macomb and Jeannette Francheville de Marentette, who left three sons: Wm. Macomb, who fought bravely and fell in battle in the war of 1860; Henry Navarre, Ex-prosecuting Attorney of Detroit; Elias Thornton connected with the Canada Railroad. 9. Monique, born 1789, was the first wife of William Macomb. She inherited the traditional loveliness of her race, and added among other accomplishments, that of a daring and superb equestrienne. She died young, leaving one son Navarre Macomb. 10. Pierre, born 1787, settled at the mouth of the Maumee in 1807. He was a trusty scout to General Harrison during the war of 1812. His thorough knowledge of the Indians and of the country enabled him to render many important services. His portrait is still possessed by his descendants, taken at the age of seventy.

4. Francois Marie, born 1759, married Marie Louise, daughter of René Godere, the children were: Robert, born 1782; Jacques, born 1788; Francois, born 1790; Archange, born 1792; Antoine, born 1796; 5. Jean Marie Alexis, born 1762, married 1789, Archange Godé; Marie, born 1793; Alexis; 4. Pluyette, born 1742; 5. Antoine, born 1745; 6. Joseph, born 1748, died young; 7. Marie Catherine, born 1749, died young; 8. Bonaventure Marie, born 1750, died 1764; 9. Catherine, born 1757, married Alexander Macomb, the great land speculator.

PELLETIER.

History states that when La Mothe Cadillac landed at Detroit he was greeted by two Coureurs des Bois, Pierre Roy and Francois Pelletier. This latter name stands very high in Canada and is found in every department of science and politics. Nicolas the first of the name came from Béance (France) and married in 1675 Jeanne Roussy. They settled at Sorrel, and left eight children to propagate their race. The eldest son Francois married Marguerite Madeleine Morrisseau by whom he had ten; one of them Marie Angelique, married 1709 Antoine de Gerlais, she was the godchild of the Baron D'Avaugour, Gov. of Canada. Her brother Francois married 1689 Madeleine Thumés Dufresne, daughter of a surgeon, whose son Francois Jean, born 1681 at Sorrel, married 1718, Marie Robert at Detroit, who afterwards married Louis Campeau. A brother (Jean) of Francois, who married Marguerite Madeleine Morrisseau, married in 1662 at Quebec, Marie Geneviève Manevely de Rainville, daughter of Charles and Francoise de Blanet, de Perche, their son Jean Francois married 1685 Geneviève Le Tendre, who was godmother for Cadillac's child, the first child baptised in Detroit. She afterwards married Etienne Volant de St. Claude. Her son by Pelletier, Jean Francois married at Quebec Catherine Arnaud with whom Cadillac later had so much trouble, and who was very influential at the Castle St. Louis, Quebec, owing to his powerful family connections.

There was another branch of Pelletier, to which belonged Michel, Sieur de la Prade and Seigneur de Gentilly, who married 1660 at Champlain, Jacqueline Chamboy.

Francois, son of Francois Antyat married 1689 Madeleine Thumés, their son Jean Bapte, born August 15, 1691 at Sorrel, married at Detroit 1718, Marie Louise Robert whose son Jean Bapte married Marie Cornet; the children were: J. Bapte, married 1769 Cath. Vallé dit Versailles; Thérèse, married 1780 Jean Bapte Chapoton; Marie Josephette; Jacques Amable, born 1746; Francois, born 1749; Andre, married 1763 Cath. Meloche; his son J. Bapte married 1809, Cath. Williams daughter of Thomas Williams and Cecile Campeau; Jacques, married 1778, Madeleine Le Vanneur at Quebec. Their children were: 1. Archange, born 1782 named after her godmother Archange Barthe, wife of Jean Askin Governor of Mackinaw. She married in 1800 Mayor John Whipple U. S. A. son of Joseph and Eliza Fairfield of Manchester, Mass. The children of this union blended the happier traits of the Puritan with the graceful charms of the dark-eyed Norman race: 1. Eunice Fairchild died in infancy; 2. James Burbick, married 1812, Sophie Godfroy, daughter of Col. Gabriel and Thérèse Douaire de Bondy; 3. John Porter; 4. Charles Whiley, the well-known lawyer and chief justice of Michigan, married Marguerite Ann

Brooks, daughter of Col. Edward Brooks, U. S. A., and Marguerite Anne May. 5. George Askin died young; 6. Caroline Hull died unmarried in 1878, leaving the memory of a most saintly life. 7. Anne Hunt married Pierre Desnoyers; 8. Henry Larned married Caroline Buckley, of Monroe, Michigan. His beautiful widow married Mr. Harvey Mixer and resides at Detroit. Sylvia Larned died young.

10. Mary Wolcott, who inherited the stately, elegant presence of her race which, added to fine conversational powers, make her a very interesting companion. 11. William Lecuyer married Louise Fairchild, he inherited his father's military talents and served with distinction in the late civil war, he died of wounds received in war. His only child, Marie Louise, married, 1882, Edgar, son of Alexander Lewis. She died in the flower of her youth and beauty, universally regretted. 12. Eliza Susan married Charles Conaghan, a prominent citizen of Cincinnati, Ohio. She died in 1882 and left three sons. 13. Margaretta Torrey married Charles Hyde and resided at Cincinnati, Ohio; 14. Catherine Sophia married Edwin Skinner. Their children were: Henry Whipple married in 1877, Mannie Avery, of Detroit; Edwin; Archange married 1881, Norton Strong, surgeon in the U. S. A., son of Norton and Ellen Chapin, of Detroit; Bernard; 2. Catherine, born 1785, died unmarried; 3. Charles married 1806, Cecile Marthe Chapoton, daughter of Louis, whose sister Catherine married Major Antoine De Quindre, a daughter by this marriage, became the wife of Louis Beaufait; a son, Charles, married Eliza Vameter Cicotte, daughter of Francois and Philis Pettier, whose children are: Marianne married Alex. Chapoton, Jr.; Charles, a prominent insurance agent of Detroit; Helena; Madeleine married Joseph Belanger, of Canada, a branch of whose family came to Detroit as early as 1715. He is well known in Detroit and deservedly popular; Agnes; Marthe married Ferdinand Zehner; 4. Antoine married 1780, Monique Bienvenu Delisle, one of the oldest families in Detroit; 5. Felice married 1811, Peter Tallman, Capt. of Artillery, U. S. A., a daugther by this marriage, Marguerite became the wife of Capt. Moyer, of the British army. In 1819 she married Francois Cicotte; 6. Marianne married Capt. John Cleves Semmes, a nephew of the famous jurist, John Cleves Semmens, whose daughter Anna married President Harris. Capt. Semmes served with gallantry at Fort Erie. He created quite a sensation in 1813 by propounding the theory that the earth was open at the poles and that the interior was accessible and habitable. He died at Hamilton, Butler County, Ohio, 1828. His descendants reside at Cincinnati; 7. Madeleine married John Askin and resided at Malden, Canada; 8. Marguerite married Dr. Davis, surgeon in the U. S. A.

REAUM.

This family counts among its descendants some of the most prominent families of Canada and the United States. Its founder was René, born 1643, son of Jean and Marie Chevalier, Diocese of La Rochelle, who married at Quebec, 1665, Marie Chevreau. They had a large family. One of their sons, Robert, born 1668, married in 1696, Elizabeth Brunet, two of whose children came to Detroit in 1730. Hyacinthe, born 1704, married in 1733, Agathe de Lacelle. Pierre, born 1709, married in 1738, Susanne Hubert de la Croix.

ELDER BRANCH.

Hyacinthe married in 1733; Agathe de Lacelle, died in 1778. Their children were: 1. Jacques, born 1737; 2. Joseph, born 1739, married in 1787, Marianne Robert; 3. Jean Baptiste, born 1741, married in 1763, Agathe Lothman de Barrois; 4. Agathe married in 1769, Joseph Poupart; 5. Catherine, born 1745; 6. Julie, born 1748, married Lieutenant Governor John Hay, she died 1794, leaving three sons and one daughter. Two of her sons were officers in the British army. Her daughter Agathe married in 1790, Pierre Montigny de Louvigny Knight, of St. Louis; his descendants occupied prominent positions in France, one serving in the body guard of the unfortunate Louis 16th, they are called Hay de Montigny; 7. Charles; 8. Marianne married in 1765, Pierre Barron; 8. Claude married in 1765, Geneviève Jaunisse; his children were: Jean Baptiste, born 1766; Agathe, born 1767; Charlotte, born 1768, married in 1795, Jacques Francheville Godé de Marautatte.

YOUNGER BRANCH.

Pierre, Hyacinthe's brother married a second time in 1738, Susanne Hubert de La Croix. The children were: 1. Charlotte, born 1738, married in 1760, Lt. Charles Deniau de Muy, a French officer, whose father was commandant of the Post Pontchartrain; 2. Susanne married in 1760, Dupèron Baby, eldest son of Raymond and Thérèse Dupré, of Montreal; 3. Bonaventure married in 1766, Jeanne Des Hestres; second, 1793, Josette Gatignon Ferton, whose descendants are numerous; 4. Veronique married Gabriel Le Grand, surgeon in the French army, widower of Madeleine Chapoton.

Louis Reaume, an officer in the British army, stationed at Detroit in 1780, was related to this family; he married in 1780, Marie Charlotte Barthe, daughter of Pierre and Charlotte Chapoton. He was killed two weeks after his marriage, leaving a young bride of seventeen, who afterwards became the wife of Louis Descomptes Labadie (Badichon).

RIOPELLE.

A branch of this family moved to Detroit shortly after the English conquest in 1760. The descendants acquired much property which many of them still possess. PIERRE, son of Pierre and Marguerite Dubois of St. Denis, Olèron, was the head of the Riopelles in America. He married, 1687, MARIE JULIEN, daughter of Jean and Madeleine Guérin. Their children were: 1. MARIE MADELEINE, B. 1688, was killed by a cannon ball; 2. BARBE, B. 1690, married 1737, Jean Dirigoyen; 3. PIERRE, B. 1691, married 1718, Marie Anne Mahew-Merchant; 4. LOUIS, B. 1693, married 1718, Ursule Vesinat; 5. NICOLAS, B. 1696, married 1721, Marguerite Garnaud; 6. MARIANNE, B. 1699, married 1st, 1716, Augustin Letartre, 2nd, in 1731, Jacques Sarcelier. AMBROISE, son of Pierre and Marie Anne Mahew-Merchant, came to Detroit and married there in 1766 Thérèse Campeau, daughter of Antoine and Angelique Pelletier. The children of this union were: 1. Pierre, B. 1767, di d in infancy; 2. Toussaint, B. 1768; 3. Pierre, married 1808, Monique Bienvenu Delisle; 4. Antoine, B. 1776; 5. Thérèse, B. 1776, died unmarried; 6. Elizabeth, B. 1778, married ——— Methé; 7. Hyacinthe, B. 1780, married 1807 Françoise Meloche, in 1812 he married again, Angelique Douaire de Bondy; 8. Archange, B. 1784, married John DIX;

9. Dominique, B. 1787, married 1818, Colette (Clotilde) Gouin, daughter of Nicolas and Archange Boyer. Colette was the widow of Antoine St. Bernard. She was universally beloved, and became a model to many who endeavored to imitate her beautiful and virtuous life. One boy and four girls were the result of this union: 1. Domique, married Elizabeth Gouin. His children are worthy representatives of the name they bear. One of them is a member of the Detroit bar. As a family they possess unusual musical talents. One of the daughters is a most brilliant pianist; 2. EDESSE, married Michel G. Payment; 3. NANCY became a nun; 4. ANGELIQUE, married Fabien Pelletier; 5. DOMITELLE, married ——— Gouin.

RIVARD.

Among the earliest marriages which were celebrated at Fort Pontchartrain is that of Francois Fafard dit Delorme, the interpreter, and Barbe Loisel, the widow of a distinguished officer, Francois Le Gautier, Sieur de la Vallée Ranée; it occurred October 30, 1713; the witnesses were, Francois de la Forêt, Commandant, Du Buisson, Lt. of Marines, J. B. Fachot, Louis Gatheau Mallet, Francois Rivard, Sieur de Montendroe, Etienne Campau, Trutard and Joseph Parent.

This family is known under various titles, Rivard de Lavigne, De la Glanderie, Loranger de St. Mars, de Montendre, de Lacoursière, &c. Its founder in this country was Nicolas Rivard, Sieur de Lavigne, born 1624, married at Batiscan, 1652.
The Hiax or Yax were of Dutch origin and settled at an early day at Fort Pontchartrain. The children of Jean Bapte were: 1. Jean Bapte, born 1763, married 1786, Irene Beaufait, daughter of Judge Louis Beaufait and Thérèse de Mersac, whose children were: André, born 1787; Monique, born 1789, married 1814, Joseph Chauvin; Antoine, born 1790, married Julie de Mersac; Jean Bapte, born 1791; Elizabeth, born 1792, married Pierre Gouin; 2. Pierre, born 1765, married 1795, Archange Séguin de Laderoute, whose son Pierre, born 1795; 3. Nicolas, born 1769; 4. Joseph, born 1772, married 1792 Agnes Chauvin; 5. Francois, born 1773, married 1799 Isabelle Chapoton, daughter of Jean Bapte and Felice Cecyre; he was an ensign in the first Regiment of Militia organized in the territory; his daughter Archange, born 1774, married 1795 Paul Plessis Bellair, son of Paul and Marianne Héry. In 1735 Rose Rivard married Oliver Plessis Bellair.

ST. AUBIN.

This family was formerly called CASSE, and is one of the very oldest in Detroit. JEAN CASSE, dit St. Aubin, came to Fort Pontchartrain as early as 1710. He brought with him his wife Marie Louise Gaultier whom he had married at Quebec in 1707. Their children were: 1. Joseph; 2. Gabriel, born 1712; 3. Jean Bapte, 1708; 4. Agathe, born 1716, married 1734 Nicolas Campau; 5. Chas; 6. Noël; 7. Thérèse; 8. Catherine, married 1751 Chas. Campeau. Jean Bapte, Jr., married 1731 Madeleine Primeau, daughter of Jean and Susanne Bellanger of Quebec; he died in 1733. Charles married 1741 Thérèse Esténe daughter of Pierre and Madeleine Frappier; she died in 1748. He married in 1750 Marie Methé. Many of his descendants reside at and around Detroit. Noël married 1731 Susanne Esténe, daughter of Pierre and Madeleine Frappier: his children were: 1. Jean Bapte, who married 1770 Thérèse Boyé, daughter of Ignace and Angelique de Cardonet whose daughters were: Archange, born 1774; Jeanne, born 1775; 2. Susanne, married 1771 Admirable Latour.

PIERRE CASSE ST. AUBIN, married Marguerite Brin d'Amour; his son LOUIS married 1775 Angelique Chevalier, daughter of Jean Bapte and Francoise Lavoine of Mackinaw, whose son FRANCOIS, born 1775, was intimately identified with the history of Detroit, and who is still remembered by many of our older citizens. He resided on his property (now known as the St. Aubin farm). To him we are indebted for many detailed accounts of incidents in the early days of the English conquest, information he had received from his father, and preserved through Judge Witherell's graphic pen. Francois married Baseline Campeau, born 1784, daughter of Jean Bapte. She survived her husband nearly forty years, dying at the advanced age of eighty-four. Francois had nine children: Louis St. Aubin, married 1st, Thérèse Chapoton, 2nd, Madeleine Cotterell; Francois, married Virginie Moran; Mrs. Louis Grosebeck; Mrs. Pierre Provençal; Mrs. Eugene W. Watson; Mrs. Richard Cornor; Mrs. John F. Godfroy (of Grand Rapids); Mrs. Henry Beaubien; Mrs. Antoine Morass.

VILLIER DIT ST. LOUIS.

Several prominent families of Detroit trace back to LOUIS VILLIER, born 1706, son of Jean and Marguerite Gatineau, of Toul, Lorraine. He had been educated for the priesthood, not finding it his vocation, determined to seek his fortune in the wilds of Canada, which offered so tempting a field to the adventurous. From Quebec he came to Detroit, where Cadillac had laid the foundation of a future city. He married there, April 26, 1746, Marguerite Morin, daughter of Pierre and Josette Drouet. Through her mother Marguerite was related to Drouet, Sieur de Richaroille, a French officer; to the Creviers and Le Neuf du Herrison, one of the oldest and most remarkable families of Canada. Louis was called St. Louis on account of his great piety. He died in 1765, leaving the following children:

1. LOUIS, born 1747, married 1770, Charlotte Requindeau, dit Joachin; family tradition relative to her is that she ran away from the Ursuline Convent at Quebec to marry Louis. She was related to Gaultier De Varennes, Governor of Three Rivers, Petit, Lefebres and many other prominent families.
2. Christopher, married 1785, Josette Suzor.
3. MARIANNE, married 1766, François Drouillard.
4. MARIE LOUISE, married 1767, Jos. Thos. Dajot.
5. JEANNE, born 1754. Louis and Charlotte Requindeau had several children: 1. LOUIS VITUS, born 1776, who served in the war of 1812, and was promoted several times for his bravery. He settled at Sandwich, and died at an advanced age;. 2. JOSETTE married Reaume; 3. HUBERT, married Thérèse Barthe, daughter of Jean Baptiste and Geneviève Cullerier de Beaubien; 4. FRANÇOIS, X.

JEANNE, married April 3, 1804, Thomas Lewis, son of Thomas and Josette De Lorme, of Three Rivers, Canada, whose children are:

JOSEPH, married Fanny Sterling, two of whose children reside at Boston, Mass., one at Detroit.

SOPHIE, married Narcissus Tourneur dit Jeannette.

THOMAS, called the good-natured, Governor of Grosse Isle,

married Jeannette Francheville de Marentette, widow of William
Macomb, whose only daughter married Dallas Norvell, son of
Senator John Norvell. He married a second time Mary Brown,
by whom he has a large and interesting family; ANNE, married
Richard Godfroy.

CHARLOTTE, married Dr. Fay, a partner of Dr. Clark. She
married a second time, Henry P. Bridge, formerly of Boston, ex-
Controller of Detroit, and one of its most prominent and respected citizens.

SAMUEL, married Jenny Fenton, sister of Gov. Fenton, of
Michigan. He died in 1878, universally regretted. He was a
successful business man, a genial companion and a Christian
gentleman.

ALEXANDER, married 1850, Elizabeth, daughter of Justus
Ingersoll and Ann Buckley. He has a large and exceptionally
charming family. He has held many offices of public trust:
mayor, fire commissioner, etc. He possesses in an eminent degree that courteous manner which was the peculiar inheritance
of the old French.

VISSIER DIT LAFERTE.

ANTOINE TERAULT dit Laferté served in the regiment of M.
de Subercasse, and was stationed at Fort Pontchartrain as early as
1710. He had married, at Montreal, Michelle Fortin, whose
mother, Louise Sommillard, was the daughter of the Sargeant at
Arms, and sister of Soeur Bourgeois, foundress of the order of
Notre Dame, at Montreal.

The children of this marriage were: Pierre, born 1707, whose
god-parents were Pierre Boucher de Boucherville and Madeleine
Lamothe Cadillac; Marianne, born 1712; Joseph, born 1724.

LOUIS VISSIER DIT LAFERTE married Louise Lafoie, by whom
he had three children. In 1771 he married Catherine L'Esprit
dit Champagne, by whom he had a large family: Louis, born
1772, married, 1800, Cath. Campeau; Alexis, born 1773, his
descendants reside at Detroit; Catherine, born 1775, married,
1794, Chas. Morand Grimard; Angelique, born 1776; Thérèse,
born 1778; Marianne, born 1779.

JOSEPH, married Mlle. Goyeau, whose son Clemence is well
known in Detroit; and the Laferté Farm takes its name from
Joseph; Pierre, born 1788, married Marie Louise Lafoie, whose
son Pierre inherits that courtesy of manner so peculiarly the gift
of the French. He married Mlle. Dauphin, of Canada.

www.ingramcontent.com/pod-product-compliance
Lightning Source LLC
Chambersburg PA
CBHW021207230426
43667CB00006B/588